THE CATHOLIC UNIVERSITY OF AMERICA
CANON LAW STUDIES
No. 249

DOMICILE OF WIFE UNLAWFULLY SEPARATED FROM HER HUSBAND

A HISTORICAL SYNOPSIS AND CANONICAL COMMENTARY

BY

REV. MARION LEO GIBBONS, C.M., LL.B., B.A., J.C.L.
PRIEST OF THE CONGREGATION OF THE MISSION

A DISSERTATION

SUBMITTED TO THE FACULTY OF THE SCHOOL OF CANON LAW OF THE CATHOLIC UNIVERSITY OF AMERICA IN PARTIAL FULFILLMENT OF THE REQUIREMENTS FOR THE DEGREE OF DOCTOR OF CANON LAW

THE CATHOLIC UNIVERSITY OF AMERICA PRESS
WASHINGTON, D. C.
1947

Imprimi Potest:
MARSHALL F. WINNE, C.M., PH.D.,
Provincialis.
Sancti Ludovici, 6 iunii, 1947.

Nihil Obstat:
EDUARDUS G. ROELKER, S.T.D., J.C.D.,
Censor Deputatus.
Washingtonii, die 7 iunii, 1947.

Imprimatur:
IOANNES M. McNAMARA, D.D.,
Episcopus Eumenensis, Administrator
Baltimorensis-Washingtonensis.
Washingtonii, die 7 iunii, 1947.

MURRAY & HEISTER—WASHINGTON, D. C.
PRINTED IN THE UNITED STATES OF AMERICA

Our Lady

of

The Miraculous Medal

TABLE OF CONTENTS

CANONICAL COMMENTARY

CHAPTER V

INTRODUCTION

Present-day philosophies of subjectivism and individualism under the guise of liberalism are in a great measure responsible for the growing conviction that marriage and its consequent obligations are purely and simply the private concern of the persons immediately involved. Concurrent with this false concept is the tenet that the contracting parties alone have any concern in the marriage contract and that the temporal happiness and convenience of the married persons alone are to be considered. Since, according to this misconception, marriage is to be regarded as a private affair, so also is the dissolution or termination of the marital union. In novels, cinemas, newspaper matrimonial bureaus, rarely is there to be found the husband or wife who when experiencing difficulty in married life feels that any one in authority has the right to determine the question of continued cohabitation with the "unjust," "incompatible" spouse. This attitude finds expression in the question so very frequently asked: "Shall I give my husband a divorce?"

The traditional concept of Christian marriage as taught by the Catholic Church is directly opposed to this modern pagan attitude. The Author of marriage, and the community which is built on this institution, each has a part in marriage, and each is vitally concerned in the rupture of the matrimonial contract. Apart from the harm committed against the moral and spiritual order and from a purely practical viewpoint, untold detriment follows from this modern conception. The spouses in time of stress and difficulty are themselves the most unqualified persons to judge of the justice of their own cause; bitterness and enmity follow in the wake of a separation, and thus reconciliation is made more difficult; remarriage follows divorce almost as naturally as the combustion of a volatile substance follows contact with heat. Thus the unchecked exercise of self-sufficiency and unrestrained private judgment in matters which vitally concern the public order break down the individual component units of society and lead to chaos and a destruction of the social order.

While there is no record of the number of Catholics who seek to release themselves from the obligations imposed by the conjugal union, and while much less is there any official source from which to determine the number of those Catholics who have separated on private authority, yet the statistics of the granted divorces indicate a strong probability that the false philosophy has been accepted and acted on by numerous Catholics.

It is not uncommon to hear the opinion expressed that a Catholic is permitted to separate from his spouse provided that he does not seek to obtain a civil decree of divorce; or that such a decree may be sought provided the Catholic does not attempt to remarry. Such an attitude is far removed from the doctrinal and juridical position of the Catholic Church.

The primary purpose of the writer is to determine what are the juridical effects of unlawful separation and, in particular, what are the legal rights and duties of a wife unlawfully separated as these rights and duties are determined by her domicile or quasi-domicile. Therefore he has sought to determine according to the present doctrinal and juridical teaching of the Church what constitutes unlawful separation of the spouses, and what, if any, juridical force private authority has in relation to the instituting of a separation of validly married persons.

The writer has divided his work into two principal parts. The first part is a historical summary concerning divorce and the institute of domicile in Roman Law and Canon Law, with special emphasis on domicile as a juridical factor in Canon Law. The second part, a canonical commentary, notes the doctrinal and juridical teaching of the Church on the unity and indissolubility of marriage; determines what constitutes unlawful separation of the spouses; analyzes the expression *"legitime non separata"* as the same is used in the Code of Canon Law; and treats in general of the juridical effects of the wife's domicile, and in particular of her domicile or quasi-domicile as a factor in the determination of judicial competency.

The writer is pleased to discharge an immense debt of gratitude by expressing his sincere thanks and appreciation to his Very

Reverend Provincial, Marshall F. Winne, C.M., for the opportunity to complete his advanced studies in Canon Law; to the Faculty of the School of Canon Law of the Catholic University of America for their profitable instruction and generous assistance. He also expresses his gratitude to his confreres, and to the members of his family for their interest, aid, and encouragement; to his benefactors for their spiritual and material benefactions; and, finally, to Her to whom this dissertation is dedicated, for help and encouragement without which this dissertation, and the course of advanced studies, would never have been completed.

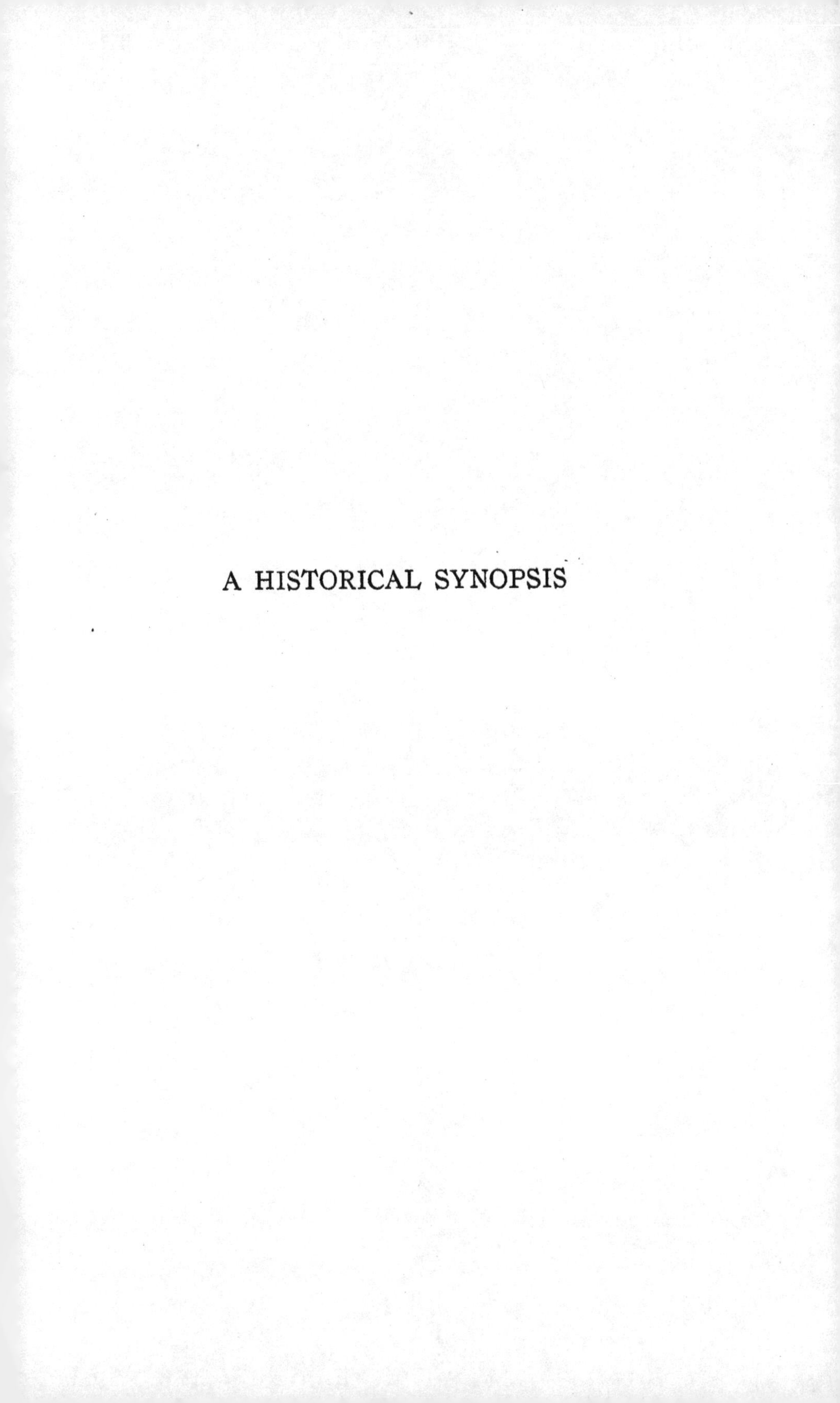

A HISTORICAL SYNOPSIS

CHAPTER I

ROMAN LAW

ARTICLE A. DOMICILE IN ROMAN LAW

SECTION 1. NATURE OF DOMICILE IN ROMAN LAW

In order to understand and appreciate the place that domicile holds in canonical jurisprudence it is necessary to review briefly the provisions made in Roman law concerning domicile. The theory of domicile was developed early in the history of Roman jurisprudence. As a determinant of local jurisdiction, of legal rights and obligations under Roman law, domicile was an outgrowth or extension of the Roman *origo.* By virtue of his local citizenship, that is, in consequence of his *origo,* a citizen owed certain duties to a particular community, and in turn enjoyed rights and privileges measured by the same fact. The citizen's *ius originis* was the sum of the privileges, laws, and obligations in a particular municipality.[1] For the non-citizen, the *incola,* there was constituted the *ius domicilii,*[2] which for all practical purposes paralleled the *ius originis* except in title and in the manner of acquisition.[3]

It suffices to note here the necessary requirements for establishing a domicile as these essential notes were finally determined. Neither prolonged and uninterrupted residence,[4] nor the mere possession of a house or property,[5] were sufficient in themselves to constitute one's domicile, but there was required, in addition to residence, an intention of permanency of residence.[6] Therefore, the mere fact of physical presence in a certain municipality did

[1] D.(50.1)(15.3).

[2] Fourneret, *Le Domicile Matrimonial* (Paris, 1906), p. 19.

[3] Voet, *Commentariorum ad Pandectas Libri Quinquaginta* (5. ed., 7 vols. in 4, Bassani: Typis Remondini, 1827), Lib. L, tit. I, n. 3; D.(50.1)29.

[4] D.(50.1)5.

[5] D.(50.1)(17.3,5).

[6] D.(50.1)23.

not automatically entitle a person to the *ius domicilii*. There was required an element of at least an intentional indefinite stability in one's municipal residence.[7]

"The intention of permanent residence placed, so to speak, upon the material habitation, changed that simple fact of residence into a juridical being—domicile."[8] Residence was proof; intention was the essential and effective cause of securing a domicile. Both elements, intention to establish a domicile and actual residence, were required; neither by itself would suffice. This was a voluntary domicile (*domicilium verum, voluntarium*). It was the first of two types of domicile known to Roman jurists.

SECTION 2. NECESSARY DOMICILE IN ROMAN LAW

The second type of domicile, the *domicilium legale,* as developed in Roman law, is the one of major concern in this present work. While much can be learned from a study of voluntary domicile, interest here lies chiefly in determining the origin, nature, and effects of the necessary or legal domicile.

While one could never strictly lose his place of origin, his *ius originis,* it was possible to remove from it and to constitute another place one's domicile. Yet, removal, even with the actual intention of not returning, did not necessarily mean the establishment of a new voluntary domicile; on the other hand, profession or state in life could require a fixation of domicile by law. A juridical fixation of domicile was imperative if proper provision was to be made for the rights and obligations of all persons.

Thus, a soldier who no longer had a domicile in his native city was judged to have a legal domicile in that place wherein he was

[7] "Sed de ea re constitutum esse eam domum unicuique nostrum debere existimari, ubi quisque sedes et tabulas haberet, suarumque rerum constitutionem fecisset."—D. (50.16) 203. With definitiveness the Code of Justinian provided: "Incolas vero . . . domicilium facit. Et in eodem loco singulos habere domicilium non ambigitur, ubi quis larem rerumque ac fortunarum suarum constituit, unde rursus non sit discessurus, si nihil avocet, unde cum profectus est, peregrinari videtur, quo si rediit, peregrinari iam destitit."—C. (10.40) 7.

[8] Costello, *Domicile and Quasi-Domicile,* The Catholic University of America Canon Law Studies, n. 60 (Washington, D. C.: The Catholic University of America, 1930), p. 15.

garrisoned.[9] Likewise, senators possessed a domicile in the city of Rome, even though by reason of privilege they were not bound to reside there.[10] A person exiled in perpetuity had a domicile only in the place of exile, while other exiled persons retained their voluntary domicile.[11] According to Ulpian (d. 228), students away from their homes did not acquire a domicile in the place of their studies.[12] But even in the time of Emperor Hadrian (117–138) such a one if he spent ten years in residence at a university was presumed to have the necessary intention to constitute his domicile in that place.[13] Minors were not regarded as retaining the domicile of their parents, or at least they were free to choose their own domiciles.[14]

Before speaking of the domicile of married women, one must note that, among the ancient Romans, persons who had the right of *connubium,* if they intermarried, contracted *iustae nuptiae,* and this according to the *ius civile;* persons who had not the right of *connubium,* by marriage with each other contracted a *matrimonium non iustum,* and this according to the *ius gentium.*[15] The form *iustae nuptiae* was with or without *manus,* depending on the nature of the ceremony. Such a marriage with *manus* dissociated the wife from her father's house, and made her subject to the *patria potestas* of her husband or to his *paterfamilias.*[16]

No doubt there was a time when *manus* was an accompaniment of all recognized marriage, but in the time of Gaius (c. 200 A.D.), and long before, it had become a mere occasional accessory transaction of increasing rarity.[17]

In the case of married women, wherever the condition of law-

---

[9] D.(50.1)23.

[10] D.(40.1)(22.6).

[11] D.(50.1)(27.3).

[12] D.(47.10)5.

[13] C.(10.40)2.

[14] D.(50.1)(3.4); D.(50.1)6.

[15] Buckland, *Elementary Principles of the Roman Private Law* (Cambridge: University Press, 1912), pp. 31–32.

[16] Muirhead, *Historical Introduction to the Private Law of Rome* (2. ed., London, 1899), p. 27; Corbett, *The Roman Law of Marriage* (Oxford: Clarendon Press, 1930), p. 223.

[17] Buckland, *op. cit.,* p. 32.

ful marriage (i.e., *iustae nuptiae*) prevailed, the rule was that she acquired the domicile of her husband.[18] However, even in the case of marriage without the formalities of the *ius civile* (i.e., *non-iustae nuptiae*), she also acquired her husband's domicile.[19]

It is conceivable that the necessary domicile could be the same municipality that had been her voluntary domicile. But it is evident that there were certain juridical effects following the acquisition of the husband's domicile, and these effects remained even after his death and as long as she did not enter upon a second marriage.[20]

Article B. Divorce in Roman Law

The Roman juridical conception of marriage together with the facility of the legal dissolution of the marriage bond brought about many situations which required juridical determination of the legal rights and obligations of separated spouses. It is true that in the case of marriage *cum manu* the wife was in a juridical status comparable to her position before marriage, i.e., she remained a *filiafamilias,* and though she might leave her husband, she could not thereby alter or change her status.

According to the conception of Roman marriage *sine manu* there existed a simple contractual relation, the essence of which was mutual consent. Withdrawal of this consent dissolved the contract.

The dissolution could take the form of a voluntary dissolution, i.e., a *divortium,* which was a private act not requiring the intervention of the court;[21] or the termination of the marital relationship could result by way of forced dissolution by either of the parties, i.e., by way of a *repudium.*[22] This latter form was divided into two classes. There was the class in which the severance of

[18] "Mulieres honore maritorum erigimus, genere nobilitamus et forum ex eorum persona statuimus et domicilia mutamus."—C. (12.1) 13.

[19] D. (50.1) (37.2).

[20] "Vidua mulier amissi mariti domicilium retinet exemplo clarissimae personae per maritum factae: Sed utrumque aliis intervenientibus nuptiis permutatur."—D. (50.1) 22.

[21] Muirhead, *op. cit.,* p. 356; Sherman, *Roman Law in the Modern World* (2. ed., 3 vols., New York: Baker, Voorhis & Co., 1924), II, 58.

[22] D. (38.11).

the marital union followed from some cause provided for in the law, but involved no blame for the person concerned, e.g., old age, sickness, sterility, insanity, and such a *repudium* was termed a *divortium bona gratia.*[23] The other class included such divorces as were purely arbitrary; those in which the cause of severance was a grave delinquency on the part of one of the spouses, e.g., the wife's adultery, an attempted murder, etc. In such a case the party responsible for the divorce was made to suffer at least something in the form of a pecuniary loss.[24]

Besides these methods of dissolution there were other ways by which marriage could come to an end, e.g., by the death of either party, by either of them becoming a slave, etc.[25]

The causes for which marriage could be dissolved varied throughout the centuries, but it suffices to note here that the Emperor Justin II (565–578) removed the restrictions which had been legislated by his uncle and predecessor, Emperor Justinian (527–565), so that liberty of divorce by mutual consent became once more a legal method.[26] Mere separation was not of itself equal to divorce any more than mutual cohabitation constituted marriage. The requirements of a manifestation of intention, as also the presence of a justifiable cause, made possible the arising of cases in which the separation of the parties might be unlawful. For the absence of one of the legal requirements made the continued separation unlawful. There were provisions made for instances of unjust divorce by one party, i.e., when the cause was not of sufficient gravity. As a rule, if the husband divorced his wife without justifiable cause, she recovered her dowry and also retained the husband's marital portion. In case a wife unjustly divorced the husband, she lost her dowry.

The *lex Julia de adulteriis* prescribed the form of *repudium,* and required the message to be delivered by a freedman of the family in the presence of seven witnesses who were above the age of

---

[23] D.(24.1).

[24] Joyce, *Christian Marriage, an Historical and Doctrinal Study* (Heythrop Series, I, New York: Sheed & Ward, 1933), p. 308. (Hereafter this work is cited *Christian Marriage.*)

[25] Leage, *Roman Private Law* (2. ed., by C. H. Ziegler, London: Macmillan & Co., 1942), p. 107.

[26] Nov.(140.1).

puberty and who likewise were citizens of Rome. The party who made a causeless *repudium,* or whose misconduct justified a *repudium,* was punished with pecuniary losses in respect to dowry and prenuptial donations. After much legislation under Christian Emperors, Justinian enacted legislation whereby a man or woman who divorced without cause should retire to a cloister and forfeit all his or her estate.[27]

Divorce among the Romans always remained a private matter. It could of course be necessary to prove in court the grounds of the separation, e.g., establishment of the fact of the wife's adultery, or that the husband was a violator of tombs, but actually the divorce was as little a matter of public or official intervention as was the marriage itself.[28]

The Romans, as also the Greeks and the Hebrew people, treating the matrimonial bond as dissoluble, had no express legislation providing for a separation from bed and board, which separation in no way touched the matrimonial bond, but these people were content to provide penal sanctions against persons guilty of the crime of adultery.[29]

---

[27] Nov. (134.11); Poste, *Gaii Institutiones* (4. ed., Oxford: Clarendon Press, 1904), p. 87.

[28] Joyce, *Christian Marriage,* p. 309.

[29] "Antiqui populi, v.g., Hebraei, Graeci, Romani cum de iure permitterent divortia plena quoad vinculum matrimonii, non habuerunt expressas leges de sola separatione a thoro et cohabitatione in ipso iure naturali fundata, sed severis *poenis* in iure *criminali* contra adulterium statutis fuerunt contenti."—Cf. Wernz-Vidal, *Ius Canonicum ad Codicis normam exactum* (7 vols. in 8, Romae: apud aedes Universitatis Gregorianae, 1923–1938), V, *Ius Matrimoniale* (2. ed., 1928), 779, nota 105.

CHAPTER II

DIVORCE IN CANON LAW

ARTICLE A. "DIVORTIUM PERFECTUM"

Divortium perfectum, i.e., an absolute dissolution of a consummated marriage contract, is distinguished from *divortium imperfectum,* wherein the bond of marriage is left intact and there is implied only a cessation of the common life between the spouses. This latter form of divorce may be either lawful or unlawful, either temporary or perpetual. The concern here is only with that form which is unlawful. To determine what constitutes an unlawful separation it is previously necessary to have a knowledge of the cases in which a separation is permitted.

In marriage, as restored by Christ, once the union has been consummated, there can be no question of an absolute divorce. Christ has so ordained, and this stands unanimously attested by the writers of the Gospels and the Epistles.[1]

That the same doctrine of indissolubility has been the constant teaching of the Catholic Church is evident from the unanimous teaching of Tradition.[2] While some of the Fathers, e.g., Tertullian (d. ca. 230), St. Basil the Great (d. 379), Epiphanius (d. 403), may seem to have allowed a second marriage during the time the other spouse was living, such is not the correct rendering of their doctrine.[3] They are to be understood as permitting the second marriage only after the death of the first spouse, and that

[1] Mark, X:11–12; Matthew, XIX:4–6, 8–9; Luke, XVI:18; I Cor., VII:7–10.

[2] Cf. St. Justin Martyr (d. ca. 165), *Apologia,* I, c. 15.—Migne, *Patrologiae Cursus Completus, Series Graeca* (161 vols., Parisiis, 1856–1866), VI, 349 (hereafter referred to as *MPG*); Athenagoras (ca. 177), *Legatio pro Christianis,* n. 33—*MPG,* VI, 965; Tertullian (d. ca. 230), *De Monogamia,* c. ix—Migne, *Patrologiae Cursus Completus, Series Latina* (221 vols., Parisiis, 1844–1864), II, 941 (hereafter referred to as *MPL*).

[3] Joyce, *Christian Marriage,* pp. 304, 306, 322.

only in the event there had been a relaxation of the prohibition of a second marriage at any time in the future, since second marriages were not regarded favorably by the Church in the early ages of its history. Epiphanius, one of those most strongly accused, did in fact speak of a second marriage after the death of the divorced wife.[4]

The declarations of the Council of Elvira (ca. 306) are cited as representative of the constant teaching of the Church in this matter. In its ninth canon this Council declared: "A faithful woman who has left an adulterous husband and is marrying another who is faithful, let her be prohibited from marrying; if she has married, let her not receive communion until the man she has left shall have departed this life, unless illness should make this an imperative necessity."[5] Declarations to the same effect are to be found in councils down through the succeeding centuries.[6]

It lies beyond the scope of this work to explain some of the apparent departures from this universal teaching of the Church.[7] As for the Penitential Books and their provisions, it suffices to note that they were not official in character, and that the Church began to proceed energetically against them in the early decades of the ninth century.[8] The entire series of cases in the nineteenth title of the IV Book of the Decretals of Gregory IX shows how

---

[4] Epiphanius, *Adversus Haereses,* LIX, n. 4—*MPG,* XLI, 1024.

[5] "Can. 8. Item foeminae, quae nulla praecedente causa relinquerint viros suos et alteris se copulaverint, nec in finem accipiant communionem. Can. 9. Item foemina fidelis, quae adulterum maritum reliquerit fidelem et alterum ducit, prohibeatur ne ducat; si duxerit, non prius accipiat communionem, nisi quem reliquit de saeculo exierit, nisi forte necessitas infirmitatis dare compulerit."—Bruns, *Canones Apostolorum et Conciliorum Saeculorum IV–VII* (2 vols., Berolini, 1839), II, 3.

[6] Council of Arles (314) c. 10—Mansi, *Sacrorum Conciliorum Nova et Amplissima Collectio* (53 vols. in 60, Paris-Arnhem-Leipzig, 1901-1927), II, 472 (hereafter referred to as Mansi); Council of Mileve (416), c. 17—Mansi, IV, 331; Council of Hereford (673), c. 10—Mansi, XI, 130; Council of Friuli (Forum Julii) in northern Italy, (791), c. 10—Mansi, XIII, 849.

[7] Cf. Council of Verberie (752), c. 9—Mansi, XII, 566-577.

[8] Council of Chalon sur Saône (813), c. 38—Mansi, XIV, 102; Hefele et Leclercq, *Histoire des Conciles* (9 vols. in 18, Parisiis, 1907-1921), III, 1143.

the complete indissolubility of Christian marriage had become firmly fixed in the juridical conscience.

In an improper sense of the term a declaration of nullity is sometimes spoken of as a divorce. This is mentioned here only for the sake of indicating another way in which there could be a lawful separation of persons who had been only apparently married. There can be no doubt that the Church has power to declare as null and void an invalid union when the postulated circumstances are duly established through proof. That the Church has exercised its authority is evidenced by the teachings of Popes Alexander III (1159–1181) and Innocent III (1198–1216).[9]

Under the dissolutions of non-Christian marriages by means of an absolute divorce in virtue of circumstances that necessitate a favoring of the Faith may be listed the exercise of the Pauline Privilege, and the dissolution under particular circumstances by papal authority of a marriage contracted by parties who were not both Christians. Since the purpose here is principally to show cases wherein lawful separation may prevail, and since a detailed treatment of these unusual cases would lead too far from the principal subject, these are solely mentioned for the sake of a complete enumeration.

It may be noted also that Christian marriage before consummation can be dissolved by virtue of a solemn profession in a Religious Order, or through an act of papal authority. But in both instances caution is necessary in the use of terms. The fact that a solemn religious profession causes the dissolution of the marriage bond, provided that the marriage had not been consummated, was distinctly taught by Pope John XXII (1316–1334).[10]

Article B. "Divortium Imperfectum"

Divortium imperfectum, also termed limited divorce, indicates some form of separation of husband and wife, but never includes a dissolution of the conjugal bond. In this historical summary there is question exclusively of a separation of the spouses from bed and cohabitation (*a toro et cohabitatione*), the marriage bond

[9] C. 3, X, *de divortiis,* IV, 19; c. 9, X, *de divortiis,* IV, 19.

[10] C. un., *de voto et voti redemptione,* tit. VI, in Extravag. Ioan. XXII.

remaining intact during the period of separation. Under requisite circumstances this separation by public or private authority could be perpetual or temporary. Depending on the causes and the manner of the separation, the departure and the absence of a spouse could be either a lawful or an unlawful one.

Prior to the Council of Trent (1545–1563) the Church had in particular instances granted legitimate perpetual separation to persons validly married: (a) when the husband or wife made a choice of evangelical perfection in religion; (b) when one of the parties had been guilty of adultery and certain conditions had been fulfilled by the innocent party; and (c) when one party had defected from the Faith, whether by the rejecting of Christianity or by the adopting of heresy.[11] The cause, "danger to soul or body," was also mentioned as a reason for a legitimate separation, which separation could be either temporary or for an indefinite period. While this cause apparently provided a very broad basis, in actuality the conditions requisite before the separation was granted greatly restricted this cause in its operation.

In practically all the foregoing cases, with only a few exceptions, e.g., evident nullity, and adultery in specified cases, the separation was not legitimate until it was granted by ecclesiastical authority. Permanent separation on private authority alone was very seldom legitimate. Even in the presence of a just and a proportionate cause the intervention of ecclesiastical authority was requisite, though a very special cause or a serious danger in delay justified a departure on private authority.[12]

The Council of Trent (1545–1563) confirmed the teaching of the Catholic Church regarding the indissolubility of the marriage bond and the separation of spouses. It also reiterated the long-standing doctrine concerning the right and the power of the Church to sanction a separation of the spouses under special conditions.[13]

---

[11] C. 4, 5, 6, 7, X, *de divortiis,* IV, 19; c. 19, X, *de conversione coniugatorum,* III, 32.

[12] C. 4, 5, X, *de divortiis,* IV, 19; c. 6, 7, 21, X, *de conversione coniugatorum,* III, 32; c. 8, 10, 13, X, *de restitutione spoliatorum,* II, 13.

[13] Conc. Trident., sess. XXIV, *de matrimonio,* can. 4. "Si quis dixerit, Ecclesiam non potuisse constituere impedimenta matrimonium dirimentia, vel in iis constituendis errasse: anathema sit."

Lawful perpetual separation of the spouses was provisionally permitted on private authority for two causes, namely, heresy and adultery. If one of the spouses defected from the Faith through apostasy or by embracing heresy, the innocent spouse was permitted to depart. A condition limited the continued use of this right. Upon the return of the spouse to his or her religious duty, the innocent party was to receive the repentant partner, provided that the faithful party had not changed his or her status in life through entrance into religion.[14] The second cause, adultery, was likewise conditioned upon several factors. Certainty of the crime, the absence of its condonation, and the innocence of the other spouse had to concur in the case.[15] If the cause for separation was adultery committed by the other spouse, the innocent party had the right to determine whether or not the common life would be restored.

The Council of Trent's definition of the right of the Catholic Church lawfully to grant a temporary separation of the spouses was directed primarily against the pseudo-reformers of the period. In this the Council was not declaring a new right, but rather giving an interpretation of the divine law, and indicating an application of a right deriving from the divine law.[16] The Council did not

---

Can. 5. "Si quis dixerit, propter haeresim, aut molestam cohabitationem, aut affectatam absentiam a coniuge, dissolvi posse matrimonii vinculum: anathema sit."

Can. 6. "Si quis dixerit, matrimonium ratum, non consummatum, per solemnem religionis professionem alterius coniugum non dirimi: anathema sit."

Can. 7. "Si quis dixerit, Ecclesiam errare, cum docuit et docet, iuxta evangelicam et apostolicam doctrinam, propter adulterium alterius coniugum matrimonii vinculum non posse dissolvi; et utrumque, vel etiam innocentem, qui causam adulterii non dedit, non posse, altero coniuge vivente, aliud matrimonium contrahere, moecharique eum, qui, dimissa adultera, aliam duxerit, et eam quae, dimisso adultero, alii nupserit: anathema sit."

Can. 8. "Si quis dixerit, Ecclesiam errare, cum ob multas causas separationem inter coniuges, quoad thorum, seu quoad cohabitationem, ad certum incertumve tempus fieri posse decernit: anathema sit."

[14] Benedictus XIV, *De Synodo Dioecesana* (2 vols., Romae: Typographia S.C. de Propaganda Fide, 1806), lib. XIII, c. 12, n. 10.

[15] Schmalzgrueber, *Ius Ecclesiasticum Universum* (5 vols. in 12, Romae, 1843–1845), lib. IV, tit. XIX, n. 110.

[16] I Cor., V: 10–11.

enumerate the causes for which a lawful temporary separation might be undertaken or allowed. Canonists subsequent to the Council agreed in their writings that the causes for which this type of separation was permissible could be divided into three main groups, namely: defection from the Faith through apostasy, heresy, or schism on the side of one of the parties; danger to the soul of the innocent party; and danger of serious bodily injury inflicted on the innocent party by the offending spouse.[17]

In addition to the problem of determining what constituted a justifying cause which would furnish sufficient grounds for instituting a separation of the spouses, several interesting questions were raised concerning the nature of the authority requisite for instituting a permanent or a temporary separation, and concerning the effects of a separation instituted solely on private authority.

Pope Alexander III (1159–1181) toward the end of the twelfth century wrote to Theobald, Bishop of Amiens, and expressed what were apparently contradictory opinions relative to the sufficiency of private authority for the instituting of separation on the part of married persons. In one of two letters Pope Alexander III stated that a separation of married persons without a judgment of the Church was not permitted on private authority, even though made under the pretext that there existed between the parties a notorious diriment impediment of affinity.[18] In a second letter,

[17] Sanchez, *Disputationum de Sancto Matrimonii Sacramento Tomi Tres* (Antverpiae, 1626), lib. X, disp. XVII (hereafter cited *De Matrimonii Sacramento*); Pirhing, *Ius Canonicum in Quinque Libros Decretalium Distributum, Nova Methodo Explicatum* (ed. novissima, 5 vols. in 4, Dilingae, 1674–1678), lib. IV. tit. XIX (hereafter cited *Ius Canonicum*); Reiffenstuel, *Ius Canonicum Universum* (5 vols. in 7, Parisiis, 1864–1870), lib. IV, tit. XIX, nn. 26–53; Schmalzgrueber, *Ius Ecclesiasticum Universum*, lib. IV, tit. XIX, nn. 137–142.

[18] "Porro de comite Pontini, qui filiam B. de sancto Valerico uxorem suam absque iudicio ecclesiae dimisit propterea, quia eam cognatam fuisse uxoris defunctae proponit, haec prudentia tua cognoscat, quod, si etiam parentela esset publica et notoria, absque iudicio ecclesiae ab ea separari non potuit, quare ipsum ad eam recipiendam, quae petit restitutionem ipsius, districte compellas. Quam si recipere noluerit, eum et superinductam vinculo excommunicationis adstringas. Si qui autem apparuerint, qui matrimonium ipsum legitime velint et possint impetere, causam audias, et eam

written to the same bishop, Pope Alexander III allowed a separation of the spouses on private authority for the cause of notorious adultery.[19]

Pope Urban III (1185–1187) in the year 1186 wrote instructions to the Bishop of Florence concerning the action to be taken in a situation involving a wife who, desiring to correct her heretical husband, had separated from him without the judgment of the Church. The husband, following the separation, rejected the heresy. Pope Urban III declared that the wife should be compelled to return to her husband.[20] The Pope added, however, that if she had separated from her husband upon a judgment of

---

fine debito decidas. Praeterea de H. qui filiam Adelmi, cognatam suam, duxit [in] uxorem, si hoc publicum est et manifestum, nec apparet aliquis, qui matrimonium velit impetere, id tibi respondemus, quod, non apparentibus accusatoribus, et parentela manifesta seu publica exsistente, quod credible non est, nisi essent consobrini in primo gradu vel secundo, tui officii interest, matrimonia illa adhibita gravitate dissolvere, quae illicite contracta noscuntur."—c. 3, X, *de divortiis,* IV, 19; Jaffé, *Regesta Pontificum Romanorum ab condita Ecclesia ad annum post Christum natum* 1198 (ed. secundam correctam et auctam auspiciis Guilelmi Wattenbach curaverunt S. Löwenfeld, F. Kaltenbrunner, P. Ewald, 2 vols. in 1, Lipsiae, 1885–1888), n. 7935 (hereafter cited Jaffé).

19 "Significasti nobis, quod quidem miles in provincia tua, uxore sua sine iudicio ecclesiae dimissa pro eo, quod suggestum sibi fuerat, ipsam incestum cum quodam consanguineo suo commisisse, vinculo fuit propter hoc excommunicationis adstrictus. Verum mulier ipsa non continuit, sed sobolem de alio viro suscepit; nec minus postulat viro restitui, asserens, se ab ipso iniuste fuisse dimissam, et eundem virum sibi materiam adulterandi dedisse. Unde, quia nos consuluisti, utrum mulier ipsa debeat viro suo restitui, et vir ad eius receptionem compelli, Consultationi tuae taliter respondemus, quod, si notorium est, mulierem ipsam adulterium commisisse, ad eam recipiendam praefatus vir cogi non debet, nisi constaret, ipsum cum alia adulterium commisisse."—c. 4, X, *de divortiis,* IV, 19.

20 "De illa vero, quae, viro suo labente in haeresim, ipsius consortium sine iudicio ecclesiae declinavit, utrum, reverente illo ad catholicam unitatem, ad redintegrandum matrimonium sit cogenda, videtur nobis, quod mulier, maxime si ea intentione decessit, ut lapsus in haeresim taedio pariter et confusione affectus se ab errore suo converteret, ei quum reversus fuerit, est reddenda, quae, etiamsi reverti noluerit, compellatur. Si vero iudicio ecclesiae ab eo sine spe matrimonii redintegrandi recessit, ad recipiendum eum nullatenus eam dicimus compellandam."—c. 6, X, *de divortiis,* IV, 19; Jaffé, n. 9873.

the Church without any hope of reconciliation she was not to be compelled to return to her husband.

The distinctions, as made by canonists of a later period, whereby the apparently conflicting opinions of Pope Alexander were reconciled, and the effects of a separation undertaken on private authority for a cause less than adultery, will be discussed in detail in a later chapter of this work.[21]

The ecclesiastical judges of the Catholic Church from the time of its beginning have been recognized as the proper and primary authorities for determining the lawfulness of a separation on the part of spouses who are members or subjects of the Church. This was confirmed by the Council of Trent in its condemnation of those who asserted the contrary.[22]

Separation *a toro et cohabitatione,* even though of temporary duration, was regarded as a matter of public concern and as contrary to the nature of matrimony. In such a case, notwithstanding the presence of a proportionately just cause, a disruption of the common life was not tolerated without the intervention of an ecclesiastical judgment. However, it was recognized that there could be cases wherein there might be a serious danger in delay, or wherein special circumstances would require an immediate departure of one of the spouses, so that the determination of its lawfulness would necessarily become a matter of subsequent judgment. Allowance was accordingly made for such special cases.[23]

---

[21] Cf. infra, Chapter V.

[22] Conc. Trident., sess. XXIV, *de matrimonio,* can. 12: "Si quis dixerit, causas matrimoniales non spectare ad iudices ecclesiasticos: anathema sit."

[23] Sixtus V (1585–1590), Const. "Ad compescendam," 30 oct. 1586: "Et propterea nefas est coniuges fideles se propria voluntate aut arbitrio a coniugali toro separare, nisi ex causa a sacris canonibus permissa, et auctoritate ac iudicio Ecclesiae cognita et probata. Idcirco, ne quis in posterum huiusmodi facinus impune committat vel attentare audeat, apostolica auctoritate statuimus et ordinamus ut coniuges, qui quaeve, indissolubilem matrimonii nexum divina lege copulatum contemnentes, sine Ecclesiae iudicio seu ecclesiastici iudicis sententia, propria temeritate, a communi cohabitatione decesserint, aut se a coniugali toro separare praesumpserint, pro excessus gravitate puniantur."—*Bullarum Diplomatum et Privilegiorum Romanorum Pontificum Taurinensis Editio* (24 vols. et Appendix, Augustae Taurinorum, 1857–1872), VIII (1572–1588), 789–794, sec. 2.

The III Plenary Council of Baltimore (1884), faced with the special problem of married persons seeking a separation before civil courts without having obtained ecclesiastical permission, saw fit to issue to such couples a warning of the grave offense they were committing and of the punishment to which at the discretion of the bishop they became liable.[24]

Even though the Church was recognized as the ultimate authority for determining whether a separation should be granted, yet at the same time it was also an acknowledged practice that within set limits a discontinuance of mutual cohabitation could lawfully take place on private authority. Thus a separation, temporary or perpetual, was permitted under certain circumstances by means of the mutual consent of the parties concerned. Likewise, when one of the parties had been guilty of adultery, of heresy, of schism, or of apostasy, the innocent party had a right to leave, provided that certain conditions were verified.[25] The right of the innocent party to separate in these cases had the character of a concession, so that the exercise of the right was not obligatory unless the foreseen consequence of scandal or the recognized danger of perversion necessitated a departure.[26]

---

[24] "Praeterea, quo magis magisque dignitati matrimonii consulatur, quod magnum in Ecclesia Sacramentum est, a quo innumera bona profluunt pro animarum salute, pro pace familiarum, pro ipsius civilis reipublicae incolumitate ac prosperitate; iis omnibus, qui matrimonio conjuncti sunt, praecipimus, ne inconsulta auctoritate ecclesiastica, tribunalia civilia adeant ad obtinendam separationem a thoro et mensa. Quod si quis attentaverit, sciat se gravem reatum incurrere et pro Episcopi judicio puniendum esse." —*Acta et Decreta Concilii Plenarii Baltimorensis Tertii,* A.D. MDCCCLXXXIV (Baltimore: John Murphy & Co., 1886), n. 126.

[25] Schmalzgrueber, *Ius Ecclesiasticum Universum,* lib. IV, tit. XIX, n. 98.

[26] Sanchez, *De Matrimonii Sacramento,* lib. X, disp. XII, n. 12; Schmalzgrueber, *op. cit.,* lib. IV, tit. XIX, n. 110; Pirhing, *Ius Canonicum,* lib. IV, tit. XIX, n. 15.

CHAPTER III

DOMICILE AS A DETERMINANT OF ECCLESIASTICAL JURIDICAL COMPETENCY TILL THE COUNCIL OF TRENT

Before any treatise regarding a wife's legal domicile in particular can be profitably undertaken, a brief general historical survey of domicile in canonical jurisprudence, as the same affected juridical competency, is in order. This treatment is divided historically as follows: (a) from the beginning to the *Decree of Gratian* (ca. 1140); (b) from the *Decree of Gratian* to the Council of Trent (1545–1563); and (c) from the Council of Trent to the enactment of the Code of Canon Law (1918).

Article A. From the Beginning to the "Decree of Gratian"

The theory of domicile as a canonical institute determining juridical competency was not applied in the early centuries of ecclesiastical legislation. The word "domicile" is said not to have been mentioned in early juridical language.[1] This does not mean that persons in any particular locality were freed from local jurisdiction. Certainly there was local residence, a fact in itself which bespoke some public authority, and even in the time of the Barbarian invasions personal supervision was not lacking. But the fact of local residence had ceased to serve for a theory of domicile.[2]

Canonical regulations concerning judicial competency were not based on domicile as such in the discipline of the early Church. The Roman theory which might have proved beneficial was lost, or at least was not adverted to, by the canonists of this period.[3]

---

[1] Costello, *Domicile and Quasi-Domicile*, pp. 29–30.

[2] Costello, *op. cit.*, p. 29.

[3] The extension of the rights of Roman citizenship to all the inhabitants

Likewise, by way of example, domicile was not the controlling factor in other ecclesiastical matters. Early legislation provided that no bishop should ordain a layman of another bishop, i.e., of a bishop of the candidate's place of origin, which legislation received subsequent confirmation.[4] But later practice led to the conclusion that a bishop was free to ordain the laymen of another bishop, that is, such as resided in his territory.[5] Previous ordination rather than domicile determined the proper ordaining minister in the case of clerics.[6] Even with the pronouncement of the Council of London (1125), "*Nullus episcopus alterius praesumat parochianum ordinare . . . ,*"[7] nothing had been determined for ascertaining what constituted one a parishioner, or what subjected a candidate to a certain bishop for ordination. Thomassinus (1619–1695) concluded that the bishop determinable by the place of the man's origin was to be recognized as the proper bishop for the candidate's ordination.[8] Since Gratian made no mention of domicile in relation to the proper bishop of ordination, Costello concludes that during the period preceding the time of Gratian "candidates for the reception of Orders became a bishop's subjects by birth or previous ordination, not by domicile."[9] It was not until the time of Pope Boniface VIII (1294–1303) that domicile became of importance in the determination of the proper bishop for ordination.[10]

Concerning the sacrament of matrimony, it was not until the publication of the decree "*Tametsi*" that domicile became a controlling element in the determination of the required competence for assistance at the marriage.[11] Yet the juridical authority of

---

of the Empire by Emperor Caracalla (d. 217) in the year 212 by the *Constitutio Antoniana* is suggested as a possible explanation for the loss of the theory of domicile during this period.

[4] Council of Sardica (343), c. 18—Mansi, III, 37; Council of Carthage (ca. 350), c. 5—Mansi, III, 47.

[5] Thomassinus, *Vetus et Nova Ecclesiae Disciplina circa Beneficia et Beneficiarios* (Magontiaci, 1787), Pars II, lib. I, cap. VII, nn. 1–5.

[6] Fourneret, *Le Domicile Matrimonial*, pp. 81–82.

[7] C. 10—Mansi, XXI, 332.

[8] Thomassinus, *op. cit.*, Pars II, lib. I, cap. VII, n. 11.

[9] Costello, *op. cit.*, p. 32.

[10] C. 3, *de temporibus ordinationum*, I, 9, in VI°.

[11] Costello, *op. cit.*, p. 30.

the Church was widely exercised during this period in connection with matrimonial cases, and that by reason of the esteemed position of the bishops.[12] The provincial councils legislated concerning the sacrament, and the bishops, as ministers of the Crown, applied the canonical rules to the cases proposed.[13]

Principles concerning juridical competence were few in number, and these were not fully developed. A bishop was limited to the judgment of his own parishioners, while a person judged by one other than his own bishop was not bound by the decision.[14] Residence was a determining factor in the election of a competent judge in a matter wherein a lay person was the defendant. This is evident from the provisions of Pope Pelagius I (555–561), found in the Decree of Gratian, as providing that the lay defendant had to appear before the judge of his own province. If the defendant was a cleric, then the matter was properly brought before the court of his bishop.[15] These were applications of the general principle: "*Actor sequitur forum rei,*" rather than a use of domicile as the guiding norm for determining competency.

It is in connection with the questions of tithes and sepulture that Gratian, in his *dictum,* for the first time in canonical history mentioned the word *domicile.*[16] He mentioned it, but did not offer any further enlightenment as to what was to be understood as constituting domicile, or as to what were its proper canonical effects. Relative to a canon of the Council of Tribur (895), which canon referred to ecclesiastical burial,[17] Gratian mentioned domicile for the second time.[18] The Council of Tribur had said: ". . . ubi quis decimas persolvebat vivus, ibi sepeliatur mortuus." Repeating these words, Gratian in his *dictum* continued: Likewise if anyone should go from one province to another and should establish in the latter place his domicile, then as one free from the jurisdiction of the prior judge, he would be subject to the

---

12 Joyce, *Christian Marriage,* p. 222.

13 Council of Agde (506), c. 25—Mansi, VIII, 329.

14 *Capitularium Caroli Magni,* lib. VIII, n. 308—Mansi, XVIIb, 1093; Council of London (1125), c. 10—Mansi, XXI, 332.

15 C. 15, 16, C. XI, q. 1.

16 C. 1, C. XIII, q. 1; c. 6, C. XIII, q. 2; Costello, *op. cit.,* p. 34.

17 Can. 16—Mansi, XVIII, 140.

18 C. 6, C. XIII, q. 2.

jurisdiction of the judge in whose province he had chosen to remain.[19] From this evident recognition of the theory of domicile, and of its juridical effect, it is only natural to expect a rapid and widespread development in the following period.

Article B. From the "Decree of Gratian" to the Council of Trent

Although the Decretals of Pope Gregory IX (1227–1241) neither gave a definition nor established any theory regarding domicile, yet a very definite advance in the meaning and importance of this institution was made during the period under consideration, and this progress was due principally to the efforts of the Glossators and Commentators on Decretal law.

Section 1. Civil Jurists of Bologna

During this period, and contemporaneous with the canonical writers, a school of civil jurists at Bologna begun by Irnerius (1050?–1130?) concerned themselves with the writing of glosses and commentaries on Roman law.[20]

Accursius (1185–1260), a glossator of this school, made several departures in the teaching of Roman law concerning domicile. For example, the "*origo*" of Roman law was taught by Accursius to be the place of birth, whether personal or paternal, whereas in reality, it signified the legal bond attaching one to a certain city, and at the same time signified the "ius originis," i.e., the sum of citizen rights in a particular city.[21] This same glossator considered domicile as the font from which flowed both the "*domicilium originis*" and the "*domicilium habitationis.*"[22] "In a word," Costello says, "Accursius sponsored and established an institution unknown in Roman law, a distortion of the Roman *origo,* the domicile of origin."[23]

---

19 "Item si quis de provincia ad provinciam transiret et ibi domicilium sibi collocaret, liber factus a ditione prioris iudicis, iurisdictioni illius iudicis, subiceretur, in cuius provincia sedem sibi eligeret."—*Dictum* ad c. 6, C. XIII, q. 2.

20 Costello, *op. cit.,* p. 36.

21 Cf. *supra,* p. 3.

22 D.(50.1) (27.2), *Glossa:* s.v. *domicilio.*

23 Costello, *op. cit.,* p. 37.

Another example of departure by Accursius was his extension to all classes of a presumption made by the Emperor Hadrian (117–138) on the part of students residing for ten years in a university town.[24] The teaching of Accursius became the accepted opinion of almost all canonical writers, and thus the correct interpretations of Roman law made by Cujas (1522–1590) in the sixteenth century were destined to serve only as matter for research.[25]

SECTION 2. DECRETALS OF POPE GREGORY IX

Domicile was definitely acknowledged in the Decretals of Pope Gregory IX (1227–1241) as a possible basis for establishing one's proper forum and judicial competency in a particular case. Pope Gregory IX, writing to the Abbot of Troyes between the years 1227–1234, specifically listed domicile as a recognized possible basis for determining one's proper forum.[26] In this letter, as in another to a bishop in England, the Pope placed domicile, in the matter of the proper forum, on a par with other determinants, e.g., the site of the commission of a crime, the particular place where the contract was sealed, and the location of the thing over which the dispute was had.[27] Hence, though neither a doctrinal theory nor a juridical definition of domicile is found in the Decretals, yet it was in the Decretals themselves that domicile received official recognition as an ecclesiastical institution.[28]

Besides being a determinant of one's proper forum, the institute of domicile became the basis for establishing other ecclesiastical rights and obligations. Pope Boniface VIII (1294–1303) pointed

---

[24] D.(47.10)(5.5); C.(10.40)2, *Glossa:* s.v. *constituerint;* Costello, *op. cit.*, pp. 21, 38.

[25] Cujas, "*Opera Omnia*" (13 vols. in 12, Venetiis, 1758–1783), III, 660.

[26] "Licet ratione delicti, seu contractus, aut domicilii, sive rei, de qua contra possessorem causa movetur, quibus forum regulariter quis sortitur, episcopus vester apud sedem apostolicam conventus non fuerit, quia tamen omnium ecclesiarum mater est eadem et magistra, rite compelli potuit, ut ibi suis adversariis responderet, nisi pro alia iusta et necessaria causa venisset, quam si tunc allegasset, ius revocandi domum salvum fuisset eidem." —c. 20, X, *de foro competenti,* II, 2.

[27] C. 17, X, *de foro competenti,* II, 2.

[28] Costello, *op. cit.*, p. 41.

out specifically that the "*proprius episcopus*" for the conferring of the sacrament of Orders was the bishop of the candidate's place of domicile,[29] and the church to which one had been attached by domicile was the proper recipient of the canonical portion that was to be paid on the occasion of the individual parishioner's burial.[30]

SECTION 3. GLOSSATORS AND COMMENTATORS ON THE DECRETALS

It is necessary to have recourse to the writings of the Glossators and the Commentators on Decretal law to discover the notion and the extent of domicile as it was accepted in canonical jurisprudence. The *Glossa ordinaria* on the *Decree of Gratian* was written by Joannes Teutonicus (Semeca or Zemecke), who died in 1245. This gloss was revised and completed shortly thereafter by Bartholomew of Brescia (d. 1258). The latter followed the teachings of Accursius on the matter of the nature of domicile.[31] Bernard of Parma (d. 1266) composed an *Apparatus* on the Decretals of Gregory IX, which composition was received as the *Glossa Ordinaria.* Concerned principally with a practical application of the factor of domicile, he noted that domicile made one a parishioner in a determined parish.[32]

In the light of the established fact of what in particular constituted one a parishioner, this same element could readily be considered as a juridical basis for the subjection of an individual to the competent jurisdiction which obtained in a specified area.[33] From this there could follow, as in reality it did, the determination of one's proper forum and competent judge.[34]

Ioannes Andreae (1272–1348), author of the *Glossa ordinaria* on the *Liber Sextus* of Pope Boniface VIII, as early as the year 1303 introduced into Canon law the concept of the domicile of

[29] C. 3, *de temporibus ordinationum,* I, 9, in VI°.

[30] C. 2, *de sepulturis,* III, 12, in VI°.

[31] C. 6, C. XIII, q. 2, *Glossa,* s.v. *liber factus;* c. 6, D. LXXI, *Glossa,* s.v. *obtinet.*

[32] C. 2, X, *de parochis et alienis parochianis,* III, 29, *Glossa,* s.v. *si alterius.*

[33] C. 5, X, *de parochis et alienis parochianis,* III, 29, *Glossa,* s.v. *habitatores iurisdictionem.*

[34] "Ratione domicilii sortitur quis forum, et ibi potest conveniri."—c. 20, X, *de foro competenti,* II, 2, *Glossa,* s.v. *aut domicilii.*

origin.[35] Likewise the application of the presumption of the ten years' residence rule was accepted as well as other points of the Bolognese theory, e.g., that of multiple domiciles held by the same individual, and that of the absence of any domicile whatever in certain circumstances of a person's life.[36]

Zenzelinus de Cassanis (d. 1334), in writing his *Glossa* on the *Extravagentes* of Pope John XXII (1316–1334), followed closely the theory of Accursius. This was particularly true in his acceptance of the domicile of origin,[37] and concerning the possibility of a person's having more than one domicile.[38]

That the canonical concept of the institution of domicile was deeply influenced by the contemporary Roman law doctrine is apparent from the commentary of Hostiensis (d. 1271). He defined domicile as follows: " Intelligitur quis ibi habere domicilium, ubi larem tenet et maiorem partem fortunarum suarum, et ubi venit, ubi emit, ubi dies festos colit, et si ab hac discedat peregrinari videtur, et cum redierit peregrinari desiit." [39] The holding of property was not a necessary qualification for the establishment of a domicile.[40] A comparison of these ideas, and even of their wording, with the concept and the pronouncement of the Emperors and of Ulpian, discloses a very marked resemblance.[41] Hostiensis accepted the generalization of the ten years' residence rule as established by the jurists of Bologna. He too recognized that one could be without a domicile, and termed such an individual a *viator*.[42]

Concerning Durantis (1238–1296) it is to be noted that he

---

[35] C. 3, *de temporibus ordinationum,* I, 9, in VIo, *Glossa,* s.v. *oriundus.*

[36] C. 3, *de sepulturis,* III, 12, in VIo, *Glossa,* s.v. *is qui;* c. 2, *de sepulturis,* III, in VIo, *Glossa,* s.v. *domicilia.*

[37] C. un., *de praebendis et dignitatibus,* tit. III, in Extravag. Ioan. XXII, *Glossa,* s.v. *commorantur.*

[38] C. un., *de praebendis et dignitatibus,* tit. III, in Extravag. Ioan. XXII, *Glossa,* s.v. *vagandi materia.*

[39] Hostiensis (Henricus de Segusio), *Commentaria in Quinque Decretalium Libros* (5 vols. in 3, Venetiis, 1581), Tom. I, lib. I, tit. 3, cap. 29, n. 7. Cf. C.(10.40)7.

[40] Hostiensis, *op. cit.,* Tom. I, lib. II, tit. 2, cap. 15, n. 3.

[41] D.(50.1)(27.1); C.(10.40)7.

[42] Hostiensis, *op. cit.,* Tom. II, lib. III, tit. 28, cap. 10, n. 8.

recognized domicile as a means of obtaining a proper forum and competent judge. He repeated the definition given by the Emperors, and he acknowledged that a person did not of necessity have a domicile. A person who had no domicile he termed a *vagabundus.*[43]

Abbas Panormitanus (Nicolaus de Tudeschis, 1386–1453) followed the theory expounded by Accursius in relation to the nature of the domicile of origin and of the ten years' residence rule.[44] On other points in connection with domicile and its effects his commentary was largely in harmony with the theory contained in Roman law. His teaching with regard to particular points, such as one's proper forum, one's parochial church, and one's relation to local jurisdictional power, was that these were determined by one's domicile.[45]

From the long list of citations furnished by Bertachinus (1448–1497) in the latter part of the fifteenth century in his *Repertorium* under the word "*Domicilium,*" it is evident that at the end of this period this institute was very much the subject of discussion among the canonists, and had taken its place among the established canonical institutes.

SECTION 4. LEGAL DOMICILE OF THE WIFE IN CANON LAW

The late acceptance and development of the theory of domicile in canon law did not prevent the early establishment of the fundamental principle that in general the wife could be said to have the duty to follow her husband.[46] As has been seen, in early Roman law the married woman had the domicile of her husband.[47] But even in the absence of this principle it seems quite natural, from the nature of the sacramental bond, and from the principal

[43] *Speculum Iuris* (3 vols., Venetiis, 1760), Pars II, lib. II, partic. I, *de competentis Iudicis Aditione,* n. 30.

[44] *Commentaria Super Quinque Libros Decretalium* (5 vols. in 7, Venetiis 1588), c. 14, X, *de foro competenti,* II, 2, n. 4 (hereafter cited *Commentaria*).

[45] Panormitanus, *Commentaria,* c. 20, X, *de foro competenti,* II, 2, n. 2; c. 10, X, *de sepulturis,* III, 28, n. 10; c. 5, X, *de parochis, et alienis parochianis,* II, 29, n. 4.

[46] "Unaquaeque mulier sequatur virum suum sive in vita sive in morte." —C. 3, C. 13, q. 2.

[47] *Supra,* pp. 5–6.

ends of the sacrament of matrimony, that the married woman should have the same place of abode as her husband, and that her intention of remaining should correspond and be subject to her husband's intention. When these two elements, residence and intention, were determined as the constitutive elements of domicile, it was natural that the Roman law principle concerning husband and wife in this matter should have been accepted together with the theory of domicile in general.

Gratian in stating the principle, ". . . *mulier sequatur virum suum, sive in vita sive in morte,*" offered no other comment than to cite examples from the Holy Scriptures in regard to the burial of the spouses of biblical personages.

As to the extension of the principle, i.e., whether or not it allowed of exceptions, and whether or not it applied only to the place of burial, the *Glossa* on the word "*sequatur*" indicated that it was not so limited, and that it did allow of exception. In the *Glossa,* Huguccio of Pisa (d. 1210) is quoted as not allowing any exception to the general rule: "Similiter dicit quod debet ipsum sequi, etiam si mittatur in carcerem, vel si cogatur ire in exercitum." It was the contention of Huguccio that a certain provision which was attributed to the Council of Verberie (756) had been abrogated. According to that provision the choice of accompanying or of not accompanying her husband was recognized for the wife, with the restriction, however, that thereafter she abstain from marrying another if she had chosen not to accompany her husband.[48] Gratian had incorporated this provision in the *Decretum.*[49]

The *Glossa ordinaria* seems not to agree with Huguccio. In the *Glossa* it seems that the wife's prenuptial knowledge of her husband's condition or state in life determined her obligation. If she had been in ignorance of his being a vagabond, she did not have to follow him; if she had been unaware of his physical

[48] *Monumenta Germaniae Historica, Legum Sectio II, Capitularia Regum Francorum,* Tom. I (ed. V. Krause, Hannoverae, 1897), p. 41.

[49] "Si quis necessitate inevitabili cogente in alium ducatum, seu provinciam fugerit, et eius uxor, cum valet, et potest, amore parentum, et rerum suarum eum sequi noluerit; ipsa omni tempore quamdiu vir eius, quem secuta non fuit, vivit, semper innupta permaneat."—c. 4, C. XXXIV, qq. 1, 2.

affliction, e.g., leprosy, likewise she did not have to go with him.[50]

This principle in its application is illustrated in the decretal legislation. In a case wherein the husband fled to escape punishment for the commission of a crime, his wife was not held to follow him.[51] In this particular case Pope Alexander III (1159–1181), addressing his words to the Bishop of Parma, held that it was proper to proceed to judgment, since the husband was absent by reason of his own fault, and the evidence showed that due diligence had been used to summon him.

Regardless of the principle—that is, concerning the duty of the wife to follow her husband—and its operation, with the acceptance of the theory of domicile in canon law, recognition was accorded to the Roman law principle that the domicile of the wife followed that of her husband.

Panormitanus furnished quite a detailed commentary on the matter of domicile, particularly in reference to it as a determinant of the competent forum.[52] According to this commentator the husband had the right to choose and to change the conjugal domicile, and the wife had the duty to follow him.[53] The wife, as it were, received her domicile from the person of the husband.[54] And yet, this was not such an absolute rule that it did not allow of exception.[55] This same commentator specifically allowed that

---

[50] " Credo, quod si sciret eum esse histrionem, tenetur eum sequi, alia non. Huggucio tamen dicit, quod semper debet ipsum sequi etiam si mittatur in carcerem, vel si cogatur ire in exercitum. Sed eadem ratione debet ipsum sequi quoties dominus petit a viro qui est servus ut serviat sibi. Lex tamen dicit, quod postquam liberta nupsit voluntate patroni, quodammodo non debet servire patrono, propter suspicionem."—*Glossa* ad c. 4, C. XXXIV, qq. 1, 2.

[51] C. 1, X, *qui matrimonium accusare possunt, vel contra illud testificari,* IV, 18.

[52] *Commentaria,* Lib. II, tit. II, cap. 9, nn. 4, 5.

[53] " Si tamen ex causa se transfert ad alia loca, vel etiam sine causa mutando domicilium, tenetur maritum sequi."—*op. cit.,* ad c. 5, X, *de sponsalibus et matrimoniis,* IV, 1, n. 5.

[54] ". . . quia uxor sortitur domicilium ex persona mariti . . ."—*op. cit.,* ad c. 20, X, *de foro competenti,* II, 2, n. 30.

[55] " In uxore distinguendum. Aut sciebat maritum vagabundum quando secum contraxit, puta quia erat iuxta locum mariti, et tenetur eum sequi. aut ignorbat vel ex post facto vagabundus est factus, et non tenetur maritum

the wife was not compelled to follow her husband if she had been ignorant of his status as a vagabond. Again, it was necessary to explore the question as to when she had come to the knowledge. If she learned of it only after the marriage, she was not held to follow the husband.

The question was raised whether or not the spouses could lawfully make a prenuptial contract that would reverse the general rule, i.e., that the husband could permit the wife to choose the place of domicile, so that he would be bound to go wherever she desired. It seems that such an agreement was regarded as lawful, but it was at the same time held that such an agreement existed in the nature of a voidable contract. In other words, it was seen that readily enough there could arise a situation in which the contract would cease to be operative. Changed circumstances could make it necessary for the husband to absent himself, and in such a case the general rule was to be preferred to the special contract.[56]

Again, if the husband decided to go on a long pilgrimage, the wife did not of necessity have to accompany him if she did not so choose, but the option thus granted to her did not affect the general rule in regard to her domicile. Panormitanus did however set down two instances wherein the wife was not obliged to continue to live with her husband, so that her departure from him did affect the status of her domicile, namely, when the marriage was claimed not to be a lawful wedlock in the face of the extant impediment of spiritual relationship, or when it became established that the husband was a vagabond.[57]

---

sequi."—*op. cit.,* ad c. 1, X, *qui matrimonium accusare possunt,* IV, 18, n. 6.

[56] *Op. cit., loc. cit.*

[57] "Primo, quia negabat matrimonium esse inter eos saltem legitimum obstante cognatione spirituali. Secundo, quod iste vir vagabatur."—*op. cit.,* c. 1, X, *qui matrimonium accusare possunt,* IV, 18, n. 3.

CHAPTER IV

DOMICILE AS A JURIDICAL FACTOR FROM THE COUNCIL OF TRENT TO THE ENACTMENT OF THE CODE OF CANON LAW

Article A. Legal Domicile of the Wife

Section 1. Nature of this Legal Domicile

The Council of Trent (1545–1563) did not legislate directly concerning the canonical institute of domicile. However, the subsequent determination of who was the proper pastor for publishing the banns of marriage, and the further determination of who was the pastor before whom the marriage could lawfully and validly be celebrated, as required by the Council, resulted in a juridical recognition of the constitutent elements of domicile. The Council had provided that the banns should be published "*a proprio contrahentium parocho*," and that the marriage should be celebrated before the "parochus."[1] Subsequent pronouncements determined that the proper pastor before whom the marriage was to be celebrated was the pastor of the place wherein the spouses or either of them had a domicile. In a response of the Sacred Congregation of the Council[2] on September 5, 1626, domicile as the determinant factor is clearly indicated. This response was confirmed on March 19, 1758, in the Letter "*Paucis abhinc*" of Pope Benedict XIV (1740–1758), and ratified by the same Pope in a decree "*Exponi Nobis fecit*" in the year of his death.[3]

---

[1] Conc. Trident., sess. XXIV, *de ref. matrim.*, c. 1.

[2] This Congregation was originally known as the "Sacra Congregatio Cardinalium Concilii Tridentini Interpretum." It was instituted by Pope Pius IV on January 26, 1563.

[3] *Bullarium Pontificium Sacrae Congregationis de Propaganda Fide* (5 vols., 2 appendices, and index. Romae: Typis Collegii Urbani, 1839–1858), Appendix II, pp. 216–222; Benedictus XIV, *Institutiones Ecclesiasticae* (3 vols., Lovanii, 1762), Inst. XXXIII, n. 5.

However, the constitutive elements of intention and of residence, so clearly evident in the establishing of a voluntary domicile, were lacking in the constitution of the legal domicile of the wife. This type of domicile in canon law continued to follow the Roman conception, and was fixed by the operation of the law itself. The wife acquired the domicile of her husband upon the celebration of the marriage, and this domicile she continued to retain even in widowhood until she might have acquired another domicile by her own free choice.[4]

SECTION 2. DETERMINATION OF THE WIFE'S PROPER FORUM

Domicile as a basis for the determination of the proper forum had been decreed by Pope Innocent III (1198–1216).[5] The Council of Trent, not speaking directly of domicile, legislated that "matrimonial and criminal causes shall not be left to the judgment of a dean, archdeacon or other inferiors, even in the course of their visitation, but shall be reserved to the examination and jurisdiction of the bishop only . . ."[6]

The Congregation of the Council clarified the issue as to what was necessary with reference to the factor of domicile in the establishment of a proper forum. On January 28, 1865, this Congregation by its decision clearly indicated that, although one was regularly said to acquire his forum in view of the place where the delict was committed, where the contract was made, where the dwelling-place was, or where the thing in dispute was situated, yet the forum of domicile could be properly termed, inasmuch as it actually also was the natural and ordinary forum, the forum of more far-reaching import, and the forum which was concurrent with all the others here mentioned; that it was sufficient that the defendant be subject to the ecclesiastical court by reason of some domicile recognized in canon law; and that the wife appropriated the forum in which her husband had his domicile.[7]

---

[4] Schmalzgrueber, *Ius Ecclesiasticum Universum,* lib. III, tit. III, nn. 147–148.

[5] C. 20, X, *de foro competenti,* II, 2.

[6] Conc. Trident., sess. XXIV, *de ref. matrim.,* c. 20; Schroeder, *Canons and Decrees of the Council of Trent* (St. Louis: Herder, 1941), p. 211.

[7] "Quamvis regulariter quis forum sortiri dicatur, iuxta caput 'Licet,'

These general principles had been recognized and confirmed by the canonical writers in the preceding centuries. For example, Schmalzgrueber (1663–1735) had stated: ". . . ubi enim maritus domicilium habet, habet et uxor, atque id etiam vidua retinet, quamdiu talis manet." [8]

The principles regarding the proper forum in matrimonial causes were incorporated in an Instruction drawn up and promulgated for the Austro-Hungarian Empire in 1855 by Joseph Cardinal Rauscher (1797–1875), Prince-Archbishop of Vienna (1853–1875).[9] The influence of this *Austrian Instruction* is clearly discernible in an Instruction of the Sacred Congregation for the Propagation of the Faith in the year 1883.[10] This Instruction, hereafter referred to as "*Causae matrimoniales*," of the Sacred Congregation for the Propagation of the Faith concerned the procedure to be followed in matrimonial causes, and incorporated verbatim several of the sections of the *Austrian Instruction.* Of particular interest is section ninety-six of the latter, which section ninety-six had provided for two exceptions to the

---

de Foro Competenti, ratione delicti, contractus, domicilii, rei sitae; tamen domicilii forum dici et esse naturalem, ordinarium, universaliorem, et cum caeteris concurrentem. II . . . Sufficit enim quod Reus conventus per aliquod domicilium iuxta canonicam doctrinam subditus evaserit alicuius ecclesiasticae Curiae, ubi conveniri possit. III. Uxorem forum sortiri in quo vir suum domicilium habet."—*Acta Sanctae Sedis* (41 vols., 1865–1908), II (1866), 137–141.

[8] *Ius Ecclesiasticum Universum,* Lib. II, tit. III, n. 12.

[9] Instructio Austriaca Josephi Cardinalis Rauscher, 4 maii, 1855—*Analecta Iuris Pontificii* (Romae, 1855–1868; Parisiis, 1869–1890), II (1857), 2546–2565 (henceforth referred to as the *Austrian Instruction*); *Acta et Decreta Sacrorum Concilionum Recentionum, Collectio Lacensis* (7 vols., Friburgi Brisgaviae: Herder, 1870–1890), V, pp. 1286–1316; Vaughan, *Constitutions for Diocesan Courts,* The Catholic University of America Canon Law Studies, n. 210 (Washington, D. C.: The Catholic University of America, 1944), pp. 3–5.

[10] S. C. de Prop. Fide, instr. a. 1883 (no other date), n. 2—*Codicis Iuris Canonici Fontes,* cura Emi Petri Card. Gasparri editi (9 vols., Romae [postea Civitate Vaticana]: Typis Polyglottis Vaticanis, 1923–1939; [Vols. VII, VIII, IX, ed. cura et studio Emi Iustiniani Card. Serédi]), n. 4901 (henceforth this collection of sources will be cited *Fontes*).

general rule for determining juridical competency based on domicile.[11]

The second paragraph of the Instruction "*Causae matrimoniales*" confirmed the general rule for determining the competent forum in marriage causes, but at the same time recognized two exceptions, namely, causes of separation *a toro et mensa* and of malicious desertion. In the prior case each party had the right of bringing the other before the diocesan court of the diocese in which the defendant (*pars rea*) resided; in the latter case, that of malicious desertion, the deserted wife was entitled to institute her cause either before the bishop of the diocese in which she resided or before the bishop of the diocese in which her deserting spouse had his domicile.[12]

The III Plenary Council of Baltimore (1884) enjoined the exact observance of the Instruction "*Causae matrimoniales.*" It recommended likewise a consultation of the *Austrian Instruction,* even though this had had authority only in the Austro-Hungarian Empire. Specifically the Council enjoined that the second paragraph of the Instruction "Causae matrimoniales" was to be the norm for the determination of competency on the part of judges in marriage cases.[13]

---

[11] "Sec. 96—Conjuges in caussis matrimonialibus subsunt Episcopo, in cujus dioecesi maritus domicilium habet. Exceptioni locus est, si conjugale vitae consortium aut per separationem a thoro et mensa aut per desertionem malitiosam a marito patratam sublatum sit. Priori casu quaelibet pars jus accusandi contra alteram ipsi competens coram Episcopo dioecesis, ubi haecce domicilium habet, exercere debet. Posteriori casu uxor apud Episcopum, intra cujus dioecesim domicilium ejus situm est, actionem instituere potest. Postquam citatio judicialis intimata est mutatio quoad conjugum domicilium facta mutationem respectu judicis competentis minime operatur."—*Analecta Iuris Pontificii,* II (1857), 2526.

[12] S. C. de Prop. Fide, instr. a. 1883 (no other date), n. 2: "Coniuges in causis matrimonialibus subsunt Episcopo in cuius dioecesi maritus domicilium habet. Exceptioni locus est si coniugale vitae consortium aut per separationem a toro et mensa, aut per desertionem malitiosam a marito patratam sublatum sit. Priori casu quaelibet pars ius accusandi contra alteram ipsi competens, coram Episcopo dioecesis, ubi haecce domicilium habet, exercere debet. Posteriori casu uxor apud Episcopum, intra cuius dioecesim domicilium eius situm est, actionem instituere potest."—*Fontes,* n. 4901.

[13] §2. *In Causis Matrimonialibus.* 304. In agendis hisce causis pro rei gravitate exacte servetur tum Constitutio Benedicti XVI, *Dei Miseratione,*

That the domicile of the husband continued to specify the proper forum for the determining of the matrimonial causes is seen from a reply of the Sacred Congregation of the Holy Office under date of June 30, 1892.[14] If the cause concerned a mixed marriage, the bishop of the diocese in which the Catholic party had his or her domicile was the proper judge to determine the cause; if both parties were Catholics, the cause was subject for its determination to the bishop in whose diocese the husband had his domicile. Continued confirmation of this juridical rule of competence may be noted in the reply of the Sacred Congregation of the Holy Office in the year 1903.[15]

Article B. Quasi-Domicile of the Wife

Quasi-domicile is mentioned here because of its ultimate bearing on the proper forum of the wife. The Decretal Collection of Pope Gregory IX (1227–1234) did not make mention of quasi-domicile; it treated only of domicile as one of the possible determinants of the proper forum. Quasi-domicile was developed as a concept and came into prominence in the works of canonists after the Council of Trent (1545–1563), particularly in relation to the validity of marriages celebrated in places where the Decree "*Tametsi*" of the Council of Trent had not been published.

Reiffenstuel's (1647–1703) definition is here chosen as indica-

---

3 Nov. 1741, tum Instructio a S. Congr. de Prop. Fide Nobis communicata quae incipit *Causae Matrimoniales.* Utiliter etiam consuli poterit Instructio pro judiciis ecclesiasticis Imperii Austriaci in causis matrimonialibus, a. 1855 a gravibus theologis et canonistis Romanis, licet solo privato suo judicio, commendata. 305. . . . Quoad competentiam judicis servetur Instr. S. C. supra cit., §2."—*Acta et Decreta Plenarii Baltimorensis Tertii,* A D. MDCCCLXXXIV, nn. 304–305.

[14] S. C. S. Off. 30 iun., 1892: "Coniuges in causis mixtarum nuptiarum subsunt Episcopo in cuius dioecesi pars catholica domicilium habet; et quando ambo sunt catholici quia pars haeretica in Ecclesiae sinum reversa est, subsunt Episcopo in cuius dioecesi domicilium habet maritus."—*Fontes,* n. 1157.

[15] S. C. S. Off. (Colonien), 23 iun., 1903: "Quando vero agitur de matrimonio mixto contrahendo cum haeretico separato per divortii sententiam tribunalis civilis ab haeretica, erit Episcopus domicilii partis catholicae, ad quem spectat iudicare an contrahentes gaudeant status libertate."—*Fontes,* 1266.

tive of the common conception of quasi-domicile. "Per quasi-domicilium intelligitur habitatio dumtaxat temporalis, longior tamen, seu per maiorem partem anni, vel etiam plures annos alicuibi continuata, absque anima ibi perpetuo commorandi." [16] In his discussion of the nature and effects of quasi-domicile, Reiffenstuel followed the conclusions reached by Sanchez (1550–1610) with regard to the rights enjoyed by those within a parish who lived under conditions necessary for the acquisition of a quasi-domicile.[17] Schmalzgrueber (1663–1735) likewise held that such persons were truly parishioners of the place and thus were entitled to receive the sacraments, to be joined in marriage, to receive burial, and to be dispensed from vows—all of which matters constituted rights peculiar to parishioners.[18]

Quasi-domicile was officially recognized by Pope Benedict XIV (1740–1758) in his Letter "*Paucis abhinc.*" [19] In so far as the question affected the validity of marriages, the Holy Office, under date of June 7, 1867, replying to a petition of the Archbishop of Baltimore, granted that residence for a period of one month would suffice to establish a presumption in favor of the necessary time for contracting a valid union.[20]

---

[16] *Ius Canonicum Universum,* lib. II, tit. II, n. 22.

[17] Sanchez, *De Matrimonii Sacramento,* lib. III, disp. 23, nn. 13–14.

[18] *Ius Ecclesiasticum Universum,* lib. I, tit. II, n. 16.

[19] ". . . adeo ut ex sententia communiter hodie recepta atque observata nullum atque irritum habendum sit matrimonium, in fraudem proprii parochi coram parocho alterius loci contractus, dummodo tamen ille qui contrahit, antequam matrimonio iungatur, legitimum domicilium vel quasi-domicilium revera in hoc altero loco adeptus non fuisset, . . ."—*Bullarium Pontificium Sacrae Congregationis de Propaganda Fide,* Append. II, pp. 216–222. Cf. *Fontes,* n. 447.

[20] Epistola Emi. Card. Patrizi de Matrimoniis Clandestinis et Quasi-Domicilio: ". . . Ad constituendum vero quasi-domicilium, quod in hisce casibus necessario adipiscendum est, duo haec simul requiruntur, habitatio nempe in eo loco ubi matrimonium contrahitur, atque animus ibidem permanendi per maiorem anni partem. Quapropter si legitime constet, vel ambos vel alterutrum ex sponsis animum habere permanendi per maiorem anni partem, ex eo primum die quo duo haec simul concurrunt, nimirum et huiusmodi animus et actualis habitatio, iudicandum est quasi-domicilium acquisitum fuisse et matrimonium quod proinde contrahatur esse validum. Verumtamen, si de praedicto animo non constet, ad indicia recurrendum est quae praesto sint, quaeque moralem certitudem pariant. In re autem occulta

et interna difficile est huiusmodi indica habere quae iudicem securum faciant: inde est quod adhiberi maxime debet regula a summo Pontifice Benedicto XIV confirmata, ut inspiciatur utrum ante matrimonium spatio saltem unius mensis vel ambo vel alteruter in matrimonii loco habitaverint. Quod si factum fuisse deprehendatur, censendum est ex praesumptione iuris intentionem permanendi per maiorem anni partem extitisse, et quasi-domicilium fuisse acquisitum, proindeque matrimonium esse validum. At si praesumptio haec iuris, quae ex menstrua habitatione oritur, contrariis elidatur probationibus, quibus certo ac liquido constet praedictum animum nullo pacto extitisse, tunc profecto contrarium proferri debere iudicum manifestum est, quia praesumptio cedere debet veritati. Praeterea manifestum quoque est, actualem habitationem ineptam esse ad quasi-domicilium pariendum, si quis in ea regione more vagi ac itinerantis commoretur, non autem vere proprieque habitantis, quemadmodum scilicet ceteri solent qui in eodem loco verum proprieque dictum domicilium habent."—*Acta et Decreta Plenarii Baltimorensis Tertii,* A.D. MDCCCLXXXIV, pp. 255–256.

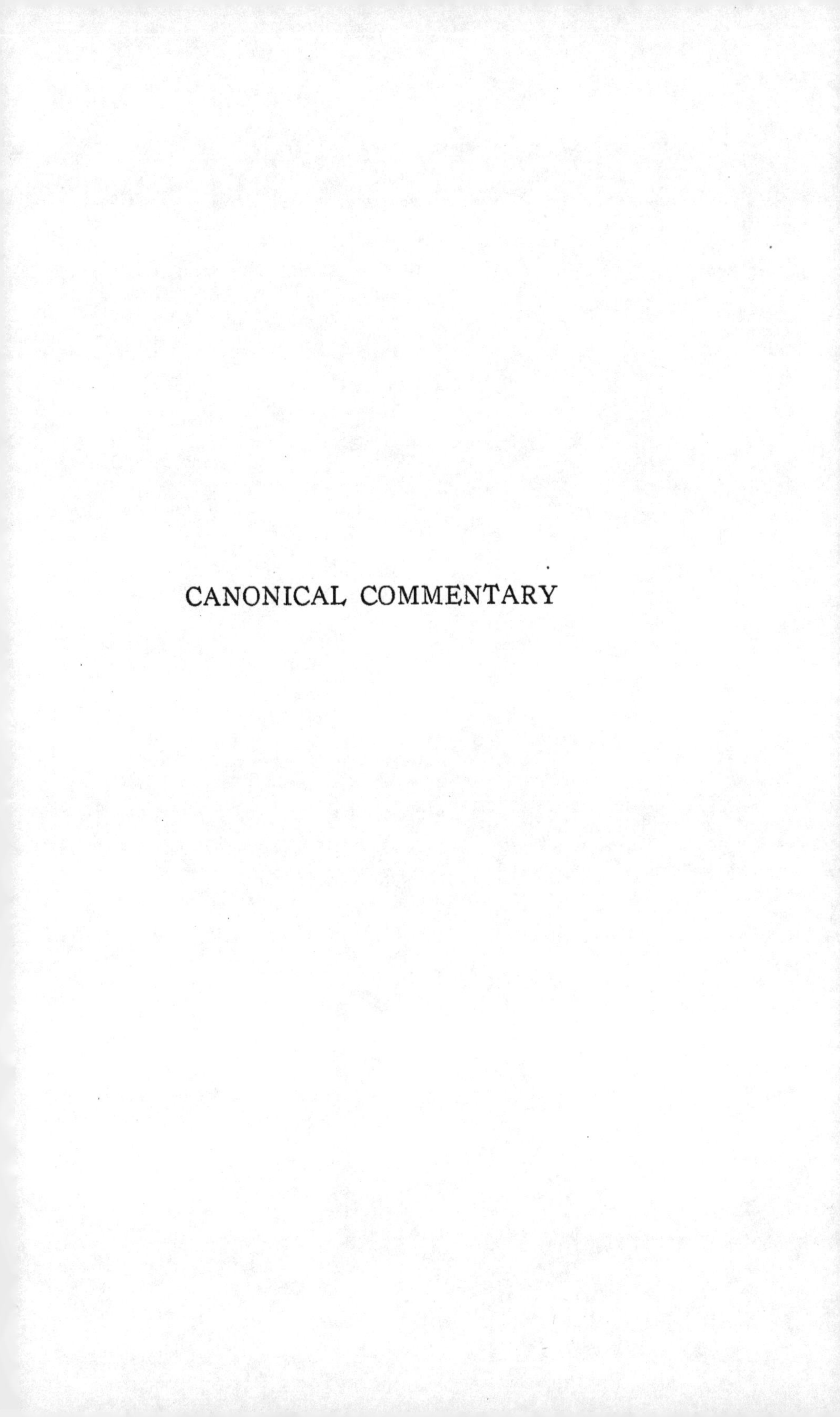

CANONICAL COMMENTARY

CHAPTER V

THE SEPARATION OF THE SPOUSES

Article A. Preliminary Notions

Never for an instant retreating from its doctrine of the indissolubility of the marriage bond of a ratified and consummated Christian marriage, the Church has ever recognized that circumstances and conditions at times may make or seem to make the attainment of the ideal most difficult. On certain occasions when the conjugal faith has been violated, when it seems impossible for the spouses to live together without manifest harm, in what the Church terms " extreme cases," imperfect separation of the parties is allowed.[1]

This granting of a separation and its juridical recognition, even in the " extreme cases," in no way weakens the firmness of the conjugal bond, and the Church in its insistence on the indissolubility of the marriage contract ever strives for a reconciliation between the parties and a restoration of the community of life.

SECTION 1. THE UNITY AND INDISSOLUBILITY OF THE MARRIAGE CONTRACT CONFIRMED BY THE CHURCH

The unity and indissolubility of the marriage contract are here spoken of because from these notes of the marital contract the element of community of life is determined as a natural consequence. This latter element must be considered in the act of adjudging the justification of the alleged cause as a factor sufficient to permit a lawful separation.

[1] Leo XIII, ep. encycl. "*Arcanum*," 10 febr. 1880, n. 25: "Quod si res eo devenerint, ut convictus ferri diutius non posse videatur, tum vero Ecclesia sinit alterum ab altera seorsum agere, adhibendisque curis ac remediis ad coniugum conditionem accomodatis, lenire studet secessionis incommoda: nec umquam committit, ut de reconcilianda concordia aut non laboret aut disperet. Verum haec extrema sunt; . . ."—*Fontes*, n. 580; *ASS* (41 vols., Romae, 1865–1908), XII (1879), 400–401.

Divine Revelation as well as the natural law are the foundations of the doctrinal position of the Church regarding the unity and indissolubility of the matrimonial contract.[2] The Code of Canon Law reaffirms this fundamental doctrine. Canon 1031, §2, of this Code establishes that unity and indissolubility are essential properties of marriage.[3]

The property of indissolubility which signalizes the valid consummated Christian marriage contract denotes the perpetuity of the marital bond whose dissolution is beyond any human power, and the Code in stating that indissolubility is an essential property of such a contract repeats the constant doctrine of the Church.[4]

The unity of marriage confirmed in the Code consists in a conjugal union of one man with one woman, and in this characteristic the Christian marital contract is opposed to polygyny and polyandry. The simultaneous possession of more than one husband is forbidden because of its inconsonance with the primary end of marriage, namely, the procreation and the education of children, and because of its absolute opposition to the secondary ends, namely, the mutual help and remedial effect against concupiscence. The practice of polygyny is not permissible since it is patently at variance with the law of the Gospel as the positively revealed word of God. Therefore neither polyandry nor polygyny can in any way be reconciled with the law of God, and hence neither of these can be tolerated in the face of the positive divine revelation which repudiates them.[5]

SECTION 2. COMMUNITY OF THE MARITAL LIFE

(a) The Nature of This Community of Life

Conjugal cohabitation implies community of roof, that is to say,

---

[2] Gen., I: 27–28; Matt., XIX: 3–9; Eph., V: 23–33.

[3] "Essentiales matrimonii proprietates sunt unitas ac indissolubilitas, quae in matrimonio christiano peculiarem obtinent firmitatem ratione sacramenti."

[4] C. 19, 39, C. XXVII, q. 2; c. 16, 26, C. XXXII, q. 7; Conc. Trident., sess. XXIV, *de ref. matrim.*, can. 5, 7.

[5] Matt., XIX: 8; Gasparri, *Tractatus Canonicus De Matrimonio* (ed. nova ad mentem Codicis I. C., 2 vols., Romae: Typis Polyglottis Vaticanis, 1932), I, nn. 553, 555. (Hereafter this work will be cited as *De Matrimonio.*)

community of table and of family life under the same roof, and this is cohabitation strictly so called. In addition to this it also includes community of the bed chamber or of bed.[6]

By its nature the conjugal bond implies and as a general rule imposes the mutual obligation to observe a community of family life under the same roof. This implication and the imposition of this mutual obligation follow directly from the mutual right and obligation that the parents have with regard to the education of their children. The moral and religious as well as the physical education of the children requires the co-operative, constant care and exertion of the father and the mother. To conduct this education properly it does not suffice for the parents to be united by a social bond, if at the same time they are living apart. It is necessary that they should have a common life and the close intimacy that springs from their relations with one another; mutual assistance, comfort, and support are natural requisites for the attainment of the Christian ideal in family life.[7]

In the matter of this obligation of family community life it is necessary to consider the situation as it exists ordinarily. Exceptional cases wherein the end can be attained without the cohabitation of the married parties are not to be patterned according to a general rule. By virtue of a natural inclination the husband and wife are led to live together, and this is the natural order of relationship that one must keep in mind when one considers the community of family life.

The *consortium tori* in the strict sense of the term means community of bed, and this is the quite general usage of the term, while in the wide sense this term denotes a community of bed chamber with separate beds. This community in the strict sense constitutes neither a right nor an obligation; the right and obligation attaches only to the *consortium tori* as considered in its wider sense. The obligation itself is based on the marriage debt, which debt may not be refused whenever one of the parties lawfully

---

[6] De Smet, *Tractatus Theologico-Canonicus De Sponsalibus et Matrimonio* (ed. quarta inde a Codice altera, Brugis: Car. Beyaert, 1927), n. 249 (hereafter cited as *De Sponsalibus et Matrimonio*).

[7] Pius XI, encycl. "*Casti connubii,*" 31 dec., 1930—*AAS,* XXII (1930), 553.

demands it; but this conjugal duty can be fulfilled perfectly without a continuous community of bed provided that there is a habitual community of bed chamber.[8]

The husband through marriage receives not a dominion over the wife as over a slave, but the *potestas maritalis,* which marital power constitutes him as the head of the woman who becomes subject to him in the government of domestic affairs. This power of the husband over the wife comprises the right to due reverence, obedience, and adequate effort toward maintaining the union. Complementary to this right of headship on the part of the husband is his office and duty of protecting and aiding his spouse. The right of the husband has its origin in the natural law and may not be arbitrarily limited. While this right may be regulated by public authority, yet no authority, whether public or private, may interfere with its substantial scope and exercise.[9]

The wife, although subject to her husband, becomes neither his concubine nor his slave, but rather a helpmate enjoying rights and privileges which are truly her own. She acquires a right to the assistance necessary to enable her to fulfill her rightful position in the family. She participates in the dignity and social standing of her husband except in those rare cases wherein there exist certain legal inequalities. Likewise by reason of her marital position there are certain canonical provisions which affect her rights and status, but these will be treated in their proper places.[10]

The respective relationship of the consorts in the family group wherein the husband is to be the head and the wife a devoted helper, and wherein mutual love, trust, and assistance should prevail, contemplates the realization of a distinct family life.[11]

---

[8] Gasparri, *De Matrimonio,* II, n. 1077; De Smet, *De Sponsalibus et Matrimonio,* n. 250.

[9] Wernz-Vidal, *Ius Canonicum,* Vol. V, *Ius Matrimoniale* (3. ed., 1946), n. 601.

[10] Wernz-Vidal, *Ius Canonicum,* V, 601.

[11] Pius XI, encycl. "*Casti connubii,*" 31 dec. 1930: "Haec sunt igitur, quae bono fidei comprehenduntur: unitas, castitas, caritas, honesta nobilisque obedientia; quae quot sunt nomina, tot sunt coniugii emolumenta, quibus pax, dignitas, felicitas matrimonii in tuto collocentur atque promoveantur."—*AAS,* XXII (1930), 550.

(b) The Obligations to Preserve This Community of Life

From the marital union so characterized by unity and indissolubility rises the mutual obligation of maintaining the common or conjugal life. This obligation derives from the virtue of justice,[12] and the Code succinctly states in canon 1128 that only a just cause excuses from the obligation: Married persons are obliged to preserve the community of conjugal life, unless a just cause excuses them from this obligation.[13]

While the essence of marriage *in facto esse*[14] consists in the conjugal union (*ligamen*), for the attainment of the Christian ideal those elements which, besides the actual consummation of marriage, pertain to the integrity of the matrimonial contract can be considered as relatively essential, namely, community of shelter, of table and of bed, which constitute the basis of conjugal life. As such it is clearly seen that their preservation merits the presence of a proportionately grave cause before a rupture of the community of life may licitly be effected.

The Church is deeply concerned over any disturbance of the ideal married state, and as a consequence is loath to countenance anything like a usurpation of its authority in maintaining the ideal. In the following articles the writer treats: (1) of the nature and divisions of imperfect divorce; (2) of unlawful separation in consequence of a deficient cause; (3) of unlawful separation for lack of adequate authorization; and (4) of the meaning of the phrase *"legitime non separata"* as the same is used in the Code of Canon Law.

---

12 "Ut quisque valeat iure suo coniugali melius uti, necnon propter mutuum vitae adiutorium, coniuges tenentur ex obligatione iustitiae ad habitandum in eadem domo et ad utendum eadem mensa eodemque toro."—Gasparri, *De Matrimonio*, II, n. 1102.

13 "Coniuges servare debent vitae coniugalis communionem, nisi iusta causa eos excuset."

14 Marriage may be considered in a twofold sense, *viz.*, marriage *in fieri*, and marriage *in facto esse*. The former is the contract in which a qualified man and woman mutually oblige themselves to an indissoluble union in which by mutual consent each becomes a co-principal in the procreation of offspring. The indissoluble union, or the marriage bond thus arising, is termed marriage *in facto esse*.

ARTICLE B. THE DEFINITION AND DIVISIONS OF IMPERFECT DIVORCE

SECTION 1. THE DEFINITION OF IMPERFECT DIVORCE

Imperfect divorce is commonly defined as a separation of the spouses from bed, board, and cohabitation, which separation effects a cessation or at least an interruption of the common life between the spouses, but in no way affects the marriage bond which is left intact. It is particularly in this latter respect that imperfect divorce is distinguished from perfect divorce.[15] In defining imperfect divorce Regatillo distinguishes it from a mere separation in fact, and limits the former to a juridic separation which is accompanied with canonical effects.[16] This distinction has merit, since it differentiates the absence of one of the parties or the mere factual separation from the departure instituted in accordance with juridic norms and sanctioned by public ecclesiastical authority. If an act is to have juridical force, surely that act must conform to the canonical norm established for its institution and continuance. Hence this definition by Regatillo is preferred by the writer in determining what constitutes a legitimate separation.

SECTION 2. THE DIVISIONS OF IMPERFECT DIVORCE

Imperfect divorce instituted in full compliance with canonical provisions is termed a juridical separation as distinguished from a non-juridical or *de facto* separation. Relative to its contemplated duration the separation may be temporary, for an indefinite period, or permanent. The separation may be total or partial depending on the extent to which it affects the common life of the spouses. Again, the separation may be the result of the mutual consent of the parties or it may come to pass against the will of one of the consorts. The authority instituting the separation may be of a public or a private character. The evident presence or absence,

---

[15] Gasparri, *De Matrimonio,* I, n. 6.

[16] "Divortium imperfectum est iuridica separatio tori, mensae, habitationis; i.e., non mera separatio *de facto,* sed *de* iure, seu cum effectibus canonicis." —Regatillo, *Ius Sacramentarium* (2 vols., Santander: Sal Terrae, 1945–1946), II, n. 585.

sufficiency or insufficiency, of the necessary justifying cause may make the resulting separation lawful or unlawful.[17]

In defining a juridical divorce Regatillo states that it is a juridical separation, temporary or permanent, pronounced through a process which has preceded the separation.[18] In the writer's opinion this distinction is important because of the canonical effect that attaches to a separation made on private authority, as will be noted later. From the arguments that can be offered in support of the distinction it seems to be a valid distinction, and appears to be in harmony with the mind of the Sacred Congregation of the Sacraments.[19]

Article C. Unlawful Separation in Consequence of a Deficient Cause

Section 1. Conditions Necessary for a Separation Because of Adultery

Having pointed out the nature and divisions of separation, the writer now proposes to demonstrate what constitutes unlawful separation in consequence of a deficient cause as offered in claim of the separation. He proceeds by showing what the alleged cause must fulfill, and concludes that anything less than the minimum requirement constitutes the resulting separation as unlawful in consequence of a deficient cause.

In consideration of the exalted dignity and sacredness of Christian marriage it is quite understandable why the Church in its present law recognizes a single reason, adultery, as a " just cause " for the *permanent* separation of the parties joined in a valid marriage, and why, moreover, in connection with this sole cause it postulates the existence of certain requisite qualifications.

Adultery, as such, has ever been a just cause for permanent separation. This is true because it intrinsically antagonizes the

---

17 Regatillo, *Ius Sacramentarium,* II, n. 585.

18 "*Divortium iuridicum* . . . est separatio *iuridica,* perpetua vel temporalis, ob delictum unius coniugis, praevio processu facta. Licet: ob adulterium, ob alia delicta."—*Op. cit.,* II, n. 585.

19 S. C. de Sacramentis, *Instructio servanda a tribunalibus diocesanis in pertractandis causis de nullitate matrimoniorum,* 15 aug. 1936, art. 6, §2—*AAS,* XXVIII (1936), 314.

unity of marriage. It is moreover the sole cause mentioned expressly in Sacred Scripture.[20] The right of separation for the reason of adultery is proper to the innocent spouse. This right derives from the divine law, both natural [21] and positive.[22]

The Code of Canon Law in legislating concerning adultery as a just cause for permanent separation provides that, in the absence of a condonation by the innocent spouse, the latter has a right to the permanent discontinuance of the community of the conjugal life.

> **On acount of adultery committed by one of the consorts, the other consort, though the bond of marriage remains, has the right to discontinue the community of life even permanently, unless he consented to the crime, or was its contributory cause, or condoned it expressly or tacitly, or committed the same crime himself. A tacit condonation obtains when the innocent consort, though informed with certainty regarding the crime of adultery, has freely continued to live with the guilty consort in marital relations. It is presumed that this tacit condonation obtains unless within six months the innocent consort has expelled the adulterous partner, left him, or brought a legal accusation against him.[23]**

The authors agree that if the adultery is to qualify as a just cause which supports a lawful separation it must be not doubtful,

---

[20] Matt., V: 19; Petrovits, *The New Church Law on Matrimony* (2. ed., Philadelphia: McVey, 1926), n. 581.

[21] Sanchez, *De Matrimonii Sacramento,* Lib. X, disp. III, n. 4; Wernz-Vidal, *Ius Canonicum,* V, n. 707.

[22] Cf. c. 9, X, *de sponsalibus et matrimoniis,* IV, 1; c. 19, X, *de conversione coniugatorum,* III, 32.

[23] Canon 1129, §1. Propter coniugis adulterium, alter coniux, manente vinculo, ius habet solvendi, etiam in perpetuum, vitae communionem, nisi in crimen consenserit, aut eidem causam dederit, vel illud expresse aut tacite condonaverit, vel ipse quoque idem crimen commiserit.

§2. Tacita condonatio habetur, si coniux innocens, postquam de crimine adulterii certior factus est, cum altero coniuge sponte, maritali affectu, conversatus fuerit; praesumitur vero, nisi sex intra menses coniugem adulterum expulerit vel dereliquerit, aut legitimam accusationem fecerit. (The translation of this canon is supplied by the writer.)

but *morally certain;* not simply inchoate, but complete and consummated; not a merely material act, but a formal sin; without approval from the innocent spouse either explicitly or implicitly; and without provocation from the second party as a contributory cause.[24]

Since in this matter of separation there is involved the deprivation of rights owing in justice, and since there follows a serious disruption of a unit of the social fabric for those who make the decision, it is of vital importance to determine whether there be present in the alleged adultery any element or circumstance which deprives the alleged cause of the force which is postulated for it if it is to serve as a *just cause* for the institution of the state of perpetual separation. To ascertain this, the writer accordingly proposes to examine in the light of canon 1129 the necessary characteristics, both positive and negative, of the alleged adultery, the doctrine of the approved authors regarding these points and the decisions of the Sacred Roman Rota insofar as the same were available.[25]

(a) Positive Conditions

1. The Adultery Must Be Morally Certain

The certainty postulated here is that of a moral certitude and not, in addition, that of a physical certitude.[26] There must not be a reasonable doubt as to the actual commission of the adultery,

---

[24] Gasparri, *De Matrimonio,* II, n. 1172; Regatillo, *Ius Sacramentarium,* II, n. 586; Genicot-Salsmans, *Institutiones Theologiae Moralis* (14. ed., 2 vols., Buenos Aires: Dedebec Ediciones Desclée, De Brouwer, 1939), II, n. 566; Noldin-Schmitt, *Summa Theologia Moralis* (3 vols., Vols. I–II, 27. ed., Vol. III, 26. ed., Oeniponte: Sumptibus et Typis F. Rauch, 1940–1941), III, *De Sacramentis,* n. 666; Merkelbach, *Summa Theologiae Moralis* (3. ed., 3 vols., Paris: Typis Desclée de Brouwer et Soc., 1939), III, 966; Cappello, *Tractatus Canonico-Moralis De Sacramentis* (3 vols., Vol. III, *De Matrimonio,* Romae: Marietti, 1923), III, n. 826. (This work is hereafter cited as *De Matrimonio.*)

[25] The writer was able to consult no more than the first 24 volumes of the *S.R.R. Decisiones seu Sententiae.* Whatever volumes were published after the year 1940 were not at his command.

[26] Regatillo, *Ius Sacramentarium,* II, n. 586; Gasparri, *De Matrimonio,* II, n. 1172.

for if such a doubt exists the accused must not be deprived of his conjugal rights.[27] The requisite certitude may result from a consideration of actual compromising circumstances which are sufficient to support a violent presumption.[28] Gasparri (1852–1934) noted that a suspicion, no matter with what degree of probability it pointed to the commission of adultery, does not suffice in proof of the act of adultery. But he likewise stated that actual visual evidence is not required for proof. He correspondingly maintained that such presumptions as the authors term " violent " presumptions suffice for the attaining of the requisite moral certitude that the crime was committed.[29]

2. The Adulterous Act Must Be Complete And Consummated

Fundamentally, adultery is a violation of conjugal faith. Therefore, if it is to constitute a just cause for a permanent separation, it must be of such a physical and moral nature that it violates the mutual right which is exclusively reserved to the spouses. Any act which lacks the completeness of a consummated intercourse will not support a contention for a permanent separation on the part of the innocent spouse. It is the common opinion of canonists and moralists that if semination does not occur then there is no consummation of the act of adultery. Correspondingly on the precise score here considered, there would not exist a sufficient basis for a permanent separation.[30]

---

[27] Kelly, "Separation and Civil Divorce"—*The Jurist* (Washington, D. C., 1941—), VI (1946), 196.

[28] Augustine, *A Commentary on the New Code of Canon Law* (8 vols., Vol. V, 5. ed., St. Louis, Herder, 1935), V, 370.

[29] *De Matrimonio*, II, n. 1172. Cf. Schmalzgrueber, *Ius Ecclesiasticum Universum*, Lib. IV, tit. XIX, n. 115.

[30] "*Consummatum*, idest copula perfecta cum seminatione completum: unde non sufficit si copula completa aut seminatio locum non habuit."—Coronata, *Institutiones Iuris Canonici . . . De Sacramentis tractatus canonicus* (3 vols., Taurini, Romae: Marietti, 1943–1946), III (*De Matrimonio et Sacramentalibus*, 1946), 918 (hereafter this work is cited as *De Sacramentis*); St. Alphonsus Maria de Ligorio, *Theologia Moralis* (ed. nova cura et studio P. L. Gaude, 4 vols., Romae: Typis Polyglottis Vaticanis, 1905–1912), Lib. VI, n. 963; Wernz-Vidal, *Ius Canonicum*, V, n. 639; Gasparri, *De Matrimonio*, II n. 1172.

Cappello states that in the event of a complete carnal union semination must be presumed.[31] Consequently, neither initiatory actions, such as embraces, kisses, touches, nor attempted but unconsummated acts of intercourse, constitute adultery in the meaning of canon 1129, §1. This remains true even though from these or similar actions pollution followed in either or in both of the parties.[32]

Semination seems to be the controlling fact regardless of the manner in which the carnal union is effected. Hence, it is the more probable opinion that adulterous onanism, as also sodomy and bestiality, may equally violate the right of the innocent spouse and thus become the basis for a perpetual separation.[33]

3. The Adultery Must Be a Formal Sin

Adultery as a basis for a permanent separation must be a formal sin, and consequently there must be present the necessary knowledge and also a freedom of the will on the part of the adulterous spouse. Otherwise there cannot be said to be a voluntary violation of conjugal faith. Therefore, good faith, error, force, and probably also grave fear, may limit the alleged adultery to a material sin, insufficient of itself to justify a permanent separation.[34] The authors are not in uniform agreement on the point whether

---

31 ". . . pro certo habemus *practice* sufficere veram copulam, etiam sine effusione seminis, tum . . . (b) quia, posita copula, semper adfuisse ex communiter contingentibus etiam seminis effusio; . . ."—*De Matrimonio,* n. 826.

32 Coronata, *De Sacramentis,* III, 918; Gasparri, *De Matrimonio,* II, n. 1172.

33 " Adulterium debet esse consummatum ipsa copula cum seminatione, etsi onanistice peracta, cui aequiparantur sodomia proprie dicta et bestialitas in quibus par est ratio iniuriae illatae; . . ."—Merkelbach, *Summa Theologiae Moralis,* III, n. 966; Cappello, *De Matrimonio,* n. 826; Coronata, *De Sacramentis,* III, 918. The contrary opinion is stated by Petrovits, *The New Church Law on Matrimony,* n. 583.

34 Gasparri, *De Matrimonio,* II, n. 1172; Regatillo, *Ius Sacramentarium,* II, n. 586; Tanquerey, *Synopis Theologiae Moralis et Pastoralis* (3 vols., Parisiis: Desclée et Socii, 1936–1939), I (*De Paenitentia, De Matrimonio et Ordine,* 12. ed., 1936), 462.

or not an adulterous intercourse effected under the influence of grave fear proves sufficient as justification for a permanent separation.[35]

Therefore, if a husband in good faith [36] believed his wife to be dead and thereupon contracted a second union, his subsequent marital acts would not be adulterous in the sense of canon 1129, §1, and would not of themselves offer a sufficient cause for instituting a permanent separation. The note of good faith would naturally cease at the moment the husband became aware that his lawful wife was actually living.

If through error or invincible ignorance a husband had sexual intercourse with a woman other than his spouse, the objective act of adultery would lack the note of volition requisite for formal adultery, and consequently it would not justify a permanent separation.[37] The adulterous consort must know that the other party is not his spouse, and must freely and willingly consent to the sin. It is not necessary, however, that the accomplice in sin should know that his or her partner in sin is a married person.[38]

(b) Negative Conditions

Postulated that the commission of the adultery was morally certain, that it was complete and consummated, and that it was a formal sin, nevertheless the crime would not offer a just cause for a permanent separation if there were present one of the four following conditions: approval, provocation, condonation, or requital in kind on the part of the other partner. The presence of any of these conditions would under the law deprive this partner of the right to a permanent separation. These four negative conditions will now be considered separately and in detail.

---

[35] Cf. Wernz-Vidal, *Ius Canonicum,* V, n. 639; Ballerini-Palmieri, *Opus Theologicum Morale* (3. ed., 7 vols., Prati, 1898–1901), VI, n. 505.

[36] For the requirements attaching to the establishment of good faith consult: Rice, *Proof of Death in Pre-Nuptial Investigation,* The Catholic University of America Canon Law Studies, n. 123 (Washington, D. C.: The Catholic University of America Press, 1940), pp. 115–116.

[37] Ballerini-Palmieri, *Opus Theologicum Morale,* VI, n. 505.

[38] Kelly, " Separation and Civil Divorce "—*The Jurist,* VI (1946), 196.

1. The Partner in Marriage Must Not Have Given Any Approval for the Crime

Canon 1129, §1, after stating the right of the innocent party to bring to an end, even perpetually, the community of conjugal life as a result of the adultery committed by the other spouse, in the first place conditions the existence of the right on the fact that the innocent spouse has not consented to the crime: *ius habet solvendi . . . vitae communionem nisi in crimen consenserit, . . .*

The consent here mentioned is synonymous with approval. The adultery must not have received the consent or the approval of the innocent spouse, given either explicitly or even implicitly. An implicit consent or approval for the crime would be present whenever the innocent spouse who knew of the proposed commission of the crime, and who could easily have prevented it, has made no effort to forestall it.[39]

Thus a wife who, in view of her illness or for some equal reason that nullifies the possible rendering of the marital debt, should instruct her husband to seek satisfaction from some other woman could not claim his sin as justification for a permanent separation. Nor could a husband who has ordered his wife to prostitute herself regard her adulterous acts as justifying a permanent separation. In either case the explicit consent to the adultery, apart from the moral culpability, destroys the note of injustice in the subsequent act in so far as that act might have been a just cause for a permanent separation.

According to a probable opinion, explicit consent to the adulterous acts removes the note of all violation of the justice that is due to the other spouse.[40]

The authors, when speaking of implicit consent to the adulterous acts, note that such consent is present when the act is not prevented. This act of prevention, however, must be understood, not inclusively of an actual prevention, but exclusively of a possible prevention, for no one is held responsible or acccountable for that which is impossible of prevention. If the innocent spouse is powerless to prevent the injustice, there is no place for a pre-

[39] Gasparri, *De Matrimonio,* II, n. 1173.

[40] Regatillo, *Ius Sacramentarium,* II, n. 586; Cappello, *De Matrimonio,* n. 826.

sumption of consent to the subsequent violation of justice. Within the sphere of this possible prevention Gasparri postulated the further note of facility in the act of prevention. This author declared that, if the innocent spouse does not prevent the adultery when he or she could have easily done so (*facile posset*), then the right to a permanent separation is lost.[41] In such a case the party, knowing of the impending crime, is considered as consenting to the commission of the adultery. However, as was stated by the same author, when there is question of obtaining evidence or conclusive proof, then the mere simulation of ignorance regarding the already executed or still proposed commission of adultery is not to be considered as an implicit consent.[42] However, in order to justify the act of simulation, the innocent spouse must be guiltless of having provoked the offending party to commit the act of adultery.

2. The Partner in Marriage Must Not Have Provoked the Crime

The notion of provocation is linked with the second of the four conditions here to be considered. Canon 1129, §1, rules out the availability of the right to a permanent separation on the part of the innocent spouse if the latter has given cause for the adultery committed by the other partner. In the words, "*aut eidem causam dederit,*" canon 1129, §1, states the second condition under which the innocent party would fail to acquire a right to a permanent separation in consequence of the adultery committed by the other party. The offended party is not permitted to profit by his or her own misconduct. Granted then that the offended party has given cause for the adultery, this party may not still point to a violation of justice that warrants a permanent discontinuance of marital cohabitation. The question naturally arises: Must the cause which is mentioned in canon 1129, §1, be regarded as implying exclusively a direct provocation, or should it be considered

---

[41] "Si adulterii malitia alteri quoque ex parte tribuenda est, e.g., si adulterium mandaverit, aut in illud consenserit seu expresse seu tacite, idest non impediens, cum sciret et facile posset."—Gasparri, *De Matrimonio,* II, 1173.

[42] "Praeterea coniux ius divortii non amittit, si, sciens alterius adulterium, simulet se illud ignorare, ut interea testes idoneos inveniat ad infidelem coniugem observandum et de adulterio convincendum."—*Loc. cit.*

as involving also an indirect provocation so that the placing of any potential occasion for the partner's act of adultery would qualify the agent as giving cause for the adultery?

Gasparri stated that if the one party impels the other, directly or indirectly, to commit the adultery, the right to a permanent separation is lost.[43] Cappello limits the loss of this right to the case wherein there has been such direct provocation that equivalently results in an effective cause; the merely indirect provocation to an act of adultery, e.g., the denial of the conjugal debt, would not in his opinion result in a loss of the right.[44] Chelodi in a brief statement seems to rule out " occasion " entirely, and requires " cause " to be given directly for the adultery, that is, by means of a direct ordering or impelling of the commission of the crime.[45]

Coronata, summarizing the teaching of the authors on this point, remarks that the more common opinion is that " occasion " is not to be considered as " cause " when a judgment is made on whether or not provocation has been given for the adultery committed.[46]

There is here a question of the loss of a right given by the law, i.e., the right of the wife to terminate, even permanently, the community of life, provided that she has not given cause for the injustice which made her right available. If the condition is

---

[43] "Hoc coniugis adulterium ius divortii alteri non tribuit . . . (b) Si alter coniux alterum ad adulterium impulerit directe vel indirecte, e.g., negans debitum aut alimenta, vel eumdem e domo expellens, vel cum eodem non cohabitans sine iusta causa, . . ."—*De Matrimonio, II,* n. 1173.

[44] "Ut *adulterium* sit causa iusta separationis, hae conditiones requiruntur: . . . 5o Ut *non fuerit* ab altero coniuge *provocatum,* i.e., ut hic *causam* delicto *non dederit,* et quidem directe, mandans vel impellens; non solum indirecte, v.g., negatione debiti coniugalis."—*De Matrimonio,* n. 826.

[45] "At *iure* divertendi cadit qui: . . . 2. aut eidem *causam dedit,* i.e., directe mandans aut impellens, non dumtaxat indirecte occasionem praebens: . . ."—*Ius Matrimoniale iuxta Codicem Iuris Canonici* (3. ed., Tridenti: Libr. Edit. Tridentum, 1921), 176.

[46] "Causam dare adulterio directe censetur coniux qui adulterium mandat aut ad illud impellit et provocat. Aliqui auctores docent causam indirecte praebentem seu occasionem considerandum esse ut causam dantem, si occasionem praebeat alimenta subtrahendo, debitum negando, e domo expellendo. Doctrina vero communior id non admittit."—*De Sacramentis,* III, 919.

proved against her, the right is lost. The condition must therefore be interpreted strictly.[47]

A strict interpretation of " cause " in the condition is therefore in order, and such an interpretation in this case leads to a restriction of the extension or content of " cause." Hence, not any provocation in general can logically be considered as a " cause " but rather only that direct provocation which results from a mandate or from some positive act of impulsion as present in the case may reasonably be included in the concept of " cause."

It has been argued that, " since here there is question of loss of right, the law must be strictly interpreted, and therefore it would seem that frequent denial of the debitum, which, it is foreseen, will lead to adultery, if it can be proved, must be regarded as provocation to adultery, and the separation denied.[48] But in this argument, so it seems to the writer, the reasoning has led to an expansion of the basis upon which the right of separation whose protection is called for could be denied. The conclusion amounts to an extension rather than a restriction of the conditions which would result in a loss of the right of separation. The introduction of the element of the foreseen probable adultery has merged the condition " of not having caused the adultery " with the condition " of not having consented to the adultery." It has been seen that the absence of prevention when accompanied with such foreknowledge may be taken for consent to the crime subsequently committed. Therefore the conclusion which denies the right to institute should be based rather on the implicitly given consent than on an indirect provocation as amounting to a " cause " in the sense of canon 1129, §1. It seems that the more common opinion, namely, that the available use of the right of separation is sacrificed only when direct provocation for the act of adultery has been given, should be supported against the view that also an indirect provocation suffices to entail a loss of the right to institute a separation. The invoked exception to the use of the right—*aut eidem causam dederit*—should consequently be understood as pointing to a case in which direct and positive cause has been given, and not as also contemplating a case in which an in-

---

[47] Canon 19.

[48] Kelly, " Separation and Civil Divorce,"—*The Jurist,* VI (1946), 196.

direct or negative cause, that is, a simple occasion, has been furnished for the guilty party's act of adultery.

3. The Partner in Marriage Must Not Have Condoned the Crime

The third condition under which the right to a permanent separation may be lost is the condonation by the innocent spouse of the adultery committed by the guilty consort: ". . . *vel illud expresse aut tacite condonaverit* . . ."[49]

Under the system of public penances prevalent in early canonical discipline, departure from the guilty partner or at least a partial cessation of the common life between the married partners was obligatory when one of the spouses had committed adultery. The present legislation does not impose an obligation of departure, but concedes a right which the innocent party is at liberty to renounce unless the claim of fraternal correction or the need of forestalling scandal should make the act of departure imperative. This right to a permanent separation is not accorded to any spouse who condones, either expressly or tacitly, the adultery of the guilty consort. Express condonation is had if the party expressly declares to the guilty consort that the committed injustice has been forgiven.[50] This express renunciation of the right to undertake a separation becomes effective regardless of the manner in which the condonation is made.[51]

Canon 1129, §2, establishes the conditions under which a tacit condonation is had, and delineates the specified circumstances under which it is presumed in law that an act of tacit condonation has preceded.[52] Tacit condonation of the crime exists if the innocent party, after having learned of the crime, has freely continued to live in marital relationship with the other party; it is presumed that this condonation obtains, unless within six months the inno-

---

[49] Canon 1129, §1.

[50] Coronata, *De Sacramentis,* III, 919.

[51] Regatillo, *Ius Sacramentarium,* II, n. 586 *f.*

[52] "Tacita condonatio habetur, si coniux innocens, postquam de crimine adulterii certior factus est, cum altero coniuge sponte, maritali affectu, conversatus fuerit; praesumitur vero, nisi sex intra menses coniugem adulterum expulerit vel derelinquerit, aut legitimam accusationem fecerit."

cent party has expelled, departed from, or brought a legal accusation against the guilty partner.

Moral certitude regarding the commission of the crime of adultery must exist on the side of the innocent party before the latter's subsequent use of the marital right in any way affects the possession of the right to institute a separation. Marital relations subsequent to this knowledge of the crime must be characterized by freedom such as would have been present had no offense intervened. The mere fact of separation does not necessarily preclude the possibility of a condonation, since a continued status of marital relations could still exist; nor is the mere living in the same house a sufficient sign of condonation, since the continued residence of the parties under the same roof does not necessarily involve the use of the marital rights.[53]

The law presumes, subject however to disproval, that a condonation of the crime has taken place after a period of six months, unless within that time the innocent spouse exercises the right accorded in the law. This period of time, according to Coronata, is to be computed from the time the innocent spouse has learned of the crime.[54] Ignorance of a notorious crime is not presumed by the law; but if the crime was not notorious, ignorance of its commission is presumed in favor of the innocent party.[55]

The process to be instituted is not understood to be a criminal process which would contemplate the infliction of a penalty, for such a course of procedure in the ecclesiastical forum is reserved to the promoter of justice.[56] Rather, the accusation spoken of in canon 1129, §2, is to be understood in the sense of the *accusatio matrimonii* mentioned in canon 1970, wherein there is question simply of a petition for a declaration of nullity, and hence in matters of separation the accusation contemplated in the law would be a petition for a separation. The right to institute a separation, if this right has been lost through an act of condona-

---

[53] Regatillo, *Ius Sacramentarium,* II, 586 *f;* Cappello, *De Matrimonio,* n. 826.

[54] "Sex menses ultra quos praesumitur condonatio ad mentem Codicis intelligendi sunt sex menses post cognitum delictum adulterii. Praesumptio haec praesumptio est simplex iuris."—*De Sacramentis,* III, 919.

[55] Canon 16, §2; Regatillo, *Ius Sacramentarium,* II, n. 586 *f.*

[56] Canon 1934.

tion, revives if the offending spouse thereafter commits a sin of adultery.[57]

4. The Partner in Marriage Must Not Have Neutralized the Effect of the Crime

The fourth negative condition through which the right to institute a separation is lost consists in the fact that a party has, with an act of adultery, neutralized the effect which otherwise can derive from the guilty partner's previous act of adultery: ". . . *vel ipse quoque idem crimen commiserit.*"[58] In such a case the law determines that the later will act of requital cancels out the earlier act of adultery in whatever right for instituting a separation it had occasioned. This rule applies then only when a legitimate separation has not as yet been instituted. For, if the spouse to whom the separation has been legitimately granted should at a later time commit adultery, then there does not ensue any loss of right of continued separation, and such a party, if recalled by the other partner, would not be held to re-establish the community of life.[59] Reiffenstuel however stated that the opposite opinion was likewise a truly probable one, and that in his judgment the ecclesiastical sanction of the previously granted separation did not alter the obligation of the originally innocent spouse to return to a community of life with his or her partner in marriage.[60]

The foregoing principles relative to the factors which in the accompaniment of adultery are requisite for supporting a petition for a permanent separation, and the conditions under which the right to invoke a separation or its continued use would be lost, were restated with approval by the Sacred Roman Rota in a decision as recently as the year 1929.[61]

---

[57] Coronata, *De Sacramentis,* III, 920.

[58] Canon 1129, §1; "Paria crimina compensatione mutua deleantur."—C. 7, X, *de adulteriis et strupo,* V, 16.

[59] Cappello, *De Matrimonio,* n. 827; Sanchez, *De Matrimonii Sacramento,* Lib. X, disp. 10, n. 30; St. Alphonsus, *Theologia Moralis,* Lib. VI, n. 967.

[60] *Ius Canonicum Universum,* Lib. IV, tit. XIX, nn. 86–87.

[61] S. R. Rota, *Separationis,* 6 dec. 1929, *coram* R.P.D. F. Morano, Dec. LXIII, n. 3: "Causa igitur quae tribuit coniugi ius separationis perpetuae est unica, nempe adulterium alterius coniugis, quod non sit ab illo provocatum vel condonatum vel compensatum. Oportet autem ut adulterium sit

SECTION 2. TEMPORARY SEPARATION

The Code of Canon Law, while recognizing specifically only a single cause as justification for a permanent separation, does not furnish an all-inclusive enumeration of the causes which justify a temporary separation, but merely lists the principal reasons for which a temporary separation may be instituted. The law of the Church relative to temporary separation, in particular with reference to the reasons for which it may be permitted, is contained in canon 1131, §1.[62]

The causes listed in canon 1131, §1—joining a non-Catholic sect; educating the children as non-Catholics; living a criminal and ignominious life; bringing grave danger to the soul or body of the other spouse; rendering the common life too difficult by reason of harsh treatment—as well as others of equal gravity are considered as legitimate causes for which the departure of the injured spouse may be justified. It is not proposed here to examine in detail each of the recognized causes for a temporary separation, since the circumstances which accompany individual cases make each case unique in its final determination. Rather, the intention of the writer is to make clear that, though from a

---

formale et consummatum. Formale dicitur, si patratum sit cum cognitione intellectus et cum libera voluntate. Ideo ex hoc capite non est causa separationis perpetuae adulterium patratum cum ignorantia ligaminis coniugalis, ex quo adulterium peculiarem accipit malitiam, neque adulterium admissum ob violentiam. Consummatum vero dicitur adulterium per actum per se aptum ad prolis generationem. Ideo ex capite hoc non sunt causae separationis perpetuae illicitae amicitiae, actus luxuriae non consummatae, immo neque ipsi actus luxuriae consummatae qui non habeant naturam copulae perfectae. Ex communi autem interpretatione sunt causa separationis perpetuae etiam sodomia et bestialitas. Cum vero adulterium sit crimen quod generatim patratur in occulto, eius probatio fieri solet per praesumptiones violentas, nempe per coniecturas ex factis quae nonnisi in casu adulterii contingere solent."—*S. R. Rotae Decisiones seu Sententiae* (Romae: Typis Vaticanis, 1912—), XXI (1937), 525-526.

[62] "Si alter coniux sectae acatholicae nomen dederit; si prolem acatholice educaverit; si vitam criminosam et ignominiosam ducat; si grave seu animae seu corporis periculum alteri facessat; si saevitiis vitam communem nimis difficilem reddat, haec aliaquae id genus, sunt pro altero coniuge totidem legitimae causae discedendi, auctoritate Ordinarii loci, et etiam propria auctoritate, si de eis certo constet, et periculum sit in mora."—Canon 1131, §1.

cursory reading of canon 1131, §1, the Church may seem to favor a wide latitude in the matter of legitimate causes which warrant a temporary separation, such is not the mind of the Church as is evidenced by its practice. However, before noting the true mind of the Church as reflected in the decisions of the Sacred Roman Rota, the writer considers it opportune to make the following observations.

While a temporary separation may be granted for a definite time or for an indefinite period for a variety of causes, in all temporary separations the obligation of cohabitation resumes its binding force immediately upon the cessation of the cause for which the separation was granted, unless a definite period was decreed by the ordinary and before the lapse of this period he has not seen fit to decree an immediate resumption of cohabitation. Concerning the individual causes listed in the law, one must necessarily consider the following points in forming a judgment regarding the justifying strength of the alleged cause.

A simple profession of heresy and a seeming apostasy are not in themselves just causes for a temporary separation; an actual enrollment in a heretical sect, or an act of formal apostasy is required.[63] If heresy or apostasy is to exist as a basis for a legitimate temporary separation, then two elements are necessary: the abandonment of the Catholic faith and the affiliation with a non-Catholic sect.[64] That those who belong to an atheistic sect are to be judged according to the same norms as those who belong to a non-Catholic sect is clear from a reply of the Pontifical Commission for the Interpretation of the Canons of the Code under date of July 30, 1934.[65]

The promise to baptize and educate in the Catholic religion any children to be born of the marriage is a condition precedent

[63] Wernz-Vidal, *Ius Canonicum,* V, n. 645.

[64] Doheny, *Canonical Procedure in Matrimonial Cases* (2 vols., Milwaukee, Bruce Publishing Co., 1938–1944), II, *Informal Procedure* (1944), 631.

[65] P.C.I., 30 iul. 1934, ad I: An ad normam Codicis iuris canonici, qui sectae atheisticae adscripti sunt vel fuerunt, habendi sint quoad omnes iuris effectus etiam in ordine ad sacram ordinationem et matrimonium ad instar eorum qui sectae acatholicae adhaerent vel adhaeserunt. R. Affirmative.—*AAS,* XXVI (1934), 494.

to the permission granted by the Church for a mixed marriage. Hence, if the non-Catholic party flagrantly violates this solemn promise by insisting on the non-Catholic education of the children, the Catholic consort may have the right to departure. It is to be noted that the guilt of educating the children in a non-Catholic sect, in the case of a mixed marriage, as a reason for separation, must attach to the non-Catholic party. But separation from a Catholic consort is likewise authorized if this Catholic consort is the cause of the non-Catholic education of the children.[66]

The criminal life or ignominious conduct proposed as a cause for a temporary separation must connote a habitual state.[67] A single isolated defection is not sufficient to justify a disruption of the conjugal life. Likewise the conduct of the offending spouse must be of a public character, since the resulting ignominy and disgrace is attributable to the notoriety of the conduct. Grave danger to the soul is verified if the action of the offending partner will draw his spouse into grave sin. Grave danger to the body may be verified when there is danger of bodily infection through the use of the matrimonial right, though generally, if cohabitation can be had without danger, a partial separation only is conceded.[68]

The actual adjudications of the Sacred Roman Rota quite logically appear to be a source from which to determine the mind of the Church regarding the sufficiency of the cause in cases wherein a temporary separation is sought. From these decisions the severity and reluctance of the Church to grant a separation is evident. Lega (1860–1935) in a decision written only thirty-seven years ago explained the reasons for this severity and reluctance on the part of the Church.[69]

---

[66] Doheny, *op. cit.*, II, 632–633.

[67] Cappello, *De Matrimonio*, n. 828.

[68] De Smet, *De Sponsalibus et Matrimonio*, n. 257; Ballerini-Palmieri, *Opus Theologicum Morale*, VI, 509.

[69] S. R. Rota, *Separationis quoad thorum et mensam*, 5 iul. 1910, *coram* R.P.D. Michaeli Lega, Decano, Dec. XXIV, n. 11: "Quare constans iurisprudentia fuit et huius S[ancti] O[fficii] et S[acrae] C[ongregationis] Concilii caute admodum procedendum esse ad indulgendam thori separationem, quippe quod separatio opponatur directe fini ipsius matrimonii (quod est coniunctio maris et foeminae, individuae vitae consuetudinem retinens) scandalum gignit, familiam pessumdat, periculo incontinentiae coniuges ex-

Lega pointed out that great caution has constantly been advised by the Sacred Roman Rota and the Sacred Congregation of the Council in the granting of separations from bed and board. The reason for this extreme caution has been the recognition that separation is directly opposed to the purpose and ends of marriage. Not only does separation offer such opposition, but it also gives rise to scandal, destroys the family, exposes the consorts to the danger of incontinence, and inflicts a severe loss on the children, if there be any. He likewise noted the conviction of the Most Reverend Auditors of the Sacred Roman Rota that this wise jurisprudence of the Holy See must be adhered to, and especially so when modern customs are tending to scuttle with facility all conjugal rights, either " through absolute divorce or through imperfect divorce." This conviction was fortified through the realization that matrimony exists also as a remedy for concupiscence and that a dissolution of the common life by means of a separation immediately opens the door to adulterous amours and illicit associations.[70]

The apparent tendency of some modern theologians to depart from the rigor of the older jurisprudence was reproved by Lega

---

ponit, prolemque, si quae sit, damnis afficit . . . (Cases are cited in which the practice of the Sacred Roman Rota has been upheld.)" "Imo etiam in dubio utrum matrimonium validum sit, maxime in dubio facti, facilior admitti potest probatio, sive per testes, sive per documenta, ad effectum evincendi nullitatem; dum e contrario in causa separationis thori, cum certa sit et incontroversa validitas matrimonii, omnia iura clamant ut coniugale consortium non disiungatur, nisi invicte comprobetur, adesse causam canonicam separationis."—*S. R. Rotae Decisiones seu Sententiae,* II (1913), 243–244.

[70] S. R. Rota, *Separationis quoad thorum et mensam,* 5 iul. 1910, *coram* R.P.D. Michaeli Lega, Decano, Dec. XXIV, n. 12: "Cui sapientissimae iurisprudentiae tum H[uius] S[ancti] O[fficii] tum S[acrae] C[ongregationis] C[oncilii] fortius adhaerendum esse considerarunt R[everendissimi] P[atres] A[uditores] quo hodierni mores ad facile pessumdanda coniugalia iura sive per divortium plenum, sive per divortium semiplenum, inclinant. Et nemo non scit quomodo, per divortii semipleni facilem concessionem, via sternatur facilis et veluti necessaria ad divortium plenum. Nam matrimonium datum est etiam in remedium concupiscentiae; dissoluto itaque semiplene maritali consortio, statim irrepunt adulterini amores et illiciti amplexus."—*S. R. Rotae Decisiones seu Sententiae,* II (1913), 244.

when he pointed to the necessity of adhering to the jurisprudence of the Holy See in view of the definite breakdown in morals and the change in the customs of our times.[71]

That the Sacred Roman Rota continues to follow the wise counsel of Lega seems evident also from more recent cases. Frequent quarrels, in themselves, are not regarded by the Holy See as a "just cause" even for a temporary separation, as is clearly seen from a decision of the Rota in the year 1928.[72] In this case the alleged cause in modern parlance would have been termed "incompatibility of temperament," and would no doubt have supported a "divorce" decree in almost any modern civil tribunal. The married life of the elderly couple had been marked by frequent quarrels and almost continual unhappiness. It was the contention of the petitioner that "implacable hatred" (*odium capitale*) existed on the part of the wife. The decision, while recognizing that the wife had used opprobrious language towards

[71] *Ibid.*, n. 13: "Considerare non praetermiserunt R[everendissimi] D[octores] quod perpendet E[menentissimus] Gennari, *Consult. Moral.*, cons. LXVII, pag. 312, nempe Theologos hodiernos aliquantisper discessisse a rigore antiquioris iurisprudentiae, docentes fas esse coniugibus quacumque ex legitima causa se ad invicem separare, abrupta in aliquod tempus mutua cohabitatione non in perpetuum, cauto dumtaxat ne subsit incontinentiae periculum." . . . "Nam, e contra, leves iniurias, saevitias aut ipsam characterum incompatibilitatem inter sponsos non haberi uti causas sufficientes ad eosdem dissociandos, definitum est a S[acra] C[ongregatione] C[oncilii] in una Sedunen., diei 2 novembris 1851, et aliis innumeris, quas recolit Pallottini, Coll. tom. XIII, v. *matrim.* §23, n. 199, ad notam."—*S. R. Rotae Decisiones seu Sententiae,* II (1913), 244–245.

[72] S. R. Rota, *Separationis,* 30 iun. 1928, *coram* R.P.D. Josepho Florazak, Decano, Dec. XIX, n. 2: "Affirmari tamen potest, omnium istarum causarum, ex quibus ius ad divortium obtinendum oriri potest, unum esse debere effectum, gravis nempe damni sive animae sive corporis periculum. Non sufficit timor cuiuscumque periculi, necessarium est ut malum quod timetur sit grave ac tale quale ad metum viri constantis requiritur. Ex his sequitur, non satis esse minas, nisi qui minatur solitus sit eas exsequi, prae oculis praesertim habito sive minitantis sive metuentis sexu, indole, ingenio, necnon minandi modo. Quod si de odio agatur, requiritur odium *capitale* ac *implacabile:* et leves iniuriae, verba probrosa aut ipsa characterum inter sponsos incompatibilitas, quae molestam cohabitationem faciant, non possunt haberi uti causae sufficientes ad eosdem dissociandos."—*S. R. Rotae Decisiones seu Sententiae,* XX (1936), 268–269.

her husband, declared that the use of such language did not prove the existence of " implacable hatred," but only proved her anger towards him because of his conduct. The Sacred Rota declared that the frequent quarrels were due to avarice rather than " implacable hatred," and refused to grant a temporary separation inasmuch as a " just cause " was not present.

The Sacred Roman Rota expressed the same teaching in another case decided in the year 1930.[73] In this decision the Sacred Roman Rota, recognizing that cohabitation was not of the essence of marriage, pointed out that separation from bed, board and cohabitation, even if temporary, is a grave matter. Such separation by its nature is public, contrary to the marriage obligations, and filled with dangers to the consorts, especially the danger of incontinence. The Sacred Roman Rota in this decision gave a norm for determining whether or not an alleged cause for a separation is legitimate. The cause, the Rota said, must be proportionate to the evils that result from the separation, i.e., the cause must contain an element of danger either to the soul or the body of the other party, and this danger must be so serious that there is an end of the obligation imposed by the law which binds the consorts to observe the community of conjugal life.

This norm of judging the legitimacy of the alleged cause is in harmony with the teachings of most of the authors who wrote before the enactment of the Code of Canon Law.[74] These authors agreed that all causes for a temporary separation must include the element of danger to the spiritual or bodily welfare of the other

---

[73] S. R. Rota, *Separationis,* 6 aug. 1930, *coram* R.P.D. Andrea Jullien, Ponente, Dec. XLVII, n. 2: " Verum, quamvis cohabitatio non sit de matrimonii essentia, separatio tamen tori, mensae et habitationis, etiam temporaria, est res gravis, utpote publica, obligationi naturali contraria, ac periculis plena pro coniugibus, specietenus de continentia servanda; quapropter separationis causa, ut sit legitima, debet esse proportionata, id. est continere periculum sive animae sive corporis ita grave, ut cedat obligatio illa, qua coniuges servare vitae coniugalis communionem iure tenentur."—*S. R. Rotae Decisiones seu Sententiae,* XXII (1938), 524.

[74] Wernz, *Ius Decretalium* (3. ed., 6 vols. in 10, Prati, 1913–1915), IV, n. 713; Schmalzgrueber, *Ius Ecclesiasticum Universum,* Lib. IV, tit. XIX, nn. 141–145; Gasparri, *De Matrimonio* (3 ed., 2 vols., Parisiis, 1904), II, n. 761. (This is the sole instance in which this particular edition is cited by the writer.)

party if they are to be regarded as sufficient causes for a temporary separation.

In addition to the causes specifically mentioned in the law, the Sacred Roman Rota has recognized among others the following as justifying causes for a temporary separation: the mental abnormality of one of the parties if it be conjoined with implacable hatred; [75] malicious desertion, done without justification but at the same time with the intention of not returning; [76] the persistent and constant practice of onanism and other irreligious and immoral acts on the part of one of the parties.[77]

Summary

The Church recognizes that a conditional right to a perpetual or a temporary separation exists in law, but, mindful of the primary obligation, namely, the preservation of the conjugal life, the Church is loath to sanction a separation unless the alleged cause either makes the legitimate concession of the right imperative by reason of a greater evil to be expected from a denial of such a separation, or is such as to demonstrate a violent disregard by one of the parties of the mutual condition supporting the conjugal life, which disregard seriously endangers the moral or physical welfare of the innocent spouse. Mindful of its mission and the fundamental notion of the family, the Church interprets strictly the right of separation; sanctions a perpetual separation for a single reason only, adultery, and a permanent departure on private authority for that single cause only when the cause is notorious and the requisite conditions on the part of the innocent spouse are fulfilled; and sanctions a temporary separation for several causes which endanger the moral or the physical welfare of the innocent spouse, but on private authority only if there is certainty regarding

[75] S. R. Rota, *Separationis quoad thorum et cohabitationem,* 20 aprilii 1912, *coram* R.P.D. Michaeli Lega, Decano, Dec. XVI, nn. 11–12—*S. R. Rotae Decisiones seu Sententiae,* IV (1917), 199–201.

[76] S. R. Rota, *Separationis,* 17 mart. 1913, *coram* R.P.D. Antonio Perathoner, Ponente, Dec. XIX, nn. 17–18—*S. R. Rotae Decisiones seu Sententiae,* V (1919), 225.

[77] S. R. Rota, *Separationis,* 4 febr. 1925, *coram* R.P.D. Iosepho Florczak, Ponente, Dec. VI, nn. 6–10—*S. R. Rotae Decisiones seu Sententiae,* XVII (1935), 39–47.

the sufficiency of the cause and if at the same time there is serious danger in the delaying of the separation.

Article D. Unlawful Separation for Lack of an Adequate Authorization

The present canonical discipline imposes no obligation on the innocent spouse to leave, to dismiss, or to bring action against the offending party, nor is there any canonical restriction against the innocent party's instituting a reconciliation. There may be instances wherein a moral obligation of departure exists by force of the natural law for the spiritual welfare of the spouse or of the children.

The separation spoken of here is the result of exercising a right claimed to have been given by the law. The consequent separation may change the canonical status of the innocent party, and therefore the separation to be juridically effective must, in addition to the presence of the requisite " just cause," have been sanctioned by or at least have the approbation of qualified ecclesiastical authority.

The legitimate authority with respect to matrimonial cases between baptized persons is properly and exclusively the Church.[78] The contract of marriage between baptized persons is governed not only by the divine law but also by the canon law, but with relation to the civil effects of the marriage contract the competency of the civil power is recognized by the Church.[79]

Even the temporary interruption as well as the perpetual cessation of the conjugal life by way of a separation of the parties, though not affecting the bond of marriage, can in no way be specifically considered a merely civil effect over which the State has any native authority. The Church may authorize the civil power to grant a sentence of temporal or of perpetual separation,[80]

---

[78] Canon 1960.

[79] Canon 1016.

[80] Cf. Art. 34 of the Concordat with Italy in the year 1929: "Quanto alle cause di separazione personale, la Santa Sede consente che siano giudicate dall' autorità giudiziaria civile."—*AAS,* XXI (1929), 291; cf. also the Concordat with Austria under date of June 5, 1933, where in the *Zusatzprotokoll,* Art. VII, 2, reads: "Der Heilige Stuhl willigt ein, dass

but it suffices to note here that the civil power, if acting without ecclesiastical approval, may not legitimately sanction a separation of baptized persons. The matter of the granting of a separation between baptized persons belongs primarily to the Church as interpreting the divine law or as giving effect to her canonical prescriptions.

As has been seen in the foregoing Article, the Church does not authorize the institution of a separation, either temporary or perpetual, except for certain "just causes." Likewise the immediate legitimate authorizing agency is designated in the law of the Church.[81] A scorning of the requisite agency, or also any action taken by an agency when the action lies beyond the scope of the agency's power necessarily marks any resulting separation as unlawful for lack of an adequate competence in the authority which sanctioned the separation.

SECTION 1. PERMANENT SEPARATION

Canon 1130, treating directly of the obligation of a reconciliation following a separation in consequence of adultery committed by one of the spouses, recognizes parenthetically that the innocent spouse may have lawfully departed either as a result of the sentence of a judge or on the initiative of his or her own authority.[82] If the sentence or decree is that of a competent ecclesiastical judge, then the presence of the authority of the Church is evident; if the sentence is that of a civil judge, then if the pronouncement is to be canonically valid and lawful, the judge must act with authority that is shared with him in virtue of a concordat with the Holy See through which the Church has previously sanctioned his intervention,[83] or the parties must appear before the civil judge with the express permission of the Church.[84]

---

das Verfahren bezüglich der Trennung der Ehe von Tisch und Bett den staatlichen Gerichten zusteht."—*AAS,* XXVI (1934), 277.

[81] Canons 1130; 1131, §1.

[82] Coniux innocens, sive iudicis sententia sive propria auctoritate legitime discesserit, nulla umquam obligatione tenetur coniugum adulterum rursus admittendi ad vitae consortium; . . .

[83] Cf. S. C. Sacramentis, instr. "*Provida Mater,*" Art. VI, §2—*AAS,* XXVIII (1936), 316.

[84] Cf. Kelly, "Separation and Civil Divorce"—*The Jurist,* VI (1946), 209.

Therefore, in either case the authority of the Church is recognized, and without such a public ecclesiastical authorization the subsequent separation would not constitute in law a legitimate separation.

Augustine (1872–1943) was authority for the statement that a civil court may indeed give a sentence of temporary divorce or separation, but that such a sentence had no other effect than that of private separation, unless the episcopal court accepted the evidence and the verdict of the civil court and made them its own.[85] The juridical effect of a separation undertaken on private authority will be treated later in this Article. For the present it may be noted briefly that the sphere in which such authority may be exercised in relation to a lawful departure is extremely limited. In relation to a permanent separation as sanctioned by the Church, a departure effected on private authority is conditioned on a single cause, namely that of adultery, which must be certain as opposed to doubtful or only probable, and *notorious* as opposed to occult.[86]

When the crime of adultery is not certain and notorious, a continued absence following upon a departure instituted solely on private authority is unlawful. This is true for the reason that as long as the right of departure remains doubtful the accused spouse is unjustly deprived of a right, the right to cohabitation, which as a certain and established right commands respect and honor until there is conclusive proof that the right has been sacrificed or lost.[87] Therefore, as long as the act of adultery remains doubtful, a special ecclesiastical sanction for the separation must be sought if the continued absence is to be a legitimate one. If the adultery is certain and truly notorious, the innocent spouse may provisionally depart on his or her own authority, but even in this case, in view of a possible deception regarding the notoriety of the crime, the intervention of ecclesiastical authority is strongly advised in order that the separation may have definitive effect.

---

[85] *A Commentary on the New Code of Canon Law,* V, 377.

[86] Gasparri, *De Matrimonio,* II, n. 1175; Chelodi, *Ius Matrimoniale,* n. 161; Coronata, *De Sacramentis,* III, 921; Cappello, *De Matrimonio,* n. 827.

[87] Wernz-Vidal, *Ius Canonicum,* V, n. 642.

As long as such an ecclesiastical sanction is lacking the alleged adulterer may at any time seek redress before an ecclesiastical court. In this regard the separation instituted solely on private authority is termed " provisional."

Lastly, if the alleged adultery is certain but occult, then there exists undoubtedly a right to institute a separation, but again the intervention of ecclesiastical authority is advised in order that every scandal may be forestalled and in order that any possible future conflict between the internal and the external forums may be prevented. Such a conflict would occur should the innocent spouse be constrained by ecclesiastical authority to return to the community of life from which a lawful departure had previously been effected on the initiation of the spouse's private authority.[88]

Hence it seems that, though the right to institute a permanent departure solely on private authority for the reason that adultery has been committed by the marriage partner is sanctioned in the common law of the Church, for all practical purposes it is restricted in its exercise to the internal forum, so that if a separation is to have canonical recognition in the external forum there is need of a direct ecclesiastical sanction. Thus a wife who departs licitly in consequence of the notorious adultery of her husband may for that cause licitly continue the separation, but so long as the Church has not juridically sanctioned the separation, she must be regarded as *legitime non separata,* and hence she retains her husband's domicile, and can at most establish a quasi-domicile of her own.[89]

---

[88] " At quaeritur num possit, si adulterium est certum, sed occultum. Communior et probabilior sententia affirmat, saltem pro foro conscientiae, contra S. Thomam in 4, dist. 35, q. 1, a. 3, aliosque, quia causa tribuens ius divortii indubia est, ac proinde coniux innocens discedere prohibebitur in hoc casu tantum lege caritatis ad evitandum scandalum, aut diffamationem coniugis culpabilis: sed lex caritatis non obligat cum magno incommodo, quod hisce in casibus numquam non aderit. Diximus *saltem in foro conscientiae,* quia in foro externo ex causa adulterii nec notorii nec legitime probati coniux dimissum coniugem recipere a iudice compellendus est, ne malis coniugibus praebeatur ansa innocentem compartem dimissione vel recessu iniuste vexandi."—Gasparri, *De Matrimonio,* II, n. 1175; Wernz-Vidal, *Ius Canonicum,* V, n. 642.

[89] Canon 93, §2.

SECTION 2. TEMPORARY SEPARATION

Canon 1131, §1, upon the recitation of the causes which may justify a temporary cessation of the conjugal life, establishes the proper authorities who may sanction such a departure.[90] The authority is quite generally vested in the local ordinary, but under specified conditions also in the innocent spouse.

The temporary nature of the separation sanctioned in canon 1131, §1, is evident from the second paragraph of this canon wherein the obligation of the restoration of the conjugal life is made mandatory when the cause for the departure has ceased. But if the separation was decreed by the local ordinary for a certain or indefinite period of time, the innocent spouse is not under any obligation to return to the conjugal community of life except in obedience to a decree of the ordinary or upon the lapse of the time determined by the ordinary.[91]

Regarding the temporary departure instituted on private authority it is to be noted that two conditions must be realized before this authority may even be exercised. On the part of the alleged cause, the same must be certain, and simultaneously, a delay in the departure must be fraught with serious danger.. Should either of these conditions be unrealized, then any departure and subsequent absence for any of the reasons alleged as sufficient under canon 1131, §2, would be unlawful, since the separation would exist as a departure not canonically authorized. Such a departure undertaken without a sufficient authorization would lack the same canonical effects that attend a separation when it is duly sanctioned by the competent ecclesiastical authority.

While the Code of Canon Law does not expressly state what degree of certainty is required regarding a crime of adultery if the latter is to justify a perpetual separation, but has left the determination of the degree of certainty to those who interpret the

---

[90] ". . . haec causae alique id genus, sunt pro altero coniuge totidem legitimae causae discedendi, auctoritate Ordinarii loci, et etiam propria auctoritate, si de eis constet, et periculum sit in mora."

[91] "In omnibus his casibus, causa separationis cessante, vitae consuetudo restauranda est; sed si separatio ab Ordinario pronuntiata fuerit ad certum incertumque tempus, coniux innocens ad id non obligatur, nisi ex decreto Ordinarii vel exacto tempore."—canon 1132, §2.

law, the Code specifically does permit a temporary departure on private authority then only when the cause is evident.[92] Here again, as in the case wherein one must judge concerning the sufficiency of the alleged cause for a permanent separation, one is confronted with a potential multitude of instances or cases which may extend from the perfectly obvious case which justifies a departure to the extremely questionable case which renders the right of departure very doubtful. Hence no attempt will be made in this work to determine a closed category of " certainly justifying circumstances." It is proposed by the writer, however, that, as the circumstances must be objective, so also must the judgment regarding these circumstances be objective; and that, as the rights which are due are owed in justice, so the judgment on the suspension of these rights must likewise be founded in justice, and hence may not be based on prejudice, partiality, or subjective emotions. Thus it seems reasonable to require for the sake of stability and justice that the temporary departure instituted on private authority be confirmed by the competent public authority before it can become entitled to recognition as a " legitimate " separation before the law.

As to the second condition, namely, the serious danger resulting from any delay, Coronata states that such a danger is recognized as being present if it is solely at the expense of grave harm for soul, body, or temporal goods that a recourse can be interposed with the local ordinary and his decision awaited.[93]

Since the requirement contemplates a " grave " danger, it seems reasonable to postulate that the danger be present, that it be objective, that of its nature it be of serious import to the threatened party, and that the aggressor be capable of executing the evil threatened. While threats that are not being executed, fears that are purely subjective, and harm that may be visited on another,

[92] ". . . si de eis certo constet . . ."—canon 1131, §1.

[93] " Periculum autem in mora esse censetur si sine gravi animae, corporis aut bonorum temporalium damno recurri non possit ad Ordinarium loci et eius sententia expectari, quia, e.g., amentia furiosa subito evasit; quia morbus contagiosus etiam vi legis civilis segregationem statim requirit; si rixae et odia subdito proruperint; si coniux coniugem armata manu minatus sit etc. etc."—*De Sacramentis,* III, p. 925.

will perhaps justify a departure from the contemplated danger, they hardly seem to justify a continued absence apart from an immediate ecclesiastical sanction.

An objection could be raised regarding the necessity of having recourse to the local ordinary on the score that a delay in obtaining a hearing prompted the lawgiver to empower the individual spouse to make the decision. This may be a valid objection in relation to the case wherein private authority deems it necessary to exercise the right of an immediate departure, but it does not carry weight for the case of a continued absence, since in cases of this nature the Church sanctions the use of the informal process, in which the time element may readily be reduced to a minimum.

In the examination of the nature, merits, and problems incident to petitions for a separation, ecclesiastical authorities, usually the local ordinary or his delegate may employ either of two different processes.[94] One process is administrative, the other judicial. The causes mentioned in canon 1131, §1, are ordinarily decided according to the administrative process, though the Sacred Roman Rota has indicated reasons which suggest the use of the judicial process even in cases of temporary separation.[95] Usually it belongs to the local ordinary to determine whether a particular case of separation is to be adjudicated in an administrative or in a judicial process. The consorts may, at times, for valid reasons request a judicial trial, even in those cases envisaged in canon 1131, §1.[96]

It is to be noted that, if the administrative process is used, the question of competency is to be determined by canon 201 rather than by canon 1964, and that the local ordinary may delegate someone else to decide the case. Unless forbidden expressly, the vicar general is competent to decide cases of separation through the administrative process by virtue of his office, while the *officialis,* if he is to use the administrative process, requires a

[94] P.C.I., 25 iun. 1922—*AAS,* XXIV (1932), 284; Doheny, *Canonical Procedure in Matrimonial Cases,* II, 642.

[95] Doheny, *op. cit.,* II, 642–643.

[96] Canon 1687; Doheny, *op. cit.,* II, 643.

special mandate of the bishop or of the vicar general since he is not competent simply by reason of his office.[97]

SECTION 3. SEPARATION BY PRIVATE AUTHORITY

It is not proposed here to treat in detail the subject of the separation of spouses on their own private authority, but it is necessary to determine what, if any, juridical effects flow from such a separation. By the term "private separation," or a separation undertaken on private authority, is meant a discontinuance of the mutual cohabitation as a result of the decision of one of the spouses to depart from the other, or of the expulsion of one by the other apart from the sanction of public ecclesiastical authority. It is presumed here that at the time of departure or expulsion there is present a cause which in law would justify a judicial sentence or decree of perpetual separation in consequence of a notorious adultery.[98]

The question of private authority in relation to the separation of spouses has been the subject of rather extensive canonical commentary.[99] A difference of opinion on this question originated in consequence of the seemingly contradictory decretal letters of Pope Alexander III (1159–1181), which letters were referred to previously.[100] In the first of these letters, "*Porro,*"[101] Pope

---

[97] Doheny, *op. cit.*, II, 644.

[98] Temporary separation is not considered in connection with this question, since obviously a spouse departing for a cause which justifies such a separation is bound to return when the cause no longer exists, and therefore could not have the intention necessary for establishing a domicile. Cf. canon 1132, §2. Likewise the situation of certain nullity is not considered, since it seems certain that in such a case an ecclesiastical sanction is necessary before a legitimate separation could be established.—Cf. Reiffenstuel, *Ius Canonicum Universum*, Lib. IV, tit. XIX, nn. 14, 15.

[99] Cf. Sanchez, *De Matrimonii Sacramento*, Lib. X, disp. XII, nn. 10–38; Reiffenstuel, *op. cit.*, Lib. IV, tit. XIX, nn. 89–100; Schmalzgrueber, *Ius Ecclesiasticum Universum*, Lib. IV, tit. XIX, nn. 108–115; Wernz-Vidal, *Ius Canonicum*, V, 782–783; Coronata, *De Sacramentis*, III, 920, 924.

[100] Cf. *supra*, pp.

[101] "Porro de comite Pontini, qui filiam B. de sancto Valerico uxorem suam absque iudicio ecclesiae dimisit propterea, quia eam cognatam fuisse uxoris defunctae proponit, haec prudentia tua cognoscat, quod, si etiam parentela esset publica et notoria, absque iudicio ecclesiae ab ea separari non

Alexander had ordered the restoring of a wife to her husband who had dismissed her because of an alleged diriment impediment of affinity. In the second decretal letter, "*Significasti,*"[102] it was denied that a husband, who had dismissed his adulterous wife whose crime was notorious, could be forced to receive her again into his home. Later commentaries harmonized the apparent difference of the effect of private authority in these two letters by pointing out that in the first letter there was question of the bond of marriage, and that in the second letter there was no question of the bond; also, that in the second letter mere possession had been denied to the wife by her husband, while in the first letter, property, a more fundamental right had been denied.[103] When it was a question that concerned the bond, the Church had exclusive jurisdiction; the presumption in such a case stood in favor of the bond until the existence or the validity of the bond was disproved.

After having commented on these two letters of Pope Alexander III, Schmalzgrueber proposed the following question: May the innocent spouse depart on his own authority from a spouse who has been guilty of a single adulterous act? He prefaced his reply by outlining the arguments of the proponents of the negative opinion, which opinion contended that the judgment of the Church was requisite before a departure was permissible.

The proponents of the negative opinion contended: (1) that such a departure on private authority had been expressly disallowed by Pope Alexander III in the decretal letter "*Porro*"; (2) that formerly a penalty of excommunication had been imposed on husbands who dismissed their wives without awaiting the judgment of the Church; (3) that one who thus dismissed his wife acted contrary to the legal maxim that no one was permitted to be a judge in his own cause; (4) that divorce was a penalty for the guilty person, which penalty the law did not impose *ipso facto,*

potuit, quare ipsum ad eam recipiendam, quae petit restitutionem ipsius, districte compellas. . . ." c. 3, X, *de divortiis,* IV, 19.

[102] ". . . respondemus, quod, si notorium est, mulierem ipsam adulterium commisisse, ad eam recipiendam praefatus vir cogi non debet, nisi constaret, ipsum cum alia adulterium commisisse."—c. 4, X, *de divortiis,* IV, 19.

[103] Schmalzgrueber, *op. cit.,* Lib. IV, tit. XIX, n. 114.

but reserved its infliction to public judicial authority; and (5) that since the celebration of marriage was under the authority of the Church, it belonged to the same authority, and not to that of the spouses, to dissolve the contract or to release the parties from its obligations.[104]

In replying to these arguments, Schmalzgrueber[105] noted the necessity of making this distinction, namely, either the commission of the adultery was known with certainty, or its commission was doubtful or only suspected. A doubt or a suspicion regarding the commission of adultery was not an adequate basis upon which to justify a separation on private authority. Moral certainty or a violent presumption was the minimum requirement for depriving a spouse of rightful possession. A further distinction[106] was made, namely, that if there was certainty regarding the commission of the crime, then the crime would be either notorious or occult, but certainly known to the innocent spouse. If the crime was notorious, whether in fact or in law, the innocent party was justified in separating, being released from the duty of rendering the marital debt and from the duty to cohabit with the guilty spouse. But if the crime was occult, yet certainly known to the innocent spouse, the authors were not in agreement as to the right of the innocent spouse to depart on her own authority.[107]

Schmalzgrueber stated that the more common opinion permitted a departure on private authority even in the case wherein the adultery was occult but certainly known to the innocent spouse,

[104] ". . . ex quorum sententia, ut coniux innocens ab adultero possit divertere, necessarium est iudicium ecclesiae. Fundatur (1) textu c. *porro* (c. 3, X, *de divortiis,* IV, 19) ubi diserte negatur coniugum separationem absque iudicio ecclesiae fieri posse, etiam cum parentela, sive consanguinitas publica, et notoria est. (2) Can. saeculares (c. 1, C. XXXIII, q. 2) ubi excommunicari iubentur viri, qui uxores suas sine iudicio ecclesiae dimittunt. (3) Quia sic recedentes sibi ius dicunt in propria causa contra 1. unic. C. ne quis in sua causa etc. (C.[3.5]). (4) Divortium est poena nocentis, quam ius ipso facto non imponit, sed iudicii remittit imponendam. (5) Matrimonium est ecclesiae authoritate celebratum; igitur authoritate ecclesiae et non ipsorum coniugum dissolvi debet."—Schmalzgrueber, *op. cit.,* Lib. IV, tit. XIX, n. 109.

[105] *Ibid.,* n. 110.

[106] *Ibid.,* n. 111.

[107] *Ibid.,* n. 112.

and he permitted such a departure at least in the forum of conscience and provided that scandal was not given.[108] He reasoned that the duties of the marriage contract are conditioned on the fidelity of the conjugal faith, which when broken released the innocent spouse from her duties. The right of departure was not based on the notoriety of the crime, but upon its actual commission. If the commission of the adultery was known with certainty, the right could be exercised. The limitation of the right of departure to the forum of conscience was necessary, for, if the cause of departure was neither notorious nor legitimately proved, the innocent spouse might be judicially compelled to return to the marriage partner.

Having proposed these arguments, Schmalzgrueber answered directly the arguments of those who denied that there was any right of departure on private authority. He denied the existence of any parity between the crime of adultery as a cause for departure and the alleged existence of a diriment impediment, e.g., consanguinity, as such a cause. A departure in consequence of adultery was a denial of possession only, while a departure because of the alleged existence of a diriment impediment was a denial of a fundamental right, property, which resulted in greater prejudice, and consequently necessitated a judicial determination of the existence of the impediment.[109]

He furthermore contended that the excommunication imposed on husbands who dismissed their wives was not applicable to the question, since the excommunication recorded by Gratian applied

[108] "Quod si vero adulterium alterius publice occultum sit, sed innocenti privatim certo cognitum, maior est controversia . . . sed communior etiam hoc casu permittit innocenti ut propria authoritate possit recedere, saltem pro foro conscientiae et secluso scandalo. Ratio est, quia matrimonium ex natura sua non aliter obligat ad thorum et redditionem debiti coniugalis, quam sub conditione, si etiam alter coniux fidem coniugalem servet."—*op. cit., loc. cit.*

[109] "Negatur paritas inter separationem matrimonii, quae fit ex causa adulterii, et inter eam, quae fit ex causa impedimenti consanguinitatis, vel alterius impedimenti dirimentis: per *primam* coniux privatur sola possessione, sive usu communis thori, et commodis obsequii coniugalis, per secundam vero deiicitur ipsa proprietate, quod cum multis maioris sit praeiudicii, merito ad separationem hanc decernendam exigitur iudicium et authoritas ecclesiae."—*Ibid.*, n. 114.

to those who dismissed their spouses without a grave cause and for ulterior motives.[110] A departure on private authority, he contended, did not violate the rule which forbade one to judge his own cause, but rather the departure was the exercise of a right given in the law.[111] Likewise the divorce instituted by the innocent party, as also the denial of the marital debt, was not properly a penalty; but rather, these factors reflected the exercise of a right allowed by the very nature of the marital contract, and it was sufficient for the exercise of the right that the innocent party knew that the conjugal faith had been broken.[112]

In reply to the final argument against the adequacy of private authority in relation to a separation for the cause of adultery, Schmalzgrueber seemed to concede that for the *external forum* the authority of the Church was requisite.[113] For the *internal forum*, however, he reasoned that the nature of the contract was to be considered, for through the contract the duties of mutual cohabitation and of rendering the marital debt on the part of one of the spouses were conditioned on the observance of the conjugal faith by the other. His concession for the external forum points perhaps to the conclusion that all his foregoing arguments were meant as so many justifying reasons for the internal forum only.

Reiffenstuel [114] and Sanchez [115] upheld the *licitness* of a separa-

---

[110] "In textu illo (c. 1, C. XXXIII, q. 2) non agitur de eo, qui uxorem suam dimisit ex causa adulterii, cuius notitiam certam habet; sed de eo, qui illam dimisit sine ulla graviori culpa, aut probabili causa, animo ad illicita consortia accedendi."—*Ibid.*, n. 114, nota 2.

[111] "Innocens discessu illo non tam sibi ius dicit, quam utitur iure, sibi ex natura matrimonii certo competente, et nulla lege adempta."—*Ibid.*, n. 114, nota 3.

[112] "Divortium non est proprie poena, sed quasi conditio inhibita in ipso matrimonii contractu, quae cum sit in favorem innocentis, satis est, ut innocens, adulterii conscius adulterum iure exigendi privet."—*Ibid.*, n. 114, nota 4.

[113] "Conceditur sequela pro foro externo, in interno spectatur natura contractus matrimonialis, qui ad debitum reddendum, et cohabitationem mutuam non obligat, nisi sub conditione servatae fidei ab altero coniuge."—*Ibid.*, n. 114, nota 5.

[114] "Si adulterium notorium est, v.g., quia maritus aliam impregnavit idque in judicio probatum, vel ab eodem confessum sit, aut si uxor, absente

tion instituted under the circumstances considered here. It appears that these commentators all were considering the question from the moral rather than from the legal point of view. In substance they seemed to say that it was licit for the innocent spouse to depart when the adultery was notorious; licit also when the adultery was occult but certainly known to the innocent spouse, and that the latter was true at least for the forum of conscience and provided that no scandal was given. Schmalzgrueber through his concession of the necessity of ecclesiastical juridical authority for the separation indicated that he knew of no definite prescription of the Church on the matter, and conceded that if there were such a prescription then the innocent spouse even in the case of notorious adultery would be required to comply with the prescription.

The Code today speaks of a *legitimate* separation,[116] of a *legitimate* accusation,[117] of a *legitimate* departure [118] and of *legitimate* causes.[119] These phrases seem to imply something more than the simple consideration of licitness in an act of separation or departure. The Instruction [120] of the Sacred Congregation of the Sacraments offers the strongest indications to the same effect. Therein, at least when there is question of an alleged nullity of the marriage, private authority is not recognized as an adequate basis for establishing a legitimate separation. Sartori, as noted by Torre,[121] considered an ecclesiastical juridical sentence or decree

---

vel impotente viro, ab alio impregnata est, in utroque foro est *licitum* propria auctoritate divortium facere."—*Ius Canonicum Universum,* Lib. IV, tit. XIX, n. 89.

115 *De Matrimonii Sacramento,* Lib. X, disp. XII, nn. 12, 25.

116 Cf. canon 93, §§1, 2.

117 Cf. canon 1129, §2.

118 Cf. canon 1130.

119 Cf. canon 1131, §1.

120 S. C. de Sacramentis, instr. "*Provida Mater,*" Art. 6, §1—*AAS,* XXVIII (1936), 314.

121 "Sartori apud Enchridion canonicum (a. 1935 pag. 24 ad can. 93) addit sequentem rationem 'quia non est legitime (idest per iudicem ecclesiasticum) a viro separata, etsi legitime discesserit proptia tantum auctoritate.' "—Cf. Torre, *Instructio servanda a tribunalibus dioecesanis in pertractandis causis de nullitate matrimoniorum a Sacra Congregatione de Disciplina Sacramentorum edita* (Neapoli: M. D'Auria, 1937), p. 12.

a requisite for the constitution of a legitimate separation. And Sartori, an auditor of the Sacred Roman Rota, had expressed this opinion before the issuance of the Instruction *"Provida Mater"* of the Sacred Congregation of the Sacraments. Regatillo is of the opinion that a private separation can have only a *moral* effect, and terms the innocent party's departure licit, but void of *juridical* effect.[122]

Article E. Concept of the Expression "Legitime non Separata"

Having treated of unlawful separation in consequence of a deficient cause and for a lack of an adequate authorization, the writer now considers the meaning and the juridical extension of the phrase *"legitime non separata"* as occurring specifically in canon 93, and by way of clarification in Section two of Article Six of the Instruction "Provida Mater," issued by the Sacred Congregation of the Sacraments under date of August 15, 1936.

> "Can. 93.—§1. Uxor, a viro legitime non separata, necessario retinet domicilium viri sui; . . .
>
> §2. Minor infantia egressus potest quasi-domicilium proprium obtinere; item uxor a viro legitime non separata, legitime autem separata etiam domicilium."
>
> "Art. 6—Sec. 2. Uxor, a viro perpetuo aut ad tempus indefinitum separata legitime, i.e., per sententiam iudicialem competentis tribunalis ecclesiastici, vel etiam civilis a S. Sede, vi concordati, recognitam, aut per Ordinarii decretum, non sequitur domicilium viri, ideoque conveniri debet vel coram Ordinario loci in quo nuptiae initiae sunt, vel coram Ordinario sui domicilii vel quasi-domicilii."[123]

In the law legitimacy or "non-legitimacy" of a separation determines whether or not the wife so separated may or may not establish her own independent voluntary domicile. By virtue of canon 93, §1, a wife not legitimately separated from her husband necessarily retains the domicile of her husband, although if she is so separated she can establish her own proper quasi-domicile; by

[122] *Ius Sacramentarium,* II, n. 588.

[123] *AAS,* XXVIII (1936), 313–361, at p. 316.

reason of canon 93, §2, a wife legitimately separated from her husband can acquire a voluntary domicile independently of her husband. The question presents itself: What is meant by a legitimate separation in ecclesiastical jurisprudence?

A valid distinction seems warranted between the terms "legitimate" and "licit," when these words are employed to describe a state of separation. Cocchi, writing shortly after the promulgation of the Code of Canon Law, in commenting on canon 93 stated briefly that a legitimate separation is one conformable to the norm of law; and that it is not required that the separation have been effected through the authority of a judge which is not invariably demanded, provided of course that the wife can conclusively prove her separation.[124]

The presence or absence of official juridical authority was, then, from the time of the promulgation of the Code of Canon Law recognized as an element which might affect the nature of the separation effected, for it is said specifically that there may be cases wherein judicial authority is not requisite. However, very shortly thereafter it was recognized that a distinction must be made between "licit" and "legitimate" in relation to separation.

In an official response by the Pontifical Commission for the Interpretation of the Canons of the Code of Canon Law under date of July 14, 1922, it was established that a wife maliciously deserted by her husband could not establish her own proper domicile unless a separation, either perpetual or for an indefinite period of time, had been obtained from an ecclesiastical judge.[125]

Malicious desertion,[126] therefore, reflects an instance wherein

---

[124] "*Uxor* a viro legitime non separata, necessario retinet domicilium viri sui; dicitur *legitime,* nempe ad normam iuris, nec requiritur separatio facta iudicis auctoritate (quae non semper postulatur), dummodo uxor demonstrare valeat suam separationem; . . ."—*Commentarium in Codicem Iuris Canonici* (8 vols. in 5, Taurinorum Augustae: Marietti, 1920–1930), II (*De Personis,* 1922), p. 20.

[125] "Utrum uxor, a viro malitiose deserta, possit, ad normam can. 93, §2, obtinere proprium ac distinctum domicilium. Resp. Negative, nisi a iudice ecclesiastico obtinuerit separationem perpetuam, aut ad tempus indefinitum."—*AAS,* XIV (1922), 526.

[126] The essential elements of malicious desertion are: (a) departure or dismissal of the spouse; (b) the intention of not fulfilling conjugal obliga-

the wife may be away from her husband licitly, i.e., without moral culpability on her part, and that even permanently, and yet the resulting separation is in law not such that intrinsically it could be characterized as a legitimate separation from which a determination of voluntary domicile might follow.

Vermeersch-Creusen recognize that the intervention of a juridical ecclesiastical authority is the controlling element of a legitimate separation when the effected separation is based upon a cause insufficient in itself to allow a legitimate separation to become effected on the initiative of private authority.[127] Separation consequent upon malicious desertion by the husband, while licit on the part of the wife, is not in and of itself a "legitimate" separation until juridical ecclesiastical authority has intervened and established the true sufficiency of the cause. In other words, truly malicious desertion merits in the common law to rank as a legitimate cause for a separation, but before the state of "legitimate" separation may be said to exist as deriving from this cause, ecclesiastical authority must examine the circumstances which attend the cause as alleged. The cause in itself (*per se*) is not sufficient; private authority cannot declare the resultant state "legitimate" before the law.

Michiels notes that previous to the year 1922 the common teaching was that a malicious desertion in and of itself constituted a cause for the establishing of a legitimate separation and therefore proved sufficient for the acquiring of a proper domicile distinct from that of the deserting husband.[128] The reason as-

---

tions; and (c) the absence of a just cause. Cf. S. R. Rota, *Separationis*, 17 mart. 1913, *coram* R.P.D. A. Perathoner, Ponente, Dec. XIX, n. 6—*S. R. Rotae Decisiones seu Sententiae*, V (1919), 219; S. R. Rota, *Separationis*, 6 dec. 1929, *coram* R.P.D. F. Morano, Ponente, Dec. LXIII, n. 4—*S. R. Rotae Decisiones seu Sententiae*, XXI (1937), 528.

127 "Ut separatio uxoris legitima esse censeatur, opus est ut intercesserit sententia iudicis ecclesiastici permittentis separationem perpetuam vel temporariam, saltem extra casus in quibus ipsi cc. 1130–1131 legitimam pronuntiant uxoris sèparationem, etiam quae propria auctoritate sit facta. Quare, si vir uxorem deseruerit, haec quidem *licite* separatim vivit, non autem legitime, per se, sine iudicis sententia."—*Epitome Iuris Canonici* (3 vols., Vol. I, 6. ed., 1937; Vol. II, 5. ed., 1934; Vol. III, 5., ed. 1936; Mechliniae-Romae: H. Dessain), I, n. 212, ad 4.

128 "Antea communiter docebatur desertionem malitiosam esse ex se

signed by Michiels for the necessity of the ecclesiastical pronouncement is to be found in canon 1960, whereby matrimonial causes between baptized persons are reserved to the judgment of the Church. He points out that a separation authorized by the civil authority without ecclesiastical approval would be *illegitimate* (italics supplied), and inept as a condition in consequence of which a distinct ecclesiastical domicile could be formed by the beneficiary of the civil decree or sentence of separation.

The writer submits that the phrase "*legitime non separata*" is not necessarily to be translated as "illegitimately separated," as Michiels seems to imply when he points to the example of a separation effected by civil authority. When such a circumstance intervenes in a case, then contempt for ecclesiastical authority is usually verified, and assuredly the action is illegitimate and unlawful. However, in the event that a husband deserts his wife, the latter may have foregone all action before public authority the while she continues to live apart from her husband licitly. But in that supposition she is constituted in the state contemplated in canon 93, §1, as "legitime non separata." Accordingly she is capable of establishing her own quasi-domicile, but lacks all capacity for establishing her own domicile as distinct from her husband's.

Ojetti (1862–1932) argued that an adulterous wife upon being expelled by her husband is, from the moment of the expulsion,

---

legitimae separationis causam, ideoque ad proprium domicilium acquirendum sufficientem. Nunc vero statuitur uxorem malitiose desertam, etsi licite vivat a viro separata (quia causa separationis non est ipsi imputabilis), per se non haberi legitime, seu ad normam iuris, separatam, nisi interveniat iudicis ecclesiastici sententia; quod si ita sit ad normam can. 93, §2, logice concluditur talem uxorem non posse sibi acquirere domicilium proprium, nisi sententia judicis pronuntiaverit separationem perpetuam aut saltem ad tempus indefinitum. Ratio cur in hoc casu, sicut in quacumque separationis causa judicialiter definienda, requiratur *ecclesiastici judicis sententia,* est quia ex can 1960 'causae matrimoniales inter baptizatos jure proprio et exclusivo ad judicem ecclesiasticum spectant.'" Quapropter separatio a judice civili pronuntiata habetur illegitima et ad domicilium ecclesiasticum distinctum permittendum inepta, nisi sane causarum separationis pronuntiatio ex explicita Ecclesiae concessione fuerit judicio civili permissa vel ex legitima consuetudine tolerata."—*Principia Generalia De Personis In Ecclesia* (Lublin, Universitas Catholica, 1932), p. 137.

" legitimately " separated in the sense of canon 93, §2, so that she may immediately establish a separate voluntary domicile.[129] He based his argument on this that the necessary domicile of the wife results from the necessity of leading a life in common with her husband and of being subject to his authority. When this obligation and subjection have become neutralized, then the reason for the necessary domicile no longer operates.

But it may be answered that such a situation does not necessarily establish a status of " legitimate separation," since the same elements are verified in the case of a truly malicious desertion of the husband. It is to be recalled that in the case of a malicious desertion the deserter has the intention of terminating the common life, and thus no more actual subjection obtains in the case of malicious desertion than in the case of expulsion for adultery. Yet, it is certain that a malicious desertion does not immediately establish for the deserted wife the status of a " mulier legitime separata."

For other cases which may justify a " legitimate " separation of the spouses there does not exist any definite authoritative pronouncement such as has been given with reference to a malicious

[129] " A viro legitime non separata.—Nam tunc, quum abrumpi possit, etiam in perpetuum aliquando, vel saltem ad tempus, durante causa separationis, vitae communio, coniuges iam non cohabitant. At nota, dici hic uxorem a viro *legitime* non separatam. Quid autem haec important? Num innuitur ad hunc effectum habendum, necessarium semper esse interventum iudicis, an contra significatur, id faciendum quidem esse ex concessione a lege facta, non tamen necessario interveniente iudice? Aliis verbis, si uxorem, ex. gr., ob adulterium vir expulerit propria auctoritate, ut fieri posse patet ex can. 1129, §2, 1130, uxor adulter amittitne statim domicilium mariti? Et videtur affirmative respondendum, tum quia domicilium hoc necessarium resultat ex necessitate communis vitae ducendae, ut dictum est, cum ex eo, quod mulier subdita est viro eique subiicitur; ex quibus deducitur ipsam vere ibi constituisse centrum suae vitae et sedem suorum negotiorum. Porro separatione legitime instituta subiectio illa de facto abrumpitur, et domicilium mariti non potest amplius pro uxore (et vicissim) constituere centrum vitae et sedes negotiorum. Ad id non obtinet, quando mulier a viro malitiose deseritur; tunc enim necesse est, ut mulier, si velit, ob hanc rationem petat et obtineat sententiam separationis perpetuae seu ad tempus indefinitum, cui non aequivalet *malitiosa* desertio viri."—*Commentarium in Codicem Iuris Canonici* (4 vols., Romae: apud sedes Universitatis Gregorianae, 1927–1931), II (1928), 53–54.

desertion as a similar cause. The authors, however, in their commentaries on the canons that treat of the necessary domicile of the wife, undertake to show what constitutes a "legitimate" separation. The commentators in general are in agreement on this point, namely, that there must intervene a sentence of an ecclesiastical judge which permits a temporary or a perpetual separation, at least outside the cases, as the commentators claim, "in which canons 1130 and 1131 pronounce the separation of a wife 'legitimate,' even though the separation is made on private authority." [130]

According to Michiels there is common agreement among the authors that a permanent separation may be effected on private authority in consequence of adultery committed by one of the spouses, and automatically upon the exercise of the right of departure or expulsion there is constituted the status of "legitimate separation" such as will permit the establishment of a voluntary domicile. But his reasoning is more from the point of view of the requirements relative to domicile than with reference to separation, inasmuch as the community of life has legitimately been discontinued, so that no obligation of a return to it on the part of the culpable spouse any longer exists in the law. Therefore, so he concludes, not only the innocent but also the culpable spouse may have the intention of remaining perpetually in a place, by which statement he seems to imply the capacity for the establishing of a domicile.[131] The writer has already on a previous

---

[130] Cf. Vermeersch-Creusen, *Epitome Iuris Canonici,* I, n. 212; Wernz-Vidal (*Ius Canonicum,* II [3. ed., 1943], 15), who merely repeat the doctrine of Vermeersch-Creusen, and counsel recourse to the local ordinary. Cf. also Michiels, *op. cit.,* p. 135; Cappello, *De Matrimonio,* nn. 827–828; Coronata, *Institutiones Iuris Canonici* (5 vols., Vol. I–IV, 2. ed., 1939–1945; Vol. V, 1936, Taurini, Romae: Marietti), I (2. ed., 1939), n. 126 (hereafter cited *Institutiones*); Ojetti, *Commentarium in Codicem Iuris Canonici,* II, 53.

[131] "Nec minus certe verificatur, juxta unanimem Doctorum sententiam," [Michiels here cites Vermeersch-Creusen, Toso, Coronata, Cappello, Ojetti, and Costello] "si, manente vinculo matrimoniali, ad normam can. 1129, 1130, vitae communio fuerit legitime soluta *propter adulterium* ab alterutro conjuge commissum nec ab altero condonatum aut compensatum; in hoc casu enim 'conjux innocens, sive judicis sententia sive propria auctoritate legitime discesserit, nulla umquam obligatione tenetur conjugem adulterum rursus admittendi ad vitae consortium,' ideoque nihil obstat, quominus uxor non

page[132] indicated his non-acceptance of this doctrine when he considered Ojetti's like doctrine that favored the potential establishment of a domicile on the part of the culpable party when permanently expelled because of adultery. On the other hand, there is no settled uniform opinion among the authors regarding the consequent status that attaches to a separation undertaken on private authority for a cause which in the law suffices for a temporary separation only.[133]

However, the very questions in point are whether the departure on private authority as sanctioned in law for the cases of a perpetual and indefinitely protracted period of separation, and the absence of any reconciliation as the result of the continued cleavage of the community of life, attach the note of stability to the separation contemplated in the notion of a "legitimate" separation as reflected in the phrase "legitime separata." It is true that, once there has been established a legal status of legitimate separation, the conditions for the acquisition of a voluntary domicile may obviously be present. But the precise point is the "legitimacy" in law of the status resulting from a separation undertaken on private authority, even when the departure was sanctioned in law. Before the official response of the year 1922 was given, the authors had concluded that a malicious desertion resulted in a status of legitimate separation. The Pontificial Commission for the Interpretation of the Canons of the Code gave no reasons for its declaration that the sentence of an ecclesiastical judge was requisite before a separate voluntary domicile could be established, which was tantamount to saying that no one is "legitimately" separated in law in consequence of a malicious desertion until that cause for separation had been juridically examined by ecclesiastical authority.

In a case wherein adultery is the reason for separation the innocent spouse is said to be released from the obligation of community of life, inasmuch as through the exercise on private

---

modo innocens sed et culpabilis ideoque a viro expulsa intentionem in alio loco perpetuo manendi foveat."—*Principia Generalia de Personis in Ecclesia,* pp. 135–136.

[132] Cf. *supra,* p. 82.

[133] Cf. Michiels, *op. cit.,* pp. 136–137.

authority of the right of departure or expulsion, such a spouse manifests an intention to discontinue the conjugal life so that the obligation of cohabitation is no longer binding. In law the act of malicious desertion likewise implies the same intention permanently to discontinue the common life, and consequently it could seem that the obligation of cohabitation incumbent on the deserted spouse should likewise no longer be binding. Yet, the act of malicious desertion, readily as capable of notoriety as the act of adultery, needs to be proved judicially before a status of "legitimate" separation exists, while adultery, according to the authors, may furnish the basis for a "legitimate" separation though the latter be undertaken solely on private authority.

It is not claimed by the writer that there is a parity between desertion and adultery as causes for the separation of consorts, for by reason of their very natures there does exist a fundamental difference between these two factors. But in relation to their possible ultimate effects there does seem to be such a similarity between these two factors that for the establishing of a status in law the same end seems attainable solely through the use of the same means. Hence a judicial confirmation of the cause, if it be adultery, seems requisite even as a similar confirmation is necessary when the cause is that of malicious desertion.

It is the general rule, it is true, that what is notorious no longer requires proof.[134] Now, an act of malicious desertion can very readily be a notorious act. Still the Official Interpretation has made no exceptions. Accordingly such a cause regardless of its notoriety, does not automatically establish the status connoted by the phrase "*legitime separata,*" which would permit the deserted spouse to establish an independent voluntary domicile. Could it be that the Pontifical Commission for the Interpretation of the Canons of the Code, in its response in relation to the act of malicious desertion, indicated that any separation when undertaken on private authority, also when such a separation was undertaken licitly, does not in itself and apart from an ecclesiastical confirmation constitute a "legitimate" separation in the law? Furthermore, could it be that any separation when undertaken licitly on the sole initiative of private authority can at most result in a

[134] Cf. canon 1747, 1°.

status connoted by the phrase "*legitime non separata,*" and will consequently permit the maliciously deserted wife no further option than that of establishing a voluntary quasi-domicile of her own? An affirmative seems indicated as the proper answer for both of the queries.

The writer proposes that the judicial pronouncement, though it simply confirms the separation which is legitimate *de facto* inasmuch as it was licitly instituted on private authority in full accordance with the provisions in the law, imparts to that separation the benefit of a public authoritative sanction. Although the matter does not thereby become a judicially closed issue (res iudicata)[135] yet the presumption of law thenceforth stands in favor of the one for whom the sentence or the decree was given. Previously to the confirmatory judicial pronouncement the innocent spouse could have been held to prove the legitimacy of the separation, even though the act of departure or of expulsion was fully justified in the law. With the making of the ecclesiastical pronouncement there attaches to the effected separation a note of legal stability, so much to be desired when matters of status are at issue. The question regarding the duty of the resumption of a community of life thenceforth is governed directly by the judicial decision; for its proper determination as an inoperative factor it no longer depends respectively on the cessation or on the continuance of the cause for which the separation was instituted. The separation, once a judicial pronouncement is made, becomes legitimate *de iure* and thus stands qualified with full recognition as a public act.

The Instruction of the Congregation of the Sacraments of August 15, 1936, has been specifically mentioned in connection with this question.[136] In this Instruction a wife is said to be separated *legitimately* from her husband either through a judicial sentence of a competent ecclesiastical tribunal, or even of a civil tribunal if recognized by the Holy See in virtue of concordat law, or finally as the result of a decree issued by the local ordinary.

[135] P.C.I., 8 apr. 1941: "An causae separationis coniugum recensendae sint inter causas nunquam transeuntes in rem iudicatam, de quibus in canonibus 1903 et 1989." Resp. "Affirmative."—*AAS,* XXXIII (1941), 173.

[136] Cf. *supra,* p. 78.

A separation undertaken on private authority is not set down by the Congregation of the Sacraments as a *legitimate* separation. Accordingly the question may be asked: Does the Instruction enumerate all the sources of a legitimate separation, so that a separation undertaken on private authority may not be considered in law as *legitimate* separation?

The purpose of the Instruction was to furnish norms of procedure to be observed by diocesan tribunals in the conducting of cases concerning an alleged nullity in marriages.[187] The specific clause regarding the legitimately separated wife is contained in the First Title of the Instruction, wherein there are set forth the norms which determine the competency of the forum as deriving from the consideration of domicile. The Instruction was issued by the Sacred Congregation of the Sacraments, not as by an agency duly authorized to make official interpretations of the Code of Canon Law, but as by an administrative authority whose regulations served the purpose of a more clearly indicated adaptation of the norms already in existence. Therefore, in the light of the purpose and origin of the Instruction, it does not seem that the Instruction alone can settle the question regarding the efficacy of private authority in the matter of establishing a legitimate separation.

It appears, however, that the Congregation of the Sacraments did intend to enumerate all the authoritative sources through which a proper sanction for a legitimate separation might ensue as a factor sufficient to establish a domicile, upon which consideration the competency of a tribunal might be based when the nullity of a marriage was to be considered. The sources of authorization are not enumerated after the manner of examples; rather, they are specifically named as the sources from which the sanction for a legitimate separation may issue. The Sacred Congregation of the

---

[187] The following is found in the introduction to the Instruction "*Provida Mater*" now under discussion: "In hisce regulis iudices ipsi et tribunalium administri praecipuos canones de processibus agentes accurate apteque dispositos reperient, necnon brevem facilemque eorundem explanationem, ex iurisprudentia praesertim erutam atque ex Normis S. R. Rotae, quo plenius ipsis iidem Codicis canones, quibus derogatum non est, sint perspecti, eosque expeditius singulis aptare possint matrimonialibus causis."—*AAS*, XXVIII (1936), 314.

Sacraments has not issued any correction or supplement which would indicate the intention was otherwise than is apparent on the record.[138]

At least one author has been influenced by the Instruction to change his opinion in regard to the sufficiency of private authority in the matter of establishing that type of separation which is requisite for giving the wife the necessary status to establish a domicile. Regatillo, when writing in the year 1941,[139] stated that a voluntary domicile could be acquired by a wife who was legitimately separated from her husband in consequence of a sentence or of a decree of perpetual or indefinite duration, or also by a wife who undertook the separation on her own private authority if the cause for the separation was adultery (citing canon 1130), but not by the wife who acted on her own private authority in view of any of the causes mentioned in canon 1131. His reason was the following: perpetual separation is permitted to the innocent spouse when the other spouse has committed adultery, but perpetual separation is not permitted for the causes listed in canon 1131, and consequently in connection with the latter there would be missing the note of. perpetuity contemplated in the notion of domicile.

When he wrote in the year 1946, Regatillo in treating of the effects of a separation effected on private authority stated that this separation has merely moral effect for the purpose of quieting conscience, so that in those cases wherein a departure is permitted on private authority the innocent party acts *licitly*, and that the departure lacks value so far as juridical effects are concerned. He stated further that, although the innocent party on her own authority separates licitly from her husband for the cause of

---

[138] Cf. S. C. de Sacramentis, *Decretum,* 20 dec. 1940—*AAS,* XXXIII (1941), 363; S. C. de Sacramentis, *Decretum,* 3 maii 1946—*AAS,* XXXVIII (1946), 285. In both of these decrees the particular article being discussed was confirmed without change.

[139] "Domicilium voluntarium habere possunt: . . . (3) uxores a maritis legitime separatae (cc. 1129–1131) per sententiam vel decretum separationis perpetuae seu indefinitae; aut propria auctoritate ob adulterium (c. 1130), non auctoritate propria ob causas c. 1131; nam ob adulterium permittitur innocenti separatio perpetua; non ob alias causas . . ."—*Institutiones Iuris Canonici* (2 vols., Santanda: Sal Terrae, 1941–1942), I, 112.

adultery, even in perpetuity, she is not able to acquire her own domicile, but necessarily retains the domicile of her husband. His authority for this doctrine is the pronouncement of the Congregation of the Sacraments in its definition of a "legitimate separation" as given in the Instruction "*Provida Mater.*" [140]

In treating ex professo of procedure in informal trials, and upon citing canons 1128–1132 and the Article of the Instruction here considered, Doheny states:

> "By the term 'legitimate separation' is understood one that is granted by a decree of the Ordinary, by a judicial sentence of a competent ecclesiastical tribunal, or even of a civil tribunal where such judgment is recognized in virtue of a concordat of the Holy See." [141]

This he states in dealing with the determination of competency of the forum in the adjudication of informal or summary cases.

But in treating of the canonical procedure in separation cases in his article concerning the domicile of the legally separated wife he states:

> "It is indeed regrettable that Article 6, §2, of the Instruction, *Provida,* seems to imply that the only two legitimate means of separation are by judicial sentence or by a decree of the Ordinary. Such is not the case. Canons 1129 and 1130 clearly grant to the innocent consort the right of perpetual separation *propria auctoritate,* at least when the crime of adultery is morally certain and either public or notorious. Similarly, Canon 1131, §1, allows the innocent consort the right of temporary separation as an exceptional means *et etiam propria auctoritate,*

---

[140] "Effectus separationis propria auctoritate factae—Haec habet effectum *mere moralem,* in ordine ad quietem conscientiae. Scilicet in casibus supra indicatis coniux innocens *licite* discedit. At valore iuridico caret, nempe quoad effectus iuris. Sic quamvis uxor innocens ob adulterium mariti se separet licite in perpetuum ab eo *propia* [propria] *auctoritate* tamen nequit acquirere domicilium proprium; sed necessario retinet mariti domicilium. Separatio legitima, qua iuxta c. 93, §2, potest uxor acquirere domicilium proprium, definitur a C. Sacram. loc. cit. art. 6, §2 quae fit *per sententiam iudicis aut per Ordinarii decretum in perpetuum vel ad tempus indefinitum.*" —*Ius Sacramentarium,* II, 398.

[141] *Canonical Procedure in Matrimonial Cases,* II, 147.

provided there is certainty as to the guilt of the other consort and there is danger in delay."

"It follows logically from the authoritative texts of canons 1130 and 1131, §1, that those innocent consorts who have separated *propria auctoritate,* from their guilty consorts in accordance with the laws of the Church are lawfully separated. Hence, they benefit from the special provisions of the law. Thus wives lawfully separated from their husbands, either permanently or for an indefinite period of time, may acquire their own domicile or quasi-domicile." [142]

In very similiar language the same author in his work treating of Formal Judicial Procedure remarks:

"A slight discrepancy appears between the text of Canon 1130 and Article 6, §2. The *Instruction* seems to imply that the only two legitimate means of separation are by judicial sentence or by a decree of the Ordinary; whereas Canon 1130 clearly states: 'Coniux innocens, sive iudicis sententia sive propria auctoritate legitime discesserit.' This clear provision of the Code is in no wise abrogated by Article 6, §2, and hence the innocent party still retains the right to separate legitimately on his or her own authority on account of the adultery of the other party." [143]

The definition of legitimate separation has inclined Bouscaren-Ellis to exclude the agency of private authority as a means of obtaining such a legitimate separation as would enable the wife to establish a domicile.

"What of a wife who leaves her husband because of adultery on his part? Since such separation is contemplated and allowed by law (c. 1130), some affirm that the woman is legally separated and acquires a domicile; but this has never been officially recognized, and we incline to the contrary opinion." [144]

The writer believes that a legitimate separation is to be dis-

---

[142] Doheny, *Canonical Procedure in Matrimonial Cases,* II, 649–650.

[143] *Canonical Procedure in Matrimonial Cases,* I, 24–25.

[144] Bouscaren-Ellis, *Canon Law, A Text and Commentary* (Milwaukee: The Bruce Publishing Company, 1946), 81–82.

tinguished from a legitimate departure. The former is based on a sufficient cause and at the same time on the instituting of the separation by the proper public authority; the latter, i.e., a legitimate departure, is based on a sufficient cause, on the innocence of the one departing, and on the instituting of the departure on private authority. An unlawful departure on private authority results from the fact that the cause for such departure was not an adequate one in itself, or that the requisite attending circumstances for the certification of the cause and of danger in delay were not verified. A legitimate departure, in the opinion of the writer, does not bestow a legal status which enables the wife to establish her own domicile.

CHAPTER VI

THE LEGAL DOMICILE OF THE WIFE AS A JURIDICAL FACTOR FROM THE ENACTMENT OF THE CODE OF CANON LAW TO THE PRESENT DAY

ARTICLE A. THE CANONICAL LEGAL DOMICILE

SECTION 1. THE NATURE, ACQUISITION, AND LOSS OF LEGAL DOMICILE

The Code of Canon Law has confirmed the general principles regarding the institute of domicile as these principles had been stated in pre-Code canonical jurisprudence. The place of one's origin is determined by the Code,[1] and thus the distinction between the place of origin and the institute of domicile is retained in present legislation. The Code preserves the distinction between a voluntary domicile and such a domicile as is acquired by operation of the law when the required conditions are present.[2]

For the acquisition of a voluntary domicile by one capable of establishing such a domicile the Code confirms the requisite of presence in a specific territory and concomitantly with such presence the intention of remaining permanently in that place unless something calls one away,[3] which intention the law supplies if simple residence is protracted for a period of ten years.[4]

---

[1] Canon 90, §1: "Locus originis filii, etiam neophyti, est ille in quo cum filius natus est, domicilium, aut, in defectu domicilii, quasi-domicilium habebat pater vel, si filius sit illegitimus aut postumus, mater.

§2. Si agatur de filio vagorum, locus originis est ipsemet nativitatis locus; si de exposito, est locus in quo inventus fuit."

[2] Canons 92, 93.

[3] Cf. canon 92, §1. "The prevision of some future possibility of changing residence does not suspend the present will to remain; it puts no term on it. On the other hand, the will is suspended if made conditional on some future event."—McBride, *Incardination and Excardination of Seculars*, The Catholic University of America Canon Law Studies, n. 145 (Washington, D. C.: The Catholic University of America Press, 1942), p. 313.

[4] Canon 92, §1; McBride, *op. cit.*, pp. 314–318.

Quasi-domicile, now officially recognized in canon law, may be acquired either by actual presence in a specific territory with an intention of remaining at least for the greater part of the year, unless something calls one away, or by an actual residence for the greater part of the year regardless of intention.[5]

Thus the formal element, the intention of remaining, and the material element, the actual residence in a specific place, are confirmed as the essential elements for the establishment of both a voluntary domicile and a voluntary quasi-domicile.

Besides voluntary domicile and quasi-domicile there is recognized in canonical legislation another type of domicile, namely, legal or necessary domicile, whose acquisition, retention, and loss are governed solely by operation of the law. The origin of this type of domicile is traceable to Roman Law.[6] Legal or necessary domicile, having been accepted in general by canonical jurisprudence,[7] is formally acknowledged for the first time in canonical legislation by the Code of Canon Law.[8]

While the Code does not specifically define legal domicile, but merely enumerates those persons upon whom the same is conferred, its provisions as to the manner in which legal domicile is acquired characterize this particular type of domicile as that which is necessarily acquired by disposition of the law. This characteristic note identifies legal domicile and distinguishes it from voluntary domicile.[9]

Therefore legal domicile, as to its acquisition, does not depend on the two requisites, actual personal presence and the intention of remaining, which are characteristic of voluntary domicile.

---

[5] Canon 92, §2.

[6] D.(50.1)(22.1),(3,6); D.(50.1)(38.3).

[7] Passerini, *Commentarium in Librum Sextum Decretalium* (3 vols., Venetiis, 1667–1680), Lib. I, tit. IX, art. ii, n. 28; Schmalzgrueber, *Ius Ecclesiasticum Universum,* Lib. II, tit. II, n. 14; D'Annibale, *Summula Theologiae Moralis* (4. ed., 3 vols., Romae, 1894–1897), I, n. 83; Alberti, *De Domicilio Ecclesiastico* (Romae, 1909), n. 5.

[8] Canon 93, §1.

[9] D'Angelo, *Del Domicilio Ecclesiastico e dei suoi effetti* (Giarre, 1917), p. 35; Wernz-Vidal, *Ius Canonicum,* II (3. ed., 1943), 12; Chelodi, *Ius De Personis juxta Codicem Iuris Canonici* (2. ed., Tridenti, 1927), n. 92; S. R. Rota, *in Causa Ravennaten.,* 15 maii 1911—*AAS,* III (1911), 487; S. R. Rota, *in Causa Parisien.,* 27 ian. 1912—*AAS,* IV (1912), 277.

"It matters not whether the person actually resides in the place, or whether he has the positive intention of not residing there; he has a domicile nevertheless, a domicile conferred by operation of the law, a *domicilium legale, necessarium.*" [10] The lack of intention or presence in a specified locality is supplied by the law itself.[11]

The retention of this legal domicile is also a matter provided for in the law. The domicile thus acquired by operation of the law is retained necessarily as long as the state or the condition to which it is annexed perdures; it does not effectively cease until that state or condition is legitimately lost or altered.[12] It can be said in general that, although this legal domicile as such ceases upon the cessation of the fact upon which it is founded, when the cessation of that fact is actualized the legal domicile is presumed to have become a voluntary domicile, unless it is apparent that there has been a definitive abandonment of the domicile.[13] Thus it is proper to state that a son on reaching his majority loses his legal domicile as a legal domicile, but he is presumed to retain it as a voluntary domicile until it is clear that he has abandoned it.[14]

When the legal domicile is termed a "fiction of the law," [15] this is not to be understood in the sense that the legal effects flowing from the possession of such a domicile are "fictional" or any the less real than those accorded to voluntary domicile. In the operation of the law, as will be seen in a later Article, the legal domicile is truly and effectively operative in law.

---

[10] Costello, *Domicile and Quasi-Domicile,* p. 160.

[11] Wernz-Vidal, *Ius Canonicum,* II (3. ed., 1943), n. 12; Wernz, *Ius Decretalium,* IV, n. 177 nota 190: "In casu legis dispositio supplet defectum habitationis vel intentionis; . . ."; D'Angelo, *Del Domicilio Ecclesiastico,* 35–36; Ojetti, *Commentarium in Codicem Iuris Canonici,* II, p. 54, n. 9.

[12] Alberti, *De Domicilio Ecclesiastico,* 9; "Amittitur vero domicilium necessarium statim ac cessat factum, quod requiritur tamquam conditio, ut lex aut legislatoris voluntas servetur."—S. R. Rota, *in Causa Ravennaten.,* 15 maii 1911—*AAS,* III (1911), 483.

[13] S. R. Rota, *in Causa Ravennaten.,* 15 maii 1911—"Domicilium necessarium censeretur transire in voluntarium, et tamdiu retineri praesumeretur, quamdiu non constaret, illi, expresse vel tacite, directe vel indirecte, fuisse renuntiatum."—*AAS,* III (1911), 487.

[14] Costello, *Domicile and Quasi-Domicile,* p. 161.

[15] Ojetti, *Commentarium in Codicem Iuris Canonici,* II, p. 54, n. 9.

SECTION 2. THE LEGAL DOMICILE OF THE WIFE

In canon 93, §1, are mentioned three classes of persons upon legal domicile is conferred by operation of the law.[16] There is question here of only one of these groups, namely, married women. The principle that the married woman acquired and retained the domicile of her husband was incorporated in the law of Rome,[17] and the acceptance of this principle by the canonists generally[18] was confirmed by ecclesiastical judicial pronounce-

---

16 "Uxor, a viro legitime non separata, necessario retinet domicilium viri sui; amens, domicilium curatoris; minor, domicilium illius cuius potestati subiicitur." "The Code's enumeration in canon 93, §1, of those who have necessary domiciles is to be considered as applying only to those which are borrowed (mutuatà) from others, according to some authors, for, they say, there are other groups who are required by other canons of the Code to dwell in a certain place independently of their own will, but it is their own and not somebody else's domicile which they thus acquire. Hence it should be called *necessarium sed proprium et personale.* In this category they enumerate the following: the beneficed cleric, in the place of his benefice; the Religious, in the convent to which they are affiliated; Cardinals, in the city of Rome (except those who are Bishops of non-suburbicarian dioceses); life prisoners, in the prison itself; and soldiers, in their stationary garrisons. One author places in this list also secular clerics in the diocese in which they are incardinated, on the strength of canon 111, where clerical *vagi* are outlawed, and of canons 143 and 144, where the secular cleric is shown to have no free will in selecting any residence outside the diocese. In addition to all these types of domiciles being proper instead of borrowed, another point of differentiation between them and those mentioned in canon 93, §1, is that only one element, the formal, is supplied by law. There is no evidence to show that any one of these categories would have a legal residence in a place where they never yet have been. It is their will alone which has been constrained by law to consent actually to go to a certain place and remain there, and since they are not free to leave on their own authority, they are considered as still belonging there even if they later leave without permission. Hence, it is not justifiable to put them in the same category with wives, the insane, and minors, for whom even the basic element of residence itself is supplied by law, nor may the same juridical effects be invoked."—McBride, *Incardination and Excardination of Seculars,* pp. 319–320.

17 D. (50.1) (22.1); D. (50.1) (38.3).

18 Panormitanus, *Commentaria,* c. 16, X, *de foro competenti,* II, 2, n. 7; Pirhing, *Ius Canonicum,* Lib. II, tit. ii, n. 11; Ojetti, *Synopsis Rerum*

ments.[19] The Code in canon 93, §1, retains this principle.[20]

The nature of marriage,[21] the natural subjection of the wife to the husband,[22] and the duty of cohabitation, although the latter is not an essential element of marriage,[23] all manifest the reasonableness of the provision of the law concerning the acquisition by the wife of her husband's domicile. The properly manifested consent of the parties juridically competent is the essential element which constitutes marriage.[24] This matrimonial consent, an act of the will whereby each of the contracting parties mutually gives and receives conjugal rights, has for its purpose the exchange between the two parties of acts which in and of themselves are suited for the generation of offspring, and when this consent is properly manifested it results immediately in an individual union called marriage, which union constitutes the man and the woman as one principle in the legitimate act of procreation.[25]

The mutual consent[26] establishes the relationship of husband and wife; from the moment this relationship is established the legal domicile of the wife is determined by operation of the law. The husband's domicile becomes the legal domicile of the wife. The wife, from the moment of the contract of marriage is no longer *sui iuris,* but by reason of the matrimonial bond which

---

Moralium et Iuris Pontificii (3 vols., and Index, Romae, 1909-1914), 580, s.v. *Domicilium.*

19 S. R. Rota, *in Causa Wledislavien,* 7 dec. 1912—*Decisiones coram Lega,* Dec. XXIX, n. 6; S. R. Rota, *in Causa Gratianopolitana,* 8 apr. 1913—*Decisiones coram Lega,* Dec. XXXVI, n. 11; S. R. Rota, *in Causa Parisien.,* 4 mart. 1916—*AAS,* VIII (1916), 367.

20 "Uxor, a viro legitime non separata, necessario retinet domicilium viri sui; . . ."

21 Cf. canons 1012, §§1, 2; 1013, §§1, 2.

22 Wernz-Vidal, *Ius Canonicum,* V, 703–704.

23 Canon 1128.

24 Canon 1081, §1.

25 Canon 1081, §2; Gasparri, *De Matrimonio,* II, n. 780.

26 When reference is made to contracts in general, the element of consent necessary to the contract is a deliberate act of the will which results in an agreement of two or more individuals regarding a well-defined object which includes within its compass all things inseparable from the essence of that object. Cf. Gasparri, *De Matrimonio,* I, n. 771.

attaches her to the husband she becomes subject to him, and her status is determined in law by the status of her husband.[27]

In the case of a valid matrimonial union the law supplies the elements ordinarily considered essential for the constituting of a domicile, but the law does not supply the deficiency when there is lacking a valid union between the parties concerned. Thus, a woman who lives in concubinage, or whose marriage is not celebrated according to the requisite form, does not acquire the domicile of her "husband," for in reality she is not his wife.[28] It is questionable whether the woman cohabiting illicitly would ordinarily acquire even a voluntary domicile, since by the nature of the case the law precludes the intention of continuing in illicit cohabitation. Yet, if the cohabitation is protracted for the requisite period of time, it seems that a voluntary domicile or a voluntary quasi-domicile would be acquired, since the law in this instance prescinds from the element of intention.[29]

Only the actual celebration of the marriage causes a woman to lose her voluntary domicile, and thus the departure of a woman from her place of domicile for the purpose of contracting marriage does not affect her previous domicile.[30] Her departure is provisional and conditional, although it is joined with the intention of following the one whom she proposes to marry.[31]

The Code makes no provision regarding pre-nuptial contracts which specifically provide that the domicile of the wife rather than that of the husband shall be the determinant in those matters wherein domicile is the controlling factor. Pre-Code commentators discussed the validity and effects of such contracts,[32] and these

[27] "Domicilium necessarium seu legale est illud quod dispositione legis necessario acquiritur ab iis qui non sunt sui juris ratione vinculi cum ea persona cujus potestati subjiciuntur."—De Meester, *Juris Canonici et Juris Canonico-Civilis Compendium* (nova editio, 3 vols. in 4, Brugis: sumptibus et typis Societatis St. Augustini, 1921–1928), I (1921), 213; De Smet, *De Sponsalibus et Matrimonio,* n. 46.

[28] Cappello, *De Matrimonio,* n. 681.

[29] Cappello, *loc. cit.*

[30] S. R. Rota, *in Causa Parisien.,* 5 maii 1914—*AAS,* VI (1914), 397–398; De Smet, *op. cit.,* n. 46, *nota,* 2.

[31] Cappello, *op. cit.,* n. 681.

[32] Panormitanus, *Commentaria,* ad c. 1, X, *qui matrimonium accusare possunt,* IV, 18, n. 6. Cf. *supra,* p. 28.

agreements seem to be permissible today.[33] The husband is at liberty to forego his right in this matter if he chooses to do so, but in a question of fact concerning the domicile of the wife the presumption of the law that the general rule is in effect stands until contrary evidence is adduced in proof of the fact that in this particular case the general rule is not to be followed.

By virtue of the subjection of the wife to the husband, and because of the husband's position as the head of the family, it is his right to determine the place of abode. Hence it is deduced that as a general rule the wife has the duty of accompanying her husband whenever the latter changes his domicile.[34] It is recognized there are instances other than those which might justify a legitimate separation wherein the wife's usual duty to follow her husband would not bind her.[35] But a mere suspension of the duty to follow her husband, which might be interpreted as a release from the duty to cohabit with him, in no way changes the original effect of the matrimonial contract for the reason that her legal domicile was determined by a public act, and, in the absence of a legitimate separation her legal domicile or quasi-domicile continues to be the same as her husband's domicile or quasi-domicile.

The wife retains her legal domicile as such until that time when death destroys the matrimonial bond, or until there intervenes a legitimate separation whereby the obligations imposed in consequence of the bond are juridically recognized as suspended. The law regards the loss of a domicile as a *res odiosa*, and does not countenance a presumption of its loss, even though in the case of a voluntary domicile the person is at liberty to abandon it.[36] If this be true of voluntary domicile which one is at liberty to abandon, it is all the more true of the legal domicile which the law itself confers and which the subject is not at liberty to change or abandon. Until either death or a legitimate separation has

---

[33] Wernz-Vidal, *Ius Canonicum,* V, 704.

[34] Wernz-Vidal, *loc. cit.*

[35] De Smet, *De Sponsalibus et Matrimonio,* p. 221, n. 249.

[36] Costello, *Domicile and Quasi-Domicile,* pp. 145–146; Costello cites: S. R. Rota, *in Causa Gratianopolitana,* 17 iul. 1912, Dec. XXI, nn. 4, 9—*S. R. Rotae Decisiones seu Sententiae,* IV (1917), 366, 368–369.

intervened, the wife is unable to establish a canonical voluntary domicile.

Mere departure from her husband, even with the intention of never returning, and even though the husband be willing that she should go away, does not enable her to establish a separate domicile. In this she is estopped by the law, for this departure in no way can be construed as a "legitimate" separation. Just as in the acquisition of her legal domicile the intention of acquiring it and the actual habitation in it were not controlling factors, so also with relation to the loss of her legal domicile a departure and the intention of not returning are insufficient to effect such a loss. The legal domicile attaches to her in a manner similar to the matrimonial bond. The law has made provision for the wife in allowing her to acquire a voluntary quasi-domicile, and thus has definitely manifested the mind of the legislator that the acquisition of a voluntary domicile by the wife is to be confined to the case wherein a legitimate separation as the same is understood in the law has intervened.[37]

A difficulty seems to be presented when the wife departs on her own authority for a cause which she judges to be sufficient under the law, for herein some of the authors seem to find the fact of a separation that enables the wife to establish her own domicile.[38] But, as has been pointed out in a previous Article,[39] a separation instituted on private authority, even though the cause for which it was instituted is sufficient, does not change the status of the wife so as to enable her to establish an independent voluntary domicile.

What is the effect of a separation when it is effected through the intervention of ecclesiastical authority? The writer is concerned here only with the external forum, and in particular with regard to the domicile of the wife. Certainly in such a case the wife may establish her own voluntary domicile if the separation is perpetual or granted for an indefinite period of time.[40] Does

---

[37] Canon 93, §2.

[38] Cf. *supra*, p. 83.

[39] Cf. *supra*, pp. 78–91.

[40] Canon 93, §2; Doheny, *Canonical Procedure in Matrimonial Cases,* I, 14.

she, by virtue of the legitimate separation as sanctioned by ecclesiastical authority, lose the legal domicile of her husband? The Code in no place specifically provides that in such a case the wife does lose her legal domicile. The writer however agrees with Ciprotti [41] that in the case of a legitimate separation the wife does lose her legal domicile.

By the sentence or the decree of separation, permanent or for an indefinite period of time, and sanctioned by ecclesiastical authority, it is true that the conjugal bond is not dissolved. But a suspension of the concomitant conjugal duties is effected by public ecclesiastical authority, and the wife gains a *sui iuris* status which enables her to establish her proper domicile, and which replaces the former state of dependency in view of which the domicile of the husband had been "borrowed" by provision of the law. The fact that a private voluntary reconciliation would restore the legal domicile independently of judicial intervention does not weaken the conclusion that a legitimate separation effects a loss of the legal domicile. For as Payen [42] notes, the decree of separation for the innocent party was issued after the manner of a favor which the innocent party was at liberty to forego at any time. The original reluctance of the court to grant such a decree or sentence would likewise argue for a presumption of the court's accord that the act of reconciliation should restore the benefit of the erstwhile domiciliary status.

Finally, the loss of the legal domicile by the wife in a case of legitimate separation seems deducible from the authoritative provision that a wife legitimately separated does not follow the domicile of her husband.[43] The Instruction "*Provida Mater*" in its sixth article provided that a wife, if legitimately separated from

---

[41] Cf. "Quaestiones de Competentia Ratione Contractus et Domicilii in Causis Matrimonialibus"—*Apollinaris* (Romae, 1928—), XI (1938), 461; *infra*, p. 135, fn. 2016.

[42] "Nec, ad restaurandum vitae consortium, necessaria est nova judicis sententia, si conjux innocens, judicis sententia, legitime decesserit; nam prior sententia, utpote lata in ejus commodum, facultatem ei praebet, quin ei onus imponat."—*De Matrimonio in Missionibus ac potissimum in Sinis* (3 vols., Zi-ka-wei: in Typographia T 'ou se'-we', 1928–1929), II, n. 2475.

[43] S. C. de Sacramentis, instr., "*Provida Mater,*" 15 aug. 1936, Art. 6, §2—*AAS,* XXVIII (1936), 316. Cf. *supra*, p. 78.

her husband, does not *follow* the domicile of her husband. This does not imperatively imply that through a decree of separation the wife *loses* the domicile of her husband; it is a simple statement that she does not *follow* his domicile. But perhaps the precise reason why she does not follow the domicile of her husband is the reason that through the legitimate separation and the acquisition of a *sui iuris* status she has lost the legal domicile she previously had.

A separation by mutual consent would ordinarily have only the effect of a private separation and would not effect a loss of the legal domicile of the wife. If however it was the purpose of the separation that one or both of the consorts might enter religion, then an ecclesiastical permission would be a pre-requisite,[44] and the resulting separation would be legitimate with the consequent ordinary juridical effects.

The wife whose husband has been committed to an institution for the insane is said to retain as her legal domicile the domicile established by her husband, until competent ecclesiastical authority has determined her legal status.[45]

There is no specific provision in the Code relative to the domicile or quasi-domicile of soldiers and prisoners. If the formal and material elements are present for the establishing of a domicile, that is, the intention of remaining unless something calls one away or the fact of a sufficiently continued actual residence, men in the armed forces may well establish a domicile in the place in which they are garrisoned.[46] Should a domicile be thus established by a soldier, it is a proper conclusion that this domicile would at the same time be the legal domicile of the soldier's wife. The wife of a prisoner sentenced and committed for life would have her legal domicile in the diocese in which the prison was located[47] until such time that her status was established by competent ecclesiastical authority.

The wife who obtains a decree of separation in the civil court does not thereby acquire the status of a "*mulier legitime separata,*"

[44] Cf. canons 542, §1; 572, §1, 3o; 987, 2o.

[45] Doheny, *Canonical Procedure in Matrimonial Cases,* I, 19.

[46] Doheny, *ibid.,* pp. 19–20.

[47] Doheny, *ibid.,* p. 20.

unless the decree had in some form the approval of ecclesiastical authority.[48]

Article B. The General Juridical Effects of the Wife's Legal Domicile

Section 1. In Relation to the General Norms of the Code

Since the wife necessarily shares the domicile of her husband unless she is legitimately separated from him,[49] those applicable rights and obligations which are determined in law by reason of one's canonical domicile will affect her even as if she were unmarried and had a voluntary domicile in that place. If she, not being legitimately separated from her husband, has her proper quasi-domicile,[50] or, being legitimately separated from her husband, has her own proper domicile,[51] the provisions of the law respecting the rights and obligations determined by reason of domicile or quasi-domicile will be equally applicable to her.

In this matter a basic provision is that made by canon 94, §1, which provides that through domicile, or quasi-domicile, each of the faithful acquires his proper pastor and ordinary. If her husband is a *vagus*[52] then, whether or not a wife be separated from her husband, it is possible for her to have the status of a *vagus*, in which case, being without a domicile or quasi-domicile, she is provided a proper pastor or ordinary by the law. In such a case the law states that her proper pastor or ordinary is the pastor or ordinary of the place where she actually stays.[53]

By virtue of her domicile or quasi-domicile the wife is subject directly to the power of jurisdiction that may be exercised by the pastor or ordinary of the place where she has a domicile or quasi-domicile.[54] Whether she is present in the territory of

---

[48] Cf. S. C. de Sacramentis, instr. "*Provida Mater,*" 15 aug. 1936—*AAS*, XXVIII (1936), 316; Kelly "Separation and Civil Divorce"—*The Jurist*, VI (1946), 209.

[49] Canon 93, §1.

[50] Canon 93, §2.

[51] Canon 93, §2.

[52] Canon 91. Person dicitur: . . . *vagus,* si nullibi domicilium habeat vel quasi-domicilium.

[53] Canon 94, §3.

[54] Canon 201, §1.

her domicile or quasi-domicile or absent from the territory, the wife by virtue of her domicile or quasi-domicile is subject to the particular laws of the territory of her domicile or quasi-domicile, unless it is apparent from the nature of things or from the law itself that she is not so obligated.[55] In this connection custom may have the force of particular law,[56] and consequently may affect the wife by reason of her domicile or quasi-domicile.

Since the limits within which privileges may be conceded follow strictly the limits of the legislative power of the ordinary, a wife by reason of her domicile or quasi-domicile may receive and enjoy privileges granted by her proper ordinary.[57] The same may be said of her in the status of a *peregrinus* [58] within the limits in which she would be subject to the legislative power of the ordinary.[59] Thus, she would not be bound by the particular laws of her own territory as long as she was absent from it, unless the transgression of the laws would be harmful to her own territory, or unless the laws were enacted as personal laws. Neither would she be bound by the laws of the territory in which she was at the time, unless these laws concerned the public order or determined the solemnity of acts. In the status of a *vagus,* however, she would be bound by both the general and the particular laws actually in force within the territory.[60]

The wife by reason of her domicile or quasi-domicile as a subject of a particular ordinary may enjoy the benefits of that ordinary's dispensing powers, whether these powers be proper or delegated.[61] Precepts given to individuals bind them wherever they go.[62] Hence, a wife by reason of her domicile or quasi-

[55] Canon 201, §3.

[56] Canon 25.

[57] Coronata, *Institutiones,* I, 100; Vindex, "Domicilium et Quasi-Domicilium eorumque effectus in Codice Juris Canonici"—Jus Pontificium (Romae, 1921--), VI (1926), 113. Hereafter this periodical will be referred to with the letters *JP.*

[58] Canon 91. Persona dicitur: . . . *peregrinus,* si versetur extra domicilium et quasi-domicilium quod adhuc retinet.

[59] Canon 14, §1, 1°, 2°.

[60] Canon 14, §2.

[61] Cf. Coronata, *Institutiones,* I, 125; Vindex, *art. cit.—JP,* VI (1926), 113.

[62] Canons 24; 201, §2.

domicile could receive from her proper pastor or ordinary a precept which would subsequently be binding on her regardless of her departure from her place of domicile or quasi-domicile. If in the status of a *vagus*[63] she should receive such a precept, then its binding force would seem to be conditioned on her continuing in the territorial limits of the preceptor's power.[64] This seems to be true for the reason that her departure from the territory would dissolve the bond of subjection which made the precept possible. However, should the precept have been imposed in virtue of a power delegated by the Supreme Pontiff, then this conclusion would not follow.

In the matter of rescripts, canon 44 alone is pertinent to the subject under consideration. The first section of this canon provides that a favor which has been refused by one's own ordinary shall not be asked from another ordinary unless the fact of the refusal of the first ordinary be made known. The note of invalidity is not however attached to the violation of this provision of the law. However, if the vicar general has refused to grant a favor to the wife, she cannot afterwards validly obtain the favor from the bishop without mentioning the fact of having been refused by the vicar general. Likewise, a favor refused to her by the bishop cannot be validly granted by the vicar general without the consent of the bishop, even though the refusal of the bishop be made known in the petition to the vicar general.[65] This provision of the Code is seen to be a particular application of the rule of law that, when something is prohibited to anyone by one way, the same thing may not be obtained through another way.[66]

SECTION 2. IN RELATION TO THE RECEPTION OF THE SACRAMENTS

Formerly the licit, and oftentimes the valid, reception of the sacraments depended upon their being administered by one's own

---

63 Cf. *supra*, p. 102.

64 Cf. Coronata, *Institutiones*, I, 50; Vindex, *art. cit.—JP*, VI (1926), 115.

65 Canon 44, §2.

66 Cf. Reg. 84, R. J., in VI°—"Quum quid una via prohibetur alicui, ad id alia non debet admitti."

proper pastor.[67] The determination of who was one's proper pastor oftentimes offered a very serious difficulty, but in the present legislation this difficulty has been largely removed. Canon 94, §1, provides a very convenient norm. One's proper pastor or ordinary is determined by one's domicile or quasi-domicile. The domicile or quasi-domicile of the wife may therefore be profitably considered in relation to the reception of the sacraments.

Since the sacrament of baptism can be administered privately by anyone,[68] its valid administration does not depend on a determination of the proper pastor as minister, but the Code of Canon Law reserves the licit administration of solemn baptism to the pastor for his parish, and in like manner to the local ordinary for his territory.[69] The particular question here has no relation to the baptism of the wife herself, since that question would be clearly settled when her domicile or quasi-domicile was established; the concern here is rather with regard to the baptism of the children of the marriage.

A minor retains the domicile of the person to whom he is subject, and this constitutes a necessary or legal domicile for the child.[70] And again, in view of this natural subjection, the minor would ordinarily be baptized in the territory of the father's domicile or quasi-domicile, and hence the minister would ordinarily be the pastor of that particular territory. If, however, the child were posthumous, he or she would be baptized in the parish which the mother retained by reason of her domicile or quasi-domicile, for clearly the subjection would then be owing to her, and thus the child's domicile would be clearly determined.[71] When the parents do not live together, but yet have not been legally separated, then a child living with the mother could be baptized by the pastor

---

[67] In particular as to the administration of the sacrament of baptism the reader may consult Waldron, *The Minister of Baptism,* The Catholic University of America Canon Law Studies, n. 170 (Washington, D. C.; The Catholic University of America Press, 1942), p. 46.

[68] Canon 742, §1.

[69] Cf. Waldron, *op. cit.,* pp. 72–73, for a complete discussion of the term "pastor" as understood in relation to the administration of baptism.

[70] Canon 93, §1.

[71] *Loc. cit.*

of the parish wherein the father has his domicile,[72] and, since in practice the child is subject to its mother, also by the pastor of the parish wherein the mother has her quasi-domicile.[73]

Waldron states that "when the parental separation has been legally constituted, it seems that the child will follow not only the mother's quasi-domicile but also her domicile." [74] Yet it seems well within the realm of possibility that, in the given case, the education of the child might be entrusted to the father by a decree of the ecclesiastical court.[75] This would be an indication that the child was to be subject to the father, and as a result the pastor to administer the solemn baptism would be determined by the domicile or quasi-domicile of the father. Then, again, it could happen, as Waldron notes,[76] that the child had already reached the age of reason before the legitimate separation, had thus become an adult in relation to baptism,[77] and accordingly was capable of establishing a quasi-domicile.[78] In such a case the child could be validly and licitly baptized in a parish of which his parents could in no sense whatsoever be considered members.[79]

With regard to the reception of the sacrament of confirmation it suffices to note that the domicile or quasi-domicile of the wife determines the proper bishop [80] or other lawfully qualified minister [81] by whom she should be confirmed, though she is not forbidden to seek its reception from any other qualified minister.[82] If however her proper pastor was not present at the conferral of the sacrament, the law requires that the fact of its reception be

---

[72] *Loc. cit.*

[73] Canon 93, §2.

[74] Cf. *op. cit.*, p. 76. Canon 93, §2, alone is cited as authority for his conclusion.

[75] Canon 1132.

[76] Cf. *op. cit.*, p. 76.

[77] Canon 745, §2, 2o.

[78] Canon 93, §2. Minor infantia egressus potest quasi-domicilium proprium obtinere . . .

[79] Waldron, *op. cit.*, p. 76.

[80] Canon 94, §1.

[81] Canon 782.

[82] Canons 783, §§1, 2; 784; 785, §§1, 2.

communicated to him by the minister of the sacrament or by some one delegated by this minister.[83]

Formerly by the legislation of the Church not only the power of sacred orders but also the power of jurisdiction was required of the one administering the Holy Eucharist.[84] But even before the time of the Code of Canon Law the pastor in his own territory could licitly administer this sacrament to all who requested it of him.[85] This was particularly true of Communion received out of devotion. As to Holy Communion received by reason of a precept, restrictions on its administration continued in effect until recent times.[86] In the Code of Canon Law the effect of domicile or quasi-domicile regarding this sacrament is practically reduced to the following, namely, that the wife should notify her pastor of the fulfillment of the paschal precept if the same has been complied with outside his territory.[87] The Paschal Communion formerly was to be received by all in their proper parish,[88] but even in former times many exceptions from this requirement were permitted.[89] The Code provides that the faithful are to be persuaded to fulfill the precept in their own proper parishes, and they have the duty of informing their proper pastor if they fulfill the precept in another parish.[90]

The bringing of holy Viaticum to the sick and infirm was

---

[83] Canon 799. Si proprius confirmati parochus praesens non fuerit, de collata confirmatione minister vel per se ipse vel per alium quamprimum eundem certiorem faciat.

[84] Gasparri, *Tractatus Canonicus de Sanctissima Eucharistia* (2 vols., Parisiis: Delhome et Briguet, 1897), II, n. 1070.

[85] Wernz, *Ius Decretalium,* III, n. 739.

[86] Coronata, *De Sacramentis,* I, 312; Vindex, *art. cit.—JP,* VI (1926), 117.

[87] Canon 859, §3.

[88] "Speciatim *communio paschalis* suscipi debet in ecclesia parochiali illius parochiae, in qua fidelis habet domicilium, nisi Episcopus vel proprius parochus dedit specialem licentiam in alia ecclesia."—Wernz, *Ius Decretalium,* III, n. 743.

[89] Wernz, *loc. cit.;* Coronata, *De Sacramentis,* I, 312; Vindex, *art. cit. —JP,* VI (1926), p. 118, n. 52.

[90] Canon 859, §3. Suadendum fidelibus ut huic praecepto satisfaciant in sua quisque paroecia; et qui in aliena paroecia satisfecerint, curent proprium parochum de adimpleto praecepto certiorem facere.

formerly a right of the proper pastor,[91] except for privileges that had been granted.[92] By virtue of the provisions of the Code the pastor of the territory in which the wife has her domicile or quasi-domicile is the one to whom it pertains to bring her holy Viaticum.[93] The right and duty to carry Holy Communion publicly to the sick within a parish, even to non-parishioners, is vested in the pastor, and other priests may do so only in a case of necessity, or with the presumed permission of the pastor or of the ordinary.[94] Any priest may bring Holy Communion privately to the sick with at least the presumed permission of the priest to whom the custody of the Blessed Sacrament is entrusted.[95]

Canon 854, § 5, seems to confirm the opinion[96] that the decree "*Quam singulari*"[97] referred only to the pastor and not to the proper pastor in its prescriptions concerning the reception of first Holy Communion, and hence domicile and quasi-domicile which would determine the proper pastor[98] need not be considered.

With regard to the question of domicile and quasi-domicile in relation to the sacrament of penance a distinction is made between the obligation of confessing and the power of absolving. The obligation of confessing to the proper pastor at least once a year, which was in effect formerly,[99] had been changed by custom even before the enactment of the Code of Canon Law.[100] Likewise,

---

[91] Cf. Vindex, *art. cit.—JP,* VI (1926), p. 118, n. 83.

[92] Alberti, *De Domicilio Ecclesiastico,* p. 25.

[93] Canon 850. Sacram communionem per modum Viatici sive publice sive privatim ad infirmos deferre, pertinet ad parochum ad normam can. 848 . . .

[94] Canon 848, §1. Ius et officium sacram communionem publice ad infirmos etiam non paroecianos extra ecclesiam deferendi, pertinet ad parochum intra suum territorium.

§2. Ceteri sacerdotes id possunt in casu tantum necessitatis aut de licentia saltem praesumpta eiusdem parochi vel Ordinarii.

[95] Canon 849, §1. Communionem privatim ad infirmos quilibet sacerdos deferre potest, de venia saltem praesumpta sacerdotis, cui custodia sanctissimi Sacramenti commissa est.

[96] Coronata, *De Sacramentis,* I, 291; Vindex, *art. cit.—JP,* VI (1926), p. 118, n. 51.

[97] S. C. de Sacramentis, 8 aug. 1910—*AAS,* II (1910), 877.

[98] Canon 94, §1.

[99] Cf. Reiffenstuel, *Ius Canonicum Universum,* Lib. III, tit. XXIX, n. 9.

[100] Cf. Alberti, *op. cit.,* p. 26.

there was no obligation for persons when confined to their homes by reason of sickness to confess to their proper pastor.[101]

As to the power of absolving, even before the advent of the present Code of Canon Law *incolae* and *advenae*[102] could be absolved validly and licitly by the pastors of the place as also by their proper pastors by reason of domicile or quasi-domicile.[103] *Peregrini* could be absolved validly and licitly both by their proper pastor, who exercised in regard to them ordinary power even though the pastor was outside his parish or diocese,[104] and by the pastor of the place in which they happened to be, except when they had gone out of their diocese to elude the penalty of a reservation.[105] A *vagus* could be absolved validly and licitly by the pastor of the place in which the *vagus* happened to be. The reservation of a sin or of a penalty placed a territorial restriction on the exercise of the power of absolving, but concerning this a note is made later.

The Code of Canon Law has retained the freedom of the individual to confess to any duly authorized priest,[106] and except for the restriction in regard to reservations, which will be noted later, the only practical effect of domicile or quasi-domicile in relation to the sacrament of penance is that the wife by reason of her domicile or quasi-domicile can validly and licitly confess to her proper pastor wherever he may be.

With regard to the reception of the sacrament of extreme unction there is question of the licitness of its reception by reason of domicile or quasi-domicile.[107] Prior to the Code of Canon Law, *incolae* and *advenae* were able to receive this sacrament from their

---

[101] Vindex, *art. cit.—JP,* VI (1926), p. 118, n. 84.

[102] Canon 91. Persona dicitur: *incola,* in loco ubi domicilium *advena,* in loco ubi quasi-domicilium habet; . . .

[103] Vindex, *art. cit.—JP,* VI (1926), 118–119.

[104] D'Angelo, *Del Domicilio Ecclesiastico e dei Suoi Effetti,* p. 90.

[105] Cf. Clemens X (1670–1676), const. "*Superna,*" §7—*Fontes,* n. 246.

[106] Canon 905. Cuivis fideli integrum est confessario legitime approbato etiam alius ritus, cui maluerit, peccata sua confiteri.

[107] Canon 938, §2. . . . minister ordinarius est parochus loci, in quo degit infirmus; in casu autem necessitatis, vel de licentia saltem rationabiliter praesumpta parochi vel Ordinarii loci, alius quilibet sacerdos hoc sacramentum ministrare potest.

pastor only, except in a case of necessity. A *peregrinus* likewise had to receive extreme unction from his proper pastor,[108] and under pain of sin, and sometimes also of some enacted penalty,[109] it was not licit for the pastor of the place or for other priests to administer this sacrament. There were, however, many exceptions and numerous contrary privileges.[110] A *vagus* could receive the sacrament from the pastor of the place where the *vagus* happened to be at the time when its administration was called for.[111]

The Code of Canon Law by virtue of canon 938, §3, removes all such restrictions. The sacrament of extreme unction may now be administered by the pastor of the place in which the sick person is at the time when he needs the administration of the sacrament. In a case of necessity, or with the permission (at least presumed) of the pastor, or of the local ordinary, any other priest may administer the sacrament validly and licitly. The effect of domicile or quasi-domicile in relation to the reception of the sacrament of extreme unction is practically irrelevant.

It may seem wholly unnecessary to mention the sacrament of holy orders in speaking of the domicile or quasi-domicile of the wife, but a question could be raised in connection with canon 956. It regards the effect of a separation between the spouses with reference to the place of origin of a legitimate son born subsequent to the separation of the parents. The place of origin could well become a factor for determining the son's proper bishop for ordination.[112]

"The place of origin of a youth, . . . is that place in which his father had a domicile, or in defect of it, a quasi-domicile at the time of his son's birth." [113] Since a wife legitimately separated

---

[108] " [Minister] competens vero sive legitimus minister est solus sacerdos capax nec aliunde prohibitus, qui ex officio sive ex potestate ordinaria in fideles sibi assignatos exercet curam animarum."—Wernz, *Ius Decretalium,* III, n. 749.

[109] Cf. Wernz, *Ius Decretalium,* III, n. 743.

[110] D'Angelo, *op. cit.,* p. 99.

[111] Cf. Vindex, *art. cit.—JP,* VI (1926), 119.

[112] Canon 956. "Episcopus proprius, quod attinet ad ordinationem saecularium, est tantum Episcopus dioecesis in qua promovendus habeat domicilium una cum origine aut simplex domicilium sine origine; . . .

[113] McBride, *Incardination and Excardination of Seculars,* p. 322.

from her husband may have her own proper domicile or quasi-domicile, and since the subjection—the element through which the law gives the father's domicile to the child as a necessary domicile—in this case might be owing entirely to the mother, would the child thereby have as his place of origin the domicile or quasi-domicile of his mother?[114]

In the case of an illegitimate or posthumous child it is the domicile of the mother which determines the place of origin.[115] In the event of an unlawful separation there is no doubt that the child's place of origin would definitely be that of the father's domicile or quasi-domicile, for in such a case the mother would continue to have a legal domicile in the place of the father's domicile, and the child would continue in law subject to the father by reason of the natural bond of subjection. It seems that even a legitimate separation between the parents would not affect the legal place of origin of the child, since it would not affect the paternal relationship, the true basis of subjection, and hence the legal place of origin would be the place of the father's domicile or quasi-domicile.

Through the celebration of marriage the wife loses her former domicile or quasi-domicile to acquire automatically and necessarily the domicile or quasi-domicile of her husband.[116] The element of subjection on the part of the wife to her husband precludes her having the intention requisite for retaining her prenuptial voluntary domicile, and likewise exchanges the necessary domicile she may have had by reason of her status as a minor.[117]

Questions pertaining to domicile or quasi-domicile in relation to the publication of the banns of marriage, of the qualified person before whom the marriage may be validly or licitly contracted, and of the place of the celebration of the marriage do not pertain to the scope of this commentary.

When there has occurred a legitimate perpetual separation the wife may establish a voluntary domicile or quasi-domicile.[118] If

---

[114] Canon 93, §1.

[115] Canon 90.

[116] Canons 93, §1; 1081, §§1, 2; 1110.

[117] Canon 93, §1.

[118] Canon 93, §2.

the cause of separation was adultery, and the wife was the innocent party, the note of perpetuity is more clearly perceptible than in the case wherein she was the guilty party. In the latter case the note of perpetuity may be weakened by her obligation to return to her husband if the innocent spouse should recall her. In this event she could no longer be said to be legitimately separated from her husband, since it would be her evident duty to return to him.[119]

This would be true even though the husband had formerly given cause sufficient in law to sustain a temporary legitimate separation. If at the time of her recall there was lacking the element of certainty regarding the presence of a cause for the separation, or also there was lacking the further element of some serious danger in abiding official instruction in the case, she could not even licitly remain away from her husband. Thus, in view of the discontinuance of the status of a legitimate separation, the voluntary domicile which she could and perhaps did establish after the granting of the legitimate perpetual separation would automatically become a quasi-domicile, and her legal domicile would be the domicile of her husband.

SECTION 3. IN RELATION TO ECCLESIASTICAL BURIAL

The church to which the body of a deceased wife when entitled to Christian burial is to be brought is by the common law the proper parish church as determined by the wife's domicile or quasi-domicile at the time of her death, unless the deceased had legitimately chosen another church for her burial.[120]

The important note here is that the wife, in her choice of a church for her funeral as well as of a cemetery for her burial, is entirely independent of the parish church to which she belongs by reason of domicile or quasi-domicile, and is limited only, by virtue of canon 1225, to the choice of some parochial church, a church of regulars, or some other church which has the right to

[119] "Pars vero rea ad vitae communionem revocata redire tenetur, quia ius separationis concessum est in favorem partis innocentis, non partis reae."—Coronata, *De Sacramentis,* III, 921.

[120] Canons 1215, 1216.

conduct funerals.[121] If however she had built a certain church or otherwise had endowed the church and enjoyed the *ius patronatus,* she could choose that church even though in fact it was not regularly entitled to hold funeral services. If she fulfilled the conditions necessary to permit her burial from a convent of nuns she would be entitled to choose it as the church for her burial.

It should be remembered however that, if at the time of her death she belonged to a certain parish church by reason of domicile or quasi-domicile, and yet is not to receive burial from that particular parish church, it is recommended that the proper pastor be informed of the death, since he is supposed to have a record of all his parishioners. "The Code, however, does not explicitly impose on the church which buries the subject of another parish this duty of informing the proper pastor." [122]

The domicile or quasi-domicile of the wife, by determining for her who is her proper pastor, indirectly affects the question of the distribution of the parochial portion as accruing through the funeral offering, for whenever one of the faithful is not buried from his own parish church, his proper pastor is to receive the parochial portion of the funeral offerings, unless particular law ordains otherwise, or unless the body of the deceased cannot be conveniently brought to the proper parish church.[123] If the deceased had several proper parishes to any of which the body could have easily been conveyed, and the funeral is held elsewhere, the parochial portion is to be divided among the various proper pastors.[124]

---

[121] Canon 1225. Ut electio ecclesiae funeris valeat, cadat necesse est vel in ecclesiam paroecialem, vel in ecclesiam regularium, non tamen monialium (nisi agatur de mulieribus quae famulatus, educationis, infirmitatis aut hospitii causa intra clausuram eiusdem monasterii non precario commorabantur), vel in ecclesiam iuris patronatus, si agatur de patrono, vel in aliam ecclesiam funerandi iure praeditam.

[122] Woywod, *A Practical Commentary on the Code of Canon Law* (7. ed., revised by Callistus Smith, 2 vols., New York: Joseph F. Wagner, Inc., 1943), I, 46.

[123] Canon 1236, §1. Salvo iure particulari, quoties fidelis non funeratur in ecclesia paroeciali propria, proprio defuncti parocho debetur portio paroecialis, excepto casu quo cadaver in ecclesiam propriae paroeciae commode asportari nequeat.

[124] Canon 1236, §2. Si quis habeat plures paroecias proprias ad quas

SECTION 4. IN RELATION TO THE COMPETENT FORUM

The competent forum as determined by the factor of domicile or quasi-domicile in the adjudication of matrimonial causes is treated in the following article; here the writer speaks in general of the competent forum by reason of the domicile or quasi-domicile of the defendant, and of the *forum hereditatis.*

Canon 1561, §1, provides that by reason of domicile or quasi-domicile anyone may be cited before the court of the local ordinary.[125] The competency here provided for is of a general nature, so that it is not lost by reason of the actual presence of the defendant in some other place,[126] nor is it affected by the location of the subject matter of the dispute, though the location of the subject matter would give rise to a separate basis of judicial competency.[127]

Hence it would be possible to cite the defendant before the local ordinary to answer for acts committed elsewhere, or in regard to a thing situated outside the territory of the local ordinary. Thus a wife, it seems, could be cited before the ordinary of the place of her domicile or quasi-domicile to answer concerning the exercise of her right of patronage also when this affects a benefice that lies outside the diocese of this ordinary.

Although the wife may be travelling outside her proper diocese, she may still be cited before her proper ordinary.[128] If she as a defendant has a plurality of domiciles or quasi-domiciles, the plaintiff could exercise a free choice of the forum to which she was to be cited. If after the fashion of a *vagus* she had no fixed abode, she could be cited before the ordinary of the place in which she was actually living at the time.[129]

Among those causes or judicial actions which look to a neces-

---

cadaver commode deferri posset, alibi funeretur, portio paroecialis dividenda est inter omnes parocho proprios.

[125] Ratione domicilii vel quasi-domicilii quilibet conveniri potest coram Ordinario loci.

[126] Canon 1561, §2. Ordinarius autem domicilii vel quasi-domicilii iurisdictionem in subditum, quamvis absentem, habet.

[127] Canon 1564.

[128] Canon 1561, §2.

[129] Canon 1563.

sary forum,[130] the Code provides that trials which concern hereditaments or legacies for pious causes must be tried before the ordinary of the domicile of the testatrix or, when there is question merely of the execution of the legacy, before that forum which is competent in accordance with the ordinary rules that determine judicial competency.[131] The norms of ordinary competency are those which are contained in canons 1561–1568. A case of the mere execution of a legacy is exemplified in the citing of the executor before an ecclesiastical tribunal for the specific purpose of compelling him to pay a legacy. The more common opinion holds that ecclesiastical, not civil, domicile is contemplated by the legislator in canon 1560, 4°.[132]

SECTION 5. IN RELATION TO DELICTS AND PENALTIES

Here the factors of domicile and quasi-domicile are considered in relation to the incurring, the inflicting, and the remitting of ecclesiastical penalties.

There is question here of particular penal laws only, since a general penal law of the Church binds everywhere all for whom the law was given,[133] unless special provision is made that the law does not have binding force in a particular place.[134] The principles set forth previously in this commentary [135] concerning particular laws are equally applicable though the law be penal in nature. Thus a wife is subject to the penal laws of a particular territory where she actually has her domicile or quasi-domicile.[136]

If after the fashion of a *peregrinus* she is absent from her own territory, then the penal laws of her territory are not obligatory on her, unless her transgression of the particular penal law would prove harmful to her own territory or unless the particular penal law was enacted as a personal law.[137] But it is contended by a

130 Canon 1560.
131 Canon 1560, 4°.
132 Coronata, *Institutiones,* III, 13.
133 Canons 13, §1; 2226, §1.
134 Canons 14, §1, 3°; 2226, §1.
135 Cf. *supra,* p. 103.
136 Canon 13, §2.
137 Canon 14, §1, 1°.

number of authors that in all likelihood she would be bound by the penal laws of the territory where she happened to be, inasmuch as to them it seems most improbable that the violation of such a law would not concern the public order.[138] However, granted that she is subject to the penal law, is it only to the ordinance of the law, or also to the attached penalty that she is subject? In penal law a strict subjection to the penalty can hardly be claimed if there be any tenable opinion that disavows such a subjection.[139] In a status or condition such as attaches to *vagi,* she would be subject to the penal laws, general or particular, which are in force in the territory where she happens to be.[140]

There is question here only of penalties which are inflicted through a judicial sentence, for the penalties which a guilty person incurs without the intervention of a judge affect in the same manner all who are subject to the penal law in question. The Code provides that the judicial forum of the place where the particular crime was committed is competent to inflict the punishment[141] even though the guilty person should have departed from the territory after committing the crime,[142] for the judge of the competent forum could cite before him the guilty person and inflict the punishment wherever she may have gone. In this matter the Code has introduced no variation from the previous law.[143]

---

[138] Canon 14, §1, 2°; "Post Codicem, opinio communior [Moroto, Cocchi, Prümmer, Toso, Cicognani, Eichmann, Ojetti are the authors cited.] peregrinos submittit legibus poenalibus, sed ob rationes quae *omni fundamento carent.* Contendunt enim peregrinos subditos fieri legibus poenalibus Ordinarii loci, qua ratione delicti reus forum sortitur in loco patrati delicti, vi can. 1566, §1. At hic canon nullo modo determinat ius secundum quod sententia contra peregrinos est proferenda, sed iudicem competentem. Sane expedit ut delicta puniantur ubi commissa sunt, modo aliquod delictum fuerit commissum. Nullo modo pari gressu procedunt forum sortiri et legibus illius territorii subesse, ut scribit Ph. Morto. Haec doctrina, olim propugnata, ad falsa ducit consectaria: iudex enim semper deberet iudicare secundum ius in suo territorio vigens et proinde in instantia appellationis secundum proprium ius, non secundum ius litigantium."—Van Hove, *Commentarium Lavaniense in Codicem Iuris Canonici,* Vol. I, Tomus II, *De Legibus Ecclesiasticis* (Mechliniae: H. Dessain, 1930), p. 224.

[139] Cf. canons 19 and 2219, §1.

[140] Canon 14, §2.

[141] Canon 1566, §1.

[142] Canon 1566, §2.

[143] Alberti, *De Domicilio Ecclesiastico,* p. 67.

From the general principles set forth in canon 2236, §§1, 2,[144] it is evident that domicile and quasi-domicile enter into a consideration of the remission of ecclesiastical penalties only in so far as the legislative power of the superior affects the allegedly guilty person. If a wife by reason of her domicile or quasi-domicile is a subject of a particular legislator, then by the same token the legislator, his superior, successor, or competent delegate may remit the punishment incurred by the wife as a proper subject. However, in addition to the general principle stated in canon 2236, the law makes other special provision for the remission of *latae sententiae* [145] penalties enacted in the common law and for the absolution of censures.[146]

Canon 2237, §3, distinguishes public cases from occult cases.[147] In public cases the ordinary may within the specifically restricted sphere of competence granted to him remit the *latae sententiae* penalties incurred in consequence of the enactments of the common law. In occult cases, without prejudice to the concessions of canons 2254 and 2290, the ordinary may personally or through another remit the *latae sententiae* penalties enacted by the common law, with the exception of the censures which for this absolution are reserved to the Apostolic See *specialissimo* or *speciali modo*.[148] The ordinary may use these faculties in behalf of all

---

[144] Remissio poenae sive per absolutionem, si agatur de censuris, sive per dispensationem, si de poenis vindicativis, concedi potest ab eo qui poenam tulit, vel ab eius competente Superiore aut successore, vel ab eo cui haec potestas commissa est. Qui potest a lege eximere, potest quoque poenam legi adnexam remittere.

[145] Canon 2217, §1, 2o. Poena dicitur: *Latae sententiae,* si poena determinata ita sit addita legi vel praecepto ut incurratur ipso facto commissi delicti; . . .

[146] Canon 2241, §1. Censura est poena qua homo baptizatus, delinquens et contumax, quibusdam bonis spiritualibus vel spiritualibus adnexis privatur, donec, a contumacia recedens, absolvatur.

[147] Canon 2197. Delictum est:

1o. *Publicum,* si iam divulgatum est aut talibus contigit seu versatur in adiunctis ut prudenter iudicari possit et debeat facile divulgatum ire; . . .

4o. *Occultum,* quod non est publicum; *occultum materialiter,* si lateat delictum ipsum; *occultum formaliter,* si eiusdem imputabilitas.

[148] Canon 2237, §2.

who are his subjects even though these be outside his territory, and also in behalf of *peregrini* in his territory.[149]

When there is question of the remission of particular censures enacted in the law, a distinction must be made between those whose remission is not reserved and those whose remission is reserved either *ab homine* or *a iure.*[150] Non-reserved censures may be absolved in the sacramental forum by any authorized confessor.[151] Moreover, the ordinary can absolve his subjects even outside his territory.[152] Though the Code does not specifically state that the local ordinary can absolve *peregrini* from non-reserved censures, such jurisdiction is implied in view of the statement of canon 2253, 1°, and the same requisite jurisdiction is deduced from the fact that it is possible for him to remit such reserved censures which by law are reserved to any bishop or ordinary.[153]

Domicile and quasi-domicile do not control in the determination of the one who is authorized to remit a censure imposed *ab homine.*[154] Censures that are reserved *a iure* are reserved either to the Apostolic See or to the ordinary or bishop. In the former case, ordinaries and confessors do not natively have any jurisdiction except in cases of necessity when the censure is likened to one that is not reserved. If the *a iure* established reservation lies within the competence of an ordinary then, regardless of her place of residence, the wife who is a subject can be absolved by

[149] Chelodi, *Ius Poenale et Ordo Procedendi in Iudiciis Criminalibus iuxta Codicem Iuris Canonici* (Tridenti: Libr. Edit. Tridentum, 1925), p. 30.

[150] Canon 2245, §1. Censurae aliae sunt *reservatae,* aliae *non reservatae.*

§2. Censura *ab homine* est reservata ei qui censuram inflixit aut sententiam tulit, eiusve Superiori competenti, vel successori aut delegato; ex censuris vero *a iure* reservatis aliae sunt reservatae *Ordinario,* aliae *Apostolicae Sedi.*

[151] Canon 2253, 1°. [Extra mortis periculum possunt absolvere:] A censura non reservata, in foro sacramentali quilibet confessarius; . . .

[152] Canon 201, §3.

[153] Canon 2253, 4°.

[154] Canon 2247, §2. Reservatio censurae in particulari territorio vim suam extra illius territorii fines non exserit, etiamsi censuratus ad absolutionem obtinendam e territorio egrediatur; censura vero ab homine est ubique locorum reservata ita ut censuratus nullibi absolvi sine debitis facultatibus possit. Cf. canon 2253, 2°.

the ordinary of her domicile or quasi-domicile.[155] If the reservation was made by a particular law, the reservation would not be binding outside the particular territory for which the law was enacted.[156] Because of this it may be said that the wife who had incurred such a penalty would, with reference to the non-reserved status of this penalty in her proper diocese, enjoy a favor in the law by reason of her domicile or quasi-domicile.

Article C. The Legal Domicile of the Wife as a Juridical Factor in the Determination of Judicial Competence in Matrimonial Cases

By virtue of canon 1561, §1, of the Code of Canon Law, domicile and quasi-domicile may serve as the basis of establishing judicial competence.[157] This is a norm applicable with reference to ecclesiastical trials in general. With reference to judicial competency in matrimonial causes one must look to those canons of the Code which treat of such causes in particular.[158]

Upon its enactment of norms concerning the nature of ecclesiastical jurisdiction in general with regard to matrimonial causes between baptized persons, and subsequent to its provisions for "mixed causes" in matrimonial trials and for the reservation of particular cases to specified tribunals, the Code legislates as follows: "In other matrimonial causes the competent judge is the judge of the place in which the marriage was celebrated, or of the place in which the defendant, or, if one party is a non-Catholic, in which the Catholic party has a domicile or quasi-domicile." [159]

Subsequent to the enactment of the Code, questions and difficulties arose concerning the proper determining of the forum for matrimonial causes between separated spouses. From the general principle governing the domicile and quasi-domicile of a wife as enunciated in canon 93, namely, that a wife not legitimately sep-

[155] Canon 2253, 3o.

[156] Canon 2247, §3.

[157] Ratione domicilii vel quasi-domicilii quilibet conveniri potest coram Ordinario loci.

[158] Cf. canons 1960–1965.

[159] Canon 1964. In aliis causis matrimonialibus iudex competens est iudex loci in quo matrimonium celebratum est aut in quo pars conventa vel, si una sit acatholica, pars catholica domicilium vel quasi-domicilium habet.

arated from her husband could establish only a quasi-domicile, there arose the problem regarding the sufficiency of this factor of quasi-domicile to serve as a basis for determining the proper competency.

The Pontifical Commission for the Interpretation of the Canons of the Code, under date of July 14, 1922, gave a series of responses,[160] some of which had a direct bearing on the problem in question, and subsequently the Sacred Congregation of the Sacraments issued an Instruction, "*Provida Mater,*" under date of August 15, 1936,[161] which Instruction together with the responses of the Pontifical Commission provides a means for determining judicial competence in the cases under discussion.

SECTION 1. MALICIOUS DESERTION BY THE HUSBAND AND ITS EFFECT ON THE LEGAL DOMICILE OF THE WIFE

The first pertinent response of the Pontifical Commission determined that malicious desertion by the husband did not entitle the deserted wife by that fact alone to acquire a domicile without having first obtained from an ecclesiastical judge a decree of separation in perpetuity or for an indefinite time.[162] It was evident from canon 93, §2, that the wife maliciously deserted by her husband could acquire at least her own proper quasi-domicile, since she was by the fact of the malicious desertion in any event at least "mulier legitime non separata," and the law provided that in such a case she could acquire a quasi-domicile.[163]

But it was determined that this quasi-domicile which the wife could thus acquire through the desertion by her husband was not sufficient to serve as a basis of judicial competency in a case wherein a Catholic wife as plaintiff sought action against her Catholic husband. The question was asked, whether the wife

[160] *AAS,* XIV (1922), 526–530.

[161] *AAS,* XXVIII (1936), 313–361.

[162] P.C.I., 14 iul. 1922, ad I: "Utrum uxor, a viro malitiose deserta, possit, ad normam can. 93, §2, obtinere proprium ac distinctum domicilium. Resp. Negative, nisi a iudice ecclesiastico obtinuerit separationem perpetuam, aut ad tempus indefinitum."—*AAS,* XIV (1922), 526.

[163] Canon 93, §2. Minor infantia egressus potest quasi-domicilium proprium obtinere; item uxor a viro legitime non separata, legitime autem separata etiam domicilium.

maliciously deserted by her husband could cite him in a matrimonial cause according to the norm of canon 1964 before the ordinary of her own proper and distinct quasi-domicile? To this question the official response was in the negative. She must, so said the Pontifical Commission for the Interpretation of the Canons of the Code, cite him before the ordinary of the domicile or quasi-domicile of her husband.[164]

Article 6, §1, of the Instruction "Provida Mater" is in full accord with this interpretation, for, according to its statement, even if the wife has been maliciously deserted by her husband, she may allowably cite her husband solely before one or the other of two ordinaries: the ordinary of the place where the marriage was celebrated, or the ordinary of the domicile or the quasi-domicile of the husband himself.[165]

There had been some uncertainty concerning this question previously. Mansella, writing in 1881, had expressed quite a contrary opinion. According to Mansella,[166] the bishop of the diocese in which the maliciously deserted party had his or her domicile was the competent judge. Furthermore, according to Mansella, wherever the actual residence of the deserting party might be, such a party remained subject to the bishop of the diocese where that party had his or her domicile at the time of the desertion, since the domicile was not changed in consequence of the desertion which implied actual residence elsewhere.[167]

---

[164] P.C.I., 14 iul., 1922, ad XIV, 1: "Utrum uxor, a viro malitiose deserta, eum in causa matrimoniali, ad normam can. 1964, convenire possit coram Ordinario proprii ac distincti quasi-domicilii; an vero convenire debeat coram Ordinario domicilii viri. Resp. Negative ad primam partem; affirmative ad secundam."—*AAS,* XIV (1922), 529.

[165] S. C. de Sacramentis, instr. 15 aug. 1936—"Uxor, etsi a viro malitiose deserta, eum convenire debet vel coram Ordinario loci in quo matrimonium celebratum est, vel coram Ordinario domicilii vel quasi-domicilii viri ipsius." —*AAS,* XXVIII (1936), 316.

[166] *De Impedimentis Matrimonium Dirimentibus ac de Processu Iudicali in Causis Matrimonialibus Notiones et Disceptationes Canonicae* (Romae: Ex Typographia Polyglotta S. C. de Propaganda Fide, 1881), p. 174.

[167] "Ut igitur matrimoniales causae in competente foro proponantur, attendendum est ad *coniugum domicilium.* Cum autem uxor sortiatur viri sui domicilium et forum, hinc coniuges in causis matrimonialibus subsunt Episcopo in cuius dioecesi maritus domicilium habet. Quod si coniugale

In accord with the official response of the Pontifical Commission for the Interpretation of the Canons of the Code to the effect that a wife maliciously deserted by her husband must cite him before the ordinary of his domicile or quasi-domicile,[168] and in harmony with the further interpretation that a Catholic woman as plaintiff, although not legitimately separated from her non-Catholic husband, but having a separate quasi-domicile of her own, follows indeed the domicile of her husband, but can cite her husband before either ordinary,[169] it was commonly taught that legal domicile was equal to voluntary domicile or quasi-domicile as a basis for determining the competency of the court in matrimonial cases.[170]

SECTION 2. A DECISION OF THE SUPREME TRIBUNAL OF THE APOSTOLIC SIGNATURA

The Apostolic Signatura on November 7, 1932, by a decision which seemed contrary to the generally accepted opinion, held that the legal domicile was not qualified as a basis for determining judicial competency. While this decision has been reported only privately [171] there seems to be no question concerning the record

---

vitae consortium per separationem a toro et mensa sublatum sit, hoc in casu iudex competens est Episcopus ille, in cuius dioecesi domicilium habet pars contra quam proceditur. Si vero sublatum sit per malitiosam viri vel uxoris desertionem, iudex competens est Episcopus, in cuius dioecesi pars deserta domicilium habet. Ubicumque enim existat transfuga coniux, manet subditus iudicis dioecesis domicilii hoc ipso quod domicilium per desertionem non mutet."—Cf. *op. cit., loc. sit.*

[168] P.C.I., 14 iul. 1922, ad XIV, 1—*AAS*, XIV (1922), 529.

[169] P.C.I., 14 iul. 1922, ad XIV, 2—*AAS* (1922), 530.

[170] Roberti, *De Processibus* (2 vols., Romae: Apud Aedes Facultatis Iuridicae ad S. Apollinaris, 1926), I, 119, n. 64; Roberti, "De Competentia Ratione Domicilii"—*Apollinaris*, III (1930), 458–459; Noval, *Commentarium Codicis Iuris Canonici Libri IV de Processibus, Pars I, De Iudiciis* (Taruini: Marietti, 1920), p. 41; Vlaming, *Praelectiones Iuris Canonici ad Normam Codicis Iuris Canonici* (3. ed., 2 vols., Bussum in Hollandia: Sumptibus Societatis Editricis Anonymae olim Paulis Brand, 1919–1921), II, 374.

[171] Cf. F. Cattani-Amadori, "Supr. Tribunal Signaturae Ap., "De Competentia ex Domicilio Legali In Causis Matrimonialibus" (*Florentina—Commissionis, seu Nullitatis matrimonii—7* nov. 1932)—*JP*, XIII (1933), 106–108; Bouscaren, *The Canon Law Digest, Officially Published Documents*

of the facts and the reasoning upon which the court based its decision.

The case, as related by F. Cattani-Amadori,[172] concerned a certain Alexander who had emigrated from Italy to New York and was practicing medicine in the latter city. Among his patients was one Clelia, whose parents were Italians living in America. As Clelia displayed a certain amorous affection for Alexander, she found occasion to visit him at his place of business under the pretext of seeking his professional services. Alexander told her plainly that he was engaged to another girl, and that he could not even think of marriage with her. As Clelia continued her advances, and found opportunity to provoke him to commit sin with her, Alexander on one occasion seduced her. Whereupon, Clelia's father, by threats, forced Alexander to marry her. Alexander intended, however, as he contended, to leave her at the first opportunity. A few months later Alexander in fact sold all his equipment and secretly sailed for Italy, where he established himself in Florence. Later he applied to the ecclesiastical court at Florence for a declaration of nullity of his marriage on the ground of fear.

The court refused to receive the petition, whereupon he had recourse to the Supreme Signatura, asking that his case be committed to the Sacred Roman Rota, according to the prescriptions of canon 1603, §2. To this the Supreme Signatura replied: "In the negative, but let the petitioner use his right in the competent tribunal; i.e., in that of the episcopal Curia of New York."

Alexander's counsel then contended, again upon recourse to the Supreme Signatura, that at least the tribunal of the Curia of Florence was competent to hear the case. But the Supreme Signatura replied in the negative: *Negative seu in decisis.*

Alexander contended that according to canon 1964 the competent judge was the judge of the place where the marriage was performed, or the judge of the place where the defendant had a domicile or quasi-domicile. Hence, although the court of New York was competent because the marriage took place there and the

Affecting the Code of Canon Law (2 vols., Milwaukee: The Bruce Publishing Company, 1934–1943), I, 804–806.

172 Cf. *art. cit.—JP,* XIII (1933), 106–108.

woman defendant had a quasi-domicile there, yet the court of Florence was also competent, on the ground that the woman had a true domicile there, namely, her legal domicile by reason of canon 93, §1, since she was not legitimately separated from her husband. The fact that Clelia, according to Alexander, was maliciously deserted by her husband made no difference, since there had been no decree of separation, and the official interpretation of canon 93 under date of July 22, 1922, was cited in substantiation of the contention. Alexander argued: Canon 1964 makes no distinction between voluntary and legal domicile; and therefore it allows the bringing of this suit in the place of Clelia's legal domicile, that, namely, which she necessarily retained in the place of her husband's domicile, i.e., in Florence. Furthermore, so he said, the fact that she was absent from that jurisdiction did not deprive the court of its competence, and cited canon 1561, §2, as authority for his contention.

F. Cattani-Amadori, in reporting the reasoning by which the Supreme Signatura reached its conclusion, noted that the proffered contention was based on a false interpretation of canon 1964, and then made the following observations.[173]

It is a general principle of the law that "the plaintiff follows the defendant's court; if the defendant has several courts, the plaintiff has his choice among them." This is declared in canon 1559, §3, which gives the defendant the right to be tried by his judge, and prevents the plaintiff from bringing the defendant before a judge of his own (plaintiff's) choosing. This is true in general. As regards the competent judge in marriage cases, the Code makes special provisions which declare in canon 1964: "In marriage cases, the competent judge is the judge of the place where the marriage was celebrated, or in which the defendant, or, if one party is a non-Catholic, in which the Catholic party has a domicile or quasi-domicile." Evidently, so Cattani-Amadori continued, the lawmaker wished by this canon to state something new in this matter by means of which the common good and the dignity of the sacrament would be safeguarded, and therefore a strict interpretation is required, since it is in fact a derogation from

[173] Cf. *JP*, XIII (1933), 107–108. This report is signed: "F. Cattani-Amadori, A Secretis Signaturae Ap."

the general principle of law. Further, it would be an injustice to permit a husband by his wrongful conduct to gain such an advantage over his deserted wife by placing her at such a disadvantage as citing her before a tribunal at the other end of the earth. This was exactly what might be done if canon 1964 were not limited in its application to the defendant's own voluntary domicile. It would in such a case be absolutely contrary to a common sense of justice.[174]

The report gives the following argument: Canon 1964 states that, if the defendant is a non-Catholic, the Catholic party may cite the other party before the judge of the place where he or she (i.e., the Catholic plaintiff) has a domicile or quasi-domicile, but if this same procedure could be followed also in cases where both parties are Catholics, the limiting words, "in case one of the parties is a non-Catholic," would be useless, and hence it is clear that this right can be exercised only against a non-Catholic defendant.[175]

---

[174] "Non igitur eo quod Commissio pro authentica Codicis interpretatione, ad quaestionem 'Utrum uxor, a viro malitiose deserta, possit obtinere, ad normam can. 93, proprium ad distinctum domicilium,' respondit: 'Negative, nisi a iudice ecclesiastico obtinuerit separationem perpetuam vel ad tempus indefinitum,' concludi potest ius esse viro, qui erga uxorem ita se gessit, eam postea trahendi coram iudice domicilii, quod sibi eligere placuerit, in ultimis etiam finibus terrae, ut ab eo sententiam nullitatis sui matrimonii audiat: quod revera evenire posset, si canon de quo supra, non ad solum domicilium proprium et reale coaractaretur, sed ad domicilium legale extenderetur. Hoc autem maxime sensui ipsi communi repugnaret, idest quod iniquitas et iniustitia viri ius parere valeat contra uxorem innocentem, quae iniustitiam passa sit."—Cf. Cattani-Amadori, *art. cit.—JP,* XIII (1933), 107.

[175] "Quod si adducta argumenta, pro stricta interpretatione canonis 1964, aliquid dubii relinquat, hoc penitus aufertur, si quis illum diligenter inspiciat. Inibi enim dicitur, quod si pars conventa sit acatholica, eam pars catholica trahere potest coram iudice loci, in quo ipsa domicilium vel quasi-domicilium habet. Ideo si hoc ius exerceri tantum potest contra partem acatholicam, dicendum omnino est, quod haberi nequeat contra partem catholicam; atqui in casu nostro pars conventa, seu uxor ab Alexandro deserta, est catholica: ergo haec ad forum mariti trahi nequit. Secus enim exceptio, quae contra partem acatholicam fit, non derogaret regulae, quod absurdum esset, utpote contradictorium. Aliis verbis, ex principio iuris: 'Inclusio unius est exclusio alterius,' si in hac canonis dispositione est inclusa pars acatholica, pars catholica exclusa esse debet."—Cf. *art. cit., loc. cit.*

An editorial comment was appended to the recital of the case and the reasoning of the court. This comment provoked a communication to the editor. In a reply to the letter, Toso sought to justify the decision by giving in detail the arguments of the Supreme Signatura.[176]

According to the reply of Toso the decision of the Supreme Signatura did not ignore the interpretation of the Pontifical Commission that the wife who was maliciously deserted could not acquire a voluntary domicile. The divergent interpretation centered in the fact that it opposed the contention that according to canon 1964 the legal domicile was to be honored as a basis of judicial competency. And since the canon was the fulcrum of the decision, an interpretation of the canon was essential, since the court could not apply the law to a particular fact without at the same time interpreting the canon, not indeed authentically, but as it appeared to the tribunal. It was necessary to study the reasoning of the Supreme Signatura to determine whether the official response had really "extended" or "limited" the sense of the canon in the application of its norm.

The initial argument of the Supreme Signatura as defended by Toso was based on the necessity of preserving the principle that the plaintiff follows the forum of the defendant, which principle had long been recognized as a safeguard against fraud on the part of a plaintiff who would seek to cite a defendant before a court wherein the defendant would be at a great disadvantage in defending his or her rights. Toso argued that the legislator in the enactment of canon 1964 had not overlooked the age-old principle; that in Catholic marriages it was necessary to beware lest the identity of the conjugal domicile overthrow this established principle; that the legislator did in fact invoke this principle, and that therefore the words used in canon 1964 must be understood exclusively of the proper and real domicile, and not of the legal domicile which in fact was derived from another.[177]

---

[176] Cf., "De Curia Romana Litteris Egregii Cujusdam Antecessoris Aequa Responsio."—*JP,* XIII (1933), 232-234.

[177] "Sed, quia introductioni causarum matrimonialium fere semper praecedit *separatio coniugum,* praecavere oportebat, ne *identitas domicilii coniugalis* (quam in aliis causis natura ipsa postulat) subverteret regulam de

To the foregoing argument it may be answered that the necessity of preventing a plaintiff from committing a fraud against the defendant, or of placing the latter at a disadvantage through a means not allowed by the law, is well recognized, but likewise this caution must not be invoked as a reason for denying the plaintiff any lawful approach to the securing of justice. Thus, it may be argued, there are dangers involved in permitting quasi-domicile to serve as a basis of judicial competency. Yet, rather than deny the right to cite a person on this basis, provision is made for determining the reality of the quasi-domicile, and thus fraud is guarded against and the just right of the petitioner recognized.[178]

When the court has been assured of the good faith on the part of the one claiming the quasi-domicile, there is no objection to permitting the use of the alleged right. Likewise, the inconvenience caused to the defendant, and the possibility of disadvantage to the latter in the particular forum, are not valid arguments against the exercise of a certain right to choose the forum in question. If therefore the particular forum corresponds to the conjugal domicile, and the law has specifically provided concerning the juridical value of the latter in relation to competency, it belongs to the court to determine whether or not it is the true conjugal domicile, and it does not pertain to the court to inquire concerning the extension of the law in relation to domicile.

Toso's second argument was to the effect that, since legal domicile was not in question when a non-Catholic marriage was the

foro rei adeundo, quum pars conventa est uxor, fraudibusque actoris viam sterneret contra uxorem absentem et, propter distantiae incommoda, aut contumacem aut vix vel nevix respondere valentem: maxime quum *non sine ratione* can. 93, §2, caveat, ut uxor, quamvis a viro legitime non separata, *quasi-domicilium proprium obtinere possit.* . . . Competentiam tribunalis ex duplici causa docet oriri posse, ex contractu et ex commoratione . . . ; ratione vero commorationis, in iudice illius territorii, in quo reus (si catholicum fuerit matrimonium) '*domicilium* vel *quasi-domicilium* habet.' . . . Quod si id ne cogitare quidem possumus," (i.e., legislatorem hic neglexisse principium), "iam statim oportet concedamus, allata verba can. 1964 exclusive intelligenda esse (prout iudex Curiae Florentinae intellexit) de domicilio et quasi-domicilio *proprio* seu *reali,* non autem legali seu ex alieno domicilio derivante."—Cf. Toso, *art. cit.—JP,* XIII (1933), 233.

[178] Cf. S. C. de Sacramentis, instr. 23 dec. 1929—*AAS,* XXII (1930), 168–171.

subject matter of a judicial trial, neither was legal domicile to be understood in canon 1964 when a Catholic marriage was impugned. He stated his argument substantially as follows. If a mixed marriage is impugned, then canon 1964 provides that the competent judge on the basis of domicile is the judge of the place in which the Catholic party has a domicile or a quasi-domicile. Therefore the Catholic party has a certain privilege of forum, by force of which privilege, whether the Catholic party is plaintiff or defendant, the non-Catholic party is held to follow the forum of the Catholic party. He asked: Was there question here of the legal domicile of the Catholic party; was the Catholic wife, if she was not legitimately separated from her non-Catholic husband in view of the fact that " she must retain the domicile of her husband," capable of being cited in a manner by which she was held to follow the forum of the husband? But then, he insisted, where was the privilege? [179]

The reply to this argument is specifically this, that in mixed marriages the exception to the general rule applies equally to voluntary domicile and legal domicile.[180] Toso argued from a privilege granted in canon 1964 in favor of the Catholic party in a mixed matrimonial case to a denial of a general rule which provides for a forum based on legal domicile when both of the parties to the matrimonial case are Catholics. The case he envisaged contemplated a non-Catholic husband citing his Catholic wife before an ecclesiastical tribunal. In such a case, Toso contended, the application of the rule that the legal domicile may serve as a

[179] "Quid, si mixtum fuerit matrimonium accusandum? Tunc, ait canon, competens est iudex loci . . . in quo pars catholica domicilium vel quasi-domicilium habet. Habet igitur, pars catholica, privilegium quoddam fori . . . , vi cuius, sive agat sive conveniatur, pars acatholica *eius forum sequi tenetur.* Num igitur hic de domicilio *legali* partis catholicae? Num uxor catholica, a viro acatholico legitime non separata, eo quod 'retineat domicilium viri sui,' *citari potest* et ideo de legali in causa matrimonii iudicem viri? Sed tunc, ubi privilegium? At si non agitur de *legali* domicilio in causa matrimonii mixti, neque de domicilio legali agitur in causa matrimonii catholici: nam verba '*domicilium vel quasi-domicilium habet*' utrique generi causae referuntur, ac proinde eodem sensu utrobique sunt accipienda."—Cf. Toso, *art. cit.*—*JP*, XIII (1933), 233.

[180] Cf. Ciprotti, "Quaestiones de Competentia Ratione Contractus et Domicilii in Causis Matrimonialibus"—*Apollinaris,* XI (1938), 458–465.

qualified basis for the determination of judicial competency would destroy the privilege in favor of the Catholic party which privilege canon 1964 had established. A case wherein a non-Catholic could act as plaintiff before a Catholic ecclesiastical tribunal is most exceptional. The writer treats of it later in his commentary,[181] but in no case may it destroy the privilege granted in the law. In mixed marriages the exception to the general rules applies equally to voluntary domicile and legal domicile.

The non-Catholic party could have a domicile or quasi-domicile other than the domicile or quasi-domicile of the Catholic party. But, if this should happen to be the case, then though according to the general norms the defendant would have to be cited in his own domicile, yet according to the special norm he can be cited in the domicile or quasi-domicile of the Catholic plaintiff.[182]

The third argument as stated by Toso was that the relationship of canon 1964 to the other canons which define judicial competency by reason of domicile was after the manner of a species to a genus. The species modifies the genus and restricts it. Therefore canon 1964, being a restriction and modification of these other canons, requires in itself a strict interpretation. But, domicile and quasi-domicile, when understood in a strict sense, do not include the notion of a legal domicile, and consequently domicile and quasi-domicile as mentioned in canon 1964 do not include a legal domicile in their concept.[183]

To this argument it is answered that, while a strict interpretation is truly in order, yet it must be understood that an interpreta-

---

181 Cf. *infra,* pp. 138–140.

182 "Attamen contra animavertendum est etiam admissa competentia ex domicilio legali haberi exceptionem in casu matrimonii mixti; nam pars acatholica potest etiam habere domicilium vel quasi-domicilium aliud ac domicilium vel quasi-domicilium partis catholicae; quod si accidat, cum iuxta normas generales citanda esset in suo domicilio vel quasi-domicilio, iuxta normam specialem citari potest etiam in domicilio vel quasi-domicilio actoris catholici."—Ciprotti, *art. cit.—Apollinaris,* XI (1938), 462–463.

183 "Praeterea, can. 1964 pro causis matrimonialibus specialiter conflatus a Legislatore: ita ergo se habet quoad canones qui in reliquis causis iudicialibus competentiam definiunt, ut species quoad genus. Jamvero species derogat generi illudque coarctat. Ergo stricte interpretanda est. At domicilium et quasi-domicilium *stricte* acceptum, non potest esse legale."—Cf. Toso, *art. cit.—JP,* XIII (1933), 233.

tion which forbids an extension of the sense of the words interpreted does at the same time demand that the words be not denied their commonly accepted extension of meaning.[184] The word "domicile" when used in the law comprehends the concept of a legal domicile if that concept is applicable in the text and context, and if the lawgiver has not expressly excepted it from his legislation.[185]

In his final argument Toso, in using the words of the Supreme Signatura contended that in canon 1964 it was provided that if the defendant were a non-Catholic party, the Catholic party could cite him before the judge of the place in which the Catholic party had a domicile. Therefore, if this right can be exercised only against the non-Catholic party, then accordingly it must be said that the right can not be exercised against the Catholic party. "In other words," Toso concluded, "the legislator saw the need of an exception from the general rule, so that in matrimonial causes a spouse should be able to cite the other spouse to the forum of his (or her) own *domicile* or *quasi-domicile*. That, however, in the light of the general rule was felt impossible of accomplishment on any score (hence also on the score of a legal domicile or quasi-domicile). Therefore the concept of a legal domicile and quasi-domicile is not comprehended in the general rule. A subtle argument, indeed, but one that along with the rest conspires ever to lead to the same conclusion." [186]

---

[184] "Verum stricta interpretatio vetat quidem quominus sensus verborum extendatur, non autem iubet ut coarctetur."—Ciprotti, *art. cit.—Apollinaris,* XI (1938), 462.

[185] Cf. canon 18.

[186] "In can. 1964 'dicitur (ut ipsius Signaturae Apost. verbis utamur), quod si pars conventa sit acatholica, eam pars catholica trahere potest coram iudice loci, in quo ipsa domicilium habet. Ideo, si hoc ius *exerceri tantum potest* contra partem acatholicam, dicendum omnino est quod haberi nequeat contra partem catholicam. Aliis verbis, Legislatori visa est *necessaria exemptio* a regula generali (can. 1964), ut in causis matrimonialibus coniux coniugem trahere possit ad forum proprii *domicilii* vel *quasi-domicilii: ergo id nulla ratione* (ac proinde *ne ratione quidem* domicilii aut quasi-domicilii legalis) fieri poterat *vi regulae generalis;* ergo domicilium et quasi-domicilium legale in regula generali (can. 1964) non comprehenditur. Argumentum subtile, sed quod ad eandem semper conclusionem ducit."—Cf. Toso, *art. cit.—JP,* XIII (1933), 234.

The "subtlety" (if such it may be called!) of this argument consists really in making an exclusion which the legislator did not make, namely, by excluding *legal domicile* from the comprehension of the term *domicile.* This exclusion does not, in the mind of the writer, seem well founded.[187]

Even if it were possible to adopt the decision of the Supreme Signatura to the effect that a legal domicile may not serve as the basis for the determination of a judge's competence in matrimonial causes, at least when such a cause concerns a non-Catholic, even apart from any consideration of Article 6 of the Instruction "*Provida Mater,*" the same decision seems beyond reconciliation with recent decisions of the Sacred Roman Rota,[188] as also with Article 7 of the aforesaid Instruction. In this Article of the Instruction the following norm is provided: A wife who has her proper quasi-domicile and who is not legitimately separated from her husband may be cited even before the ordinary of the domicile of her husband, but not of his quasi-domicile, except when the husband has no domicile.[189]

This norm of procedure is directly contrary to the ruling of the Supreme Signatura. If the wife who is not legitimately separated from her husband can be cited before the judge of the domicile of

[187] For other arguments against the decision of the Supreme Signatura consult, Badii, "Se il domicilio legale possa essere un criterio de competenza matrimoniale"—*Il Dritto Ecclesiastico* (Romae, 1890—), XLIV (1933), 208-215.

[188] S. R. R., ". . . II—Causae quae eodem anno 1934 transactae fuerunt, vel peremptae, vel quae absque definitiva sententia, ex peculiaribus circumstantiis, finem habuerunt; quibus adduntur decreta quoad recursus contra libellarum reiectionem . . . IX. Liburen.—*Nullitatis matrimonii super reiectione libelli coram R. P. D. U. Mannucci.* Recurrente actore adversus decretum Curiae Liburnen.—ubi ipse domicilium—quo reiectus fuerat libellus ab eo oblatus, pro declaratione nullitatis matrimonii obtinenda, adversus uxorem, tantum de facto, non legitime ad normam can. 93, §2, separatam, Turnus decrevit, die 29 Ianuarii, reiectionem libelli in casu non sustineri." —*AAS,* XXVII (1935), 190. Cf. etiam: X, Fanen.—*Nullitatis matrimonii super reiectione libelli, AAS,* XXVII (1935), 190.

[189] "Uxor, a viro non legitime separata, quae proprium quasi-domicilium habeat, conveniri potest etiam coram Ordinario domicilii viri, non autem quasi-domicilii eiusdem viri, nisi in casu quo hic domicilio careat."—*AAS,* XXVIII (1936), 316.

her husband, and it is a case of determining the judicial competency by reason of domicile, there seems to be only one conclusion as to the nature of legal domicile as a possible determinant, namely, that the legal domicile is to be considered as on a par with voluntary domicile and quasi-domicile.

SECTION 3. THE COMPETENT FORUM WHEN ONLY ONE OF THE PARTIES IS A CATHOLIC

After the enactment of the Code of Canon Law several questions were raised concerning judicial competency by reason of domicile in those marriage causes in which only one of the parties was a Catholic. Canon 1964 provides that in matrimonial causes the judge of the place in which the defendant, or if one of the parties is a non-Catholic, in which the Catholic party has a domicile or quasi-domicile, is the competent judge to adjudicate the cause.[190] By virtue of this canon there is an evident derogation in favor of the Catholic party from the principle of law that the plaintiff must follow the forum of the defendant. This opinion, as expressed by canonical authors [191] who wrote shortly after the enactment of the Code of Canon Law, was confirmed by the Pontifical Commission for the Interpretation of the Canons of the Code in a response of July 22, 1922.[192]

The Pontifical Commission for the Interpretaton of the Canons of the Code was asked [193] whether a Catholic wife as plaintiff, if she was not legitimately separated from her husband, but if she

[190] Canon 1964. In aliis causis matrimonialibus iudex competens est iudex loci in quo matrimonium celebratum est aut in quo pars conventa vel, si una sit acatholica, pars catholica domicilium vel quasi-domicilium habet.

[191] Cappello, *De Matrimonio,* n. 868; Chelodi, *Ius Matrimoniale,* p. 188.

[192] Cappello in his opinion does not cite the response in confirmation of his opinion, but bases it apparently on canon 98, §4, and therefore it is concluded that his opinion was written prior to the response, even though the date of the publication of his book is later than that of the response.

[193] P.C.I., 14 iul. 1922, ad XIV, 2: "Utrum actrix catholica, a viro non legitime separata, quae proprium ac distinctum quasi-domicilium habet, virum acatholicum in causa matrimoniali, ad normam can. 1964, convenire possit tantum coram Ordinario proprii ac distincti quasi-domicilii; an vero etiam coram Ordinario domicilii viri." Resp. "Cum uxor in casu habeat proprium ac distinctum quasi-domicilium, et sequatur domicilium viri, potest virum convenire coram alterutro Ordinario."—*AAS,* XIV (1922), 530.

had her own proper and distinct quasi-domicile, could cite the non-Catholic husband exclusively before the ordinary of her quasi-domicile, according to the norm of canon 1964; or whether she also could cite the non-Catholic spouse before the ordinary of the place wherein he, the husband, had his domicile. The Pontifical Commission responded that, since the wife in the case had her own proper and distinct quasi-domicile, but followed still the domicile of her husband, she could cite her husband before either ordinary.

The effect of this interpretation was the following. When a legitimate separation had not taken place, the judge of the place wherein either the Catholic or the non-Catholic party had his or her domicile or quasi-domicile was competent to accept the petition of the Catholic wife who cited her non-Catholic husband as the defendant. Article 6, §3, of the Instruction " Provida Mater " cites this interpretation when it provides for the same circumstance.[194] However, by reason of the addition of the word "*etsi*" in the text of the Instruction, canonical writers found occasion for a divergence of opinion relative to the full import of the provision of the law in the case wherein only one of the parties is a Catholic.

The question as presented to the Pontifical Commission for the Interpretation of the Canons of the Code had phrased the circumstance which pointed to the absence of a legitimate separation with the following words: "*a viro non legitime separata.*" This phrase was used with reference to a Catholic wife as the plaintiff. Article 6, §3, of the Instruction provided: " Uxor catholica, *etsi a viro non legitime separata,* virum acatholicum convenire potest vel coram Ordinario proprii ac distincti quasi-domicilii vel coram ordinario domicilii viri." (Italics supplied.)

The interpretation given by the Pontifical Commission for the Interpretation of the Canons of the Code to the effect that a Catholic wife who was not legitimately separated from her hus-

---

[194] S. C. de Sacramentis, instr. 15 aug. 1936—" Uxor catholica, etsi a viro non legitime separata, virum acatholicum convenire potest vel coram Ordinario proprii ac distincti quasi-domicilii, vel coram Ordinario domicilii viri (Comm. Pont., 14 iulii 1922, ad can. 93 et 1964)."—*AAS,* XXVIII (1936), 316.

band could still cite her non-Catholic husband in his own domicile was contrary to the opinion held by some canonists of the time, among whom were Vidal (1867–1938)[195] and Roberti.[196] Gasparri (1852–1934),[197] contrary to the opinion later expressed by Ciprotti,[198] quite definitely subscribed to the conclusion established by the Pontifical Commission for the Interpretation of the Canons of the Code.

Ciprotti[199] admitted that before the issuance of the Instruction "*Provida Mater*"[200] the opinion which maintained that exclusive competency resided in the judge of the place of the Catholic party's domicile was tenable. For the law revealed nothing which favored the opinion of a concurrent competency between the judges of the Catholic and the non-Catholic parties' domiciles. Further, the official interpretation of the year 1922 admitted the competency of the judge of the non-Catholic party's domicile, and so in reality the official response simply recognized the wife's legal domicile as a basis for judicial competency. If, however, the competency had been concurrent, the judge of the non-Catholic party's domicile would have been recognized as competent independently of a consideration of the wife's legal domicile. Ciprotti contends that in view of the present wording of Article 6, §3, of the Instruction "*Provida Mater*" the competency of the judge of the Catholic party's domicile or quasi-domicile may no longer be considered as exclusive, but must be recognized as concurrent.

It is Ciprotti's opinion that the words, "*etsi a viro non legitime separata,*" evidently signify "whether separated, or not," and that consequently a Catholic wife, even one who is separated legitimately from her non-Catholic husband, can cite the latter either

---

[195] ". . . quod si una tantum pars sit catholica causa semper proponenda est in domicilio vel quasi-domicilio partis catholicae."—*Ius Canonicum,* V (2. ed., 1928), n. 689.

[196] ". . . quod si alterutra pars sit acatholica causa semper proponenda est in domicilio vel quasi-domicilio partis catholicae."—"De Competentia Ratione Domicilii," *Apollinaris,* III (1930), 458.

[197] *De Matrimonio,* II (1932), n. 1240.

[198] Cf. "Quaestiones de Competentia Ratione Contractus et Domicilii in Causis Matrimonialibus"—*Apollinaris,* XI (1938), 460.

[199] Cf. *ibid.,* p. 461.

[200] S. C. de Sacramentis, instr. 15 aug. 1936—*AAS,* XXVIII (1936), 316.

before the judge of her own proper and distinct domicile or quasi-domicile, or before the judge of her non-Catholic husband's domicile or quasi-domicile.[201]

This interpretation rather than the contrary opinion of exclusive competency in the judge of the Catholic party's domicile, so Ciprotti reasoned, is more in harmony with the end and purpose of the law. According to his view the legislator desired to favor the Catholic party by giving her the choice of citing the non-Catholic husband in his forum, and this is in harmony with the principle that the plaintiff must follow the forum of the defendant. But it is a greater favor to be able to choose between two jurisdictions than to be restricted to one only, even though this latter one be the plaintiff's proper and personal forum. So far as the actual conduct of the process is concerned, advantages for expediting the administration of justice are clearly perceptible if the process is conducted in the defendant's forum.

It is the observation of Doheny that the choice of the word "*etsi*" in Article 6, §3, is somewhat infelicitous. For to him it seems to connote that what follows this word would be true *a fortiori* if the wife were legitimately separated. It is his contention that this connotation would tend to imply more than was really intended in the reply of the Pontifical Commission for the Interpretations of the Canons of the Code, and would appear to confirm the opinion of those canonists who maintained that the word *vel* in canon 1964 was selective rather than exclusive in the case wherein the defendant was a non-Catholic. Doheny contends that the reply of the Pontifical Commission does not create this ambiguity, and that, consequently, the carefully phrased text of

---

[201] "In responso igitur Commissionis legebatur: '*a viro non legitime separata*,' pro quibus verbis nunc habetur: '*etsi a viro non legitime separata*,' quae evidenter significant: '*sive separata, sive non*,' ita ut iam actrix catholica, etiam legitime a viro separata, virum acatholicum convenire possit vel coram Ordinario proprii ac distincti domicilii vel quasi-domicilii (i.e., in domicilio vel quasi-domicilio partis catholicae), vel coram Ordinario domicilii vel quasi-domicilii viri (i.e., in domicilio vel quasi-domicilio partis conventae acatholicae), quod, si adsit legitima inter coniuges separatio, non est mulieris domicilium legale, cum mulier, ex separatione, amittat viri domicilium."—Cf. "art. cit.," *Apollinaris*, XI (1938), 461.

the Pontifical Commission's response is to furnish the true interpretation of what in reality was intended.[202]

It seems to the writer that the Instruction "*Provida Mater*" in Article 6, §3, intended to cover both situations, i.e., the cases wherein the Catholic wife was or was not legitimately separated from her non-Catholic husband. If she was legitimately separated, then she is enabled to cite him before an ecclesiastical tribunal in her own domicile or quasi-domicile by virtue of the exception granted in favor of the Catholic spouse; or, she may cite him before an ecclesiastical tribunal in his own domicile or quasi-domicile, not by reason of her legal domicile or quasi-domicile, but by virtue of the well established principle of law that the plaintiff follows the forum of the defendant. If she was not legitimately separated from her non-Catholic husband, then she is enabled to cite him before an ecclesiastical tribunal in her own quasi-domicile by virtue of the exception made in favor of the Catholic party; or, she may cite him before an ecclesiastical tribunal in her non-Catholic husband's domicile or quasi-domicile by virtue of her own legal domicile or quasi-domicile. The implication as arising *a fortiori* which Doheny detects in Article 6, §3, does seem verified, as Ciprotti has stated. The present writer, too, believes that it reflects a correct statement of the law in the matter.

Kay [203] in his treatment of the competency of ecclesiastical tribunals in matrimonial procedure makes the following conclusion concerning the proper forum by reason of domicile when there is question of a mixed marriage. "If the marriage in question is a mixed marriage the proper forum is determined according to the domicile of the Catholic party, whether defendant or plaintiff. When the husband is the Catholic, no difficulty is found in determining the properly competent tribunal. When the wife is the Catholic the selection of the proper court may cause some doubt. If the marriage is one of mixed religion the proper court is determined in the same manner as it would be in cases between two Catholics when the wife is the defendant (reus)." The writer

[202] Doheny, *Canonical Procedure in Matrimonial Cases,* I, 25.

[203] *Competence in Matrimonial Procedure,* The Catholic University of America Canon Law Studies n. 53 (Washington, D C.: The Catholic University of America, 1929), 96.

of the present commentary believes that to this last statement of Kay there should be added the following: "and no legitimate separation has intervened."[204]

The question is asked by Kay:[205] "What of cases where the husband is an infidel? Would the infidel husband be considered as having a canonical residence and the Catholic wife, as a consequence, a necessary domicile in the place where the husband has his domicile?" He notes that the question is possible should there occur a separation of the parties which was not legitimate. He was of the opinion that apparently the infidel husband is to be considered as having a canonical domicile and the wife therefore a necessary domicile in the place where the husband resides. The natural law does suppose that the wife should follow the domicile of her husband. Further, the determination of residence as outlined in the Code[206] is applied even to the non-baptized, inasmuch as canon 738, §2, mentions the proper pastor of an unbaptized "peregrinus."[207]

Marx[208] points out that the Code does not state that only those who are baptized can acquire a domicile or quasi-domicile, but that it rather seems to include anyone who has taken up residence in a particular territory, whether it be in a parish or in a diocese. Hence, he reasons, as far as domicile or quasi-domicile is concerned, these are not determined through whatever religion may be professed by the person who has taken up residence. An infidel, therefore, can establish a domicile as well as a baptized person, provided that the infidel resides within the territorial limits of a parish or of a diocese, and provided that all the other elements of the law are fulfilled. The Church, so Marx con-

---

[204] Kay is of the opinion that a court sentence is not always necessary for a legitimate separation. Cf. *loc. cit.*

[205] *Loc. cit.*

[206] Cf. canons 90–95.

[207] "Etiam peregrinus a parocho proprio in sua paroecia sollemniter baptizetur, . . ."

[208] *The Declaration of Nullity of Marriages Contracted Outside the Church*, The Catholic University of America Canon Law Studies, n. 182 (Washington, D. C.: The Catholic University of America Press, 1943), p. 66.

cludes,[209] while not making a law for the unbaptized, merely recognizes a juridical fact which can attach to the lives of the unbaptized as well as to the lives of the baptized.

It seems, therefore, that if the plaintiff is a Catholic, it would not make any material difference whether the defendant were a non-Catholic or an infidel so far as the determination of judical competency by reason of domicile is concerned. Even granted that the non-Catholic or infidel were incapable of establishing a canonical domicile, this situation would not affect the determination of competency in matrimonial causes wherein the Catholic party is the defendant. The handling of any such cause has been completely excluded by the Holy Office from the competency of the diocesan matrimonial court.

The Sacred Congregation of the Holy Office on January 27, 1928, declared that a non-Catholic, whether baptized or unbaptized, can not be a plaintiff in a matrimonial cause without the permission of that Congregation.[210] This declaration of the Sacred Congregation of the Holy Office is repeated in the Instruction "*Provida Mater*" in Title III thereof entitled: "The Right to Attack the Marriage." The particular provision is contained in Article 35, §3, which states: "Non-Catholics, whether baptized or unbaptized cannot be plaintiffs in matrimonial cases; but if special reasons arise in favor of admitting them as such, recourse must be had in each case to the Holy Office." [211] This

---

[209] Cf. *ibid.*

[210] The following questions were answered by the Holy Office: "I. Utrum in causis matrimonialibus acatholicus, sive baptizatus sive non baptizatus, actoris partis agere possit? II. Utrum in quibuslibet causis matrimonialibus inter partem catholicam et partem acatholicam, sive baptizatam sive non baptizatam, quocumque modo ad Sanctam Sedem delatis, Suprema Sacra Congregatio Sancti Officii exclusivam habeat competentiam?" The replies were: "Ad I. Negative, seu standum Codici I. C. praesertim can. 87. Siquidem autem speciales occurrant rationes ad admittendas acatholicos ut actores in huiusmodi causis, recurrendum ad Supremam Sacram Congregationem Sancti Officii in singulis casibus. Ad II. Affirmative, habita ratione can. 247, §3, et salvo praescripto can. 1557, §1, n. 1."—*AAS,* XX (1928), 75.

[211] "Itidem actoris partes agere nequeunt in causis matrimonialibus acatholici sive baptizati sive non baptizati; si quidem speciales occurrant rationes ad eosdem admittendos, recurrendum est in singulis casibus ad

provision in Article 35, §3, serves to exclude definitely any interpretation which might contend that non-Catholics were permitted to act as plaintiffs in matrimonial cases by virtue of Article 12 of the same Instruction which provides: "Cases between a Catholic party and a non-Catholic party whether baptized or not, can be tried in the first and second instance by diocesan tribunals; but if they are referred to the Holy See, they belong exclusively to the Holy Office, which may however, if it chooses to do so in a proper case, remit the case to the Tribunal of the Sacred Roman Rota (cf. can. 247, §3, and the reply of the Holy Office, of 27 Jan. 1928, ad II)."[212] The basis for the exclusion of non-Catholics from acting as plaintiffs in matrimonial causes before ecclesiastical courts is the presence of an obstacle, heresy or infidelity, which impedes the bond of communion with the Church and excludes them from a participation in the rights reserved to those persons who are not so impeded.[213]

If an ecclesiastical judge should admit a non-Catholic as plaintiff without the proper authorization of the Holy Office, it would be the duty of the defender of the bond to place an exception against the procedural capacity of such a plaintiff.[214] This duty of the defender of the bond would correspondingly become the right of

---

S. C. S. Officii (cfr. responsionem S. C. S. O., diei 27 ianuarii 1928).—*AAS,* XXVIII (1936), 321.

212 "Causae inter partem catholicam et partem acatholicam, sive baptizatam sive non baptizatam, in prima et in altera instantia cognosci possunt a tribunalibus dioecesanis; attamen, si ad Sanctam Sedem deletae fuerint, exclusive competunt ad S. C. S. Officii, quae tamen potest, si ita censeat et casus ferat, causam remittere ad Tribunal S. R. Rotae (cfr. can. 247, §3 et resp. S. C. S. Officii, 27 Ian. 1928 ad II)"—*AAS,* XXVIII (1936), 321. (The translation is that of Bouscaren, *The Canon Law Digest,* Vol. II, 475.)

213 "Baptismate homo constituitur in Ecclesia Christi persona cum omnibus christianorum iuribus et officiis, nisi, ad iura quod attinet, obstet obex, ecclesiasticae communionis vinculum impediens, vel lata ab Ecclesia censura."—canon 87.

214 Coyle, *Judicial Exceptions,* The Catholic University of America Canon Law Studies, n. 193 (Washington, D. C.: The Catholic University of America Press, 1944), p. 115.

any legally competent interested party in a matrimonial cause which did not affect the marriage bond.[215]

SECTION 4. A SUMMARY OF POSSIBLE CASES

Articles 6 and 7 of the Instruction "*Provida Mater*" make particular application to marriage cases of the general canonical principles governing the determination of the proper forum by reason of domicile in matrimonial cases in which a separation of the consorts is a circumstance. It is to be remembered that by reason of the contract of marriage the ecclesiastical tribunal of the place where the marriage was celebrated is always initially competent to decide a case arising out of that particular contract. As a means of summarizing this matter on the determination of the proper forum by reason of domicile in matrimonial cases, there is here presented the possible cases in outline form, together with a determination of the proper judicial forum by reason of domicile. The "Articles" referred to are contained in the Instruction "*Provida Mater.*"[216]

I. When there has been a legitimate separation:

Plaintiff	Defendant	Forum by Reason of Domicile or Quasi-Domicile
1. Catholic wife	Catholic husband	By virtue of canon 1964 she may choose either the forum of the husband's domicile or the forum of his quasi-domicile; but she may not choose either the forum of her own distinct domicile or the forum of her own distinct quasi-domicile.
2. Catholic wife	Non-Catholic husband	By virtue of Article 6, §3, she may choose either the forum of her own distinct voluntary domicile or quasi-domicile, or the

[215] For a satisfactory treatment of the question of non-Catholics acting as plaintiffs in matrimonial causes the reader should consult the following: Schaaf, "Diocesan Tribunal Lacks Competence Over Marriages Between Non-Catholics."—*The Ecclesiastical Review* (originally *The American Ecclesiastical Review* [Philadelphia, 1889-1943; Baltimore, 1944—]), XCI (1934), pp. 75-84.

[216] S. C. de Sacramentis, instr. 15 aug. 1936—*AAS,* XXVIII (1936), 316.

		forum of the domicile or quasi-domicile of her non-Catholic husband.
3. Non-Catholic wife	Catholic husband	Such a case is not regulated by the factor of domicile or quasi-domicile but is reserved to the Sacred Congregation of the Holy Office.
4. Catholic husband	Catholic wife	By virtue of canons 93, §2, and 1964 the plaintiff may choose the forum of the defendant's voluntary domicile or voluntary quasi-domicile. He may not choose the forum of his own voluntary domicile or voluntary quasi-domicile since the defendant has ceased to have a necessary legal domicile by reason of the legitimate separation.
5. Catholic husband	Non-Catholic wife	By virtue of canon 1964 the plaintiff may choose either the forum of the defendant's voluntary domicile or the forum of her voluntary quasi-domicile, or the forum of his own voluntary domicile or quasi-domicile. Article 6, §2, does not apply to a non-Catholic wife because the exception detailed in this section applies only to a Catholic wife.
6. Non-Catholic husband	Catholic wife	Such a case is not regulated by the factor of domicile or quasi-domicile but is reserved to the Sacred Congregation of the Holy Office.

II. When there has not been a legitimate separation:

Plaintiff	Defendant	Forum by Reason of Domicile or Quasi-Domicile
7. Catholic wife	Catholic husband	By virtue of Article 6, §1, she may choose either the forum of the husband's domicile or the forum of his quasi-domicile, but she may not choose the forum of her own quasi-domicile.

8. Catholic wife	Non-Catholic husband	By virtue of Article 6, §3, she may choose either the forum of her own proper and distinct quasi-domicile, or the forum of the domicile or quasi-domicile of her non-Catholic husband.
9. Non-Catholic wife	Catholic husband	Not regulated by domicile or quasi-domicile. Such a case is reserved to the Sacred Congregation of the Holy Office.
10. Catholic husband	Catholic wife	By virtue of Article 7 he may choose: (a) the wife's proper quasi-domicile; or, (b) the wife's legal domicile, which is his own domicile; or, (c) his own quasi-domicile, but only when he does not have a domicile.
11. Catholic husband	Non-Catholic wife	By virtue of canon 1964 the plaintiff may choose either the forum of his own voluntary domicile or quasi-domicile, and by virtue of Article 7 he may choose the forum of her voluntary quasi-domicile.
12. Non-Catholic husband	Catholic wife	Not regulated by domicile or quasi-domicile. Such a case is reserved to the Sacred Congregation of the Holy Office.

CONCLUSIONS

1. A legitimate separation is to be distinguished from a legitimate departure. The former is based on a sufficient cause and at the same time on the instituting of the separation by the proper public authority; the latter, i.e., a legitimate departure, is based on a sufficient cause, on the innocence of the one departing, and on the instituting of the departure on private authority.

2. A legitimate departure does not bestow a legal status which enables the wife to establish her own domicile.

3. An unlawful departure on private authority results from the fact that the cause for such a departure was not an adequate one in itself, or that the requisite attending circumstances for the certification of the cause and of danger in delay were not verified.

4. The words "*legitime non separata*" of canon 93, §2, point, with reference to parties joined in a presumptively valid marriage contract, to a state of separation unsanctioned by qualified authority. This state of separation relates to all departures, licit or illicit, of a spouse, and continues so long as the resulting separation lacks the sanction of a qualified authority.

5. The domicile acquired by a wife legitimately separated from her husband is changed to a quasi-domicile when upon being directed by qualified ecclesiastical authority to resume cohabitation with her husband she has refused to do so.

6. When in the case of a separation between two Catholics the husband seeks to cite his wife before an ecclesiastical tribunal, the factor of her quasi-domicile is not allowed to supplant the factor of her domicile when the place of trial is to be chosen.

7. Even though the cause of the legitimate departure be an alleged notorious act of adultery committed by the husband, the departing wife retains the legal domicile or quasi-domicile of her husband. Until such time when she will have acquired the status of being "*legitime separata*" she may be cited by him in the

judicial forum of his own domicile or quasi-domicile, since it constitutes at the same time her necessary domicile or quasi-domicile.

8. As long as the law of a Concordat does not provide for the contrary, a decree of separation when issued by a civil court is not the act of an adequate authority capable of establishing the status of a legitimate separation.

9. Even though the cause of the legitimate expulsion be an alleged notorious act of adultery committed by the wife, the wife so expelled retains the legal domicile or quasi-domicile of her husband. Until such time when she will have acquired the status of being "*legitime separata*" she may be cited by him in the judicial forum of his own domicile or quasi-domicile since it constitutes at the same time her necessary domicile or quasi-domicile.

10. A wife loses her legal domicile or quasi-domicile through the act of a legitimate separation, but she may re-acquire this legal domicile or quasi-domicile through a private reconciliation with her husband, since an ecclesiastically approved decree of separation granted in her behalf when she was the innocent party partakes of the nature of a favor which she may at any time freely renounce.

11. The Church, while most desirous of preserving the unity and indissolubility of the marital union, has not with reference to its unlawful rupture by way of separation on private authority invoked any penalty in its universal law.

BIBLIOGRAPHY

SOURCES

Acta Apostolicae Sedis, Commentarium Officiale, Romae, 1909–

Acta et Decreta Concilii Plenarii Baltimorensis Tertii, A.D. MDCCCLXXXIV, Baltimore: John Murphy & Co., 1886.

Acta et Decreta Sacrorum Conciliorum Recentionum, Collectio Lacensis, 7 vols., Friburgi Brisgoviae: Herder, 1870–1890.

Acta Sanctae Sedis, 41 vols., Romae, 1865–1908.

Bullarum Diplomatum et Privilegiorum Sanctorum Romanorum Pontificum Taurinensis Editio, 24 vols. et Appendix, Augustae Taurinorum, 1857–1872.

Bullarium Pontificium Sacrae Congregationis de Propaganda Fide, 5 vols., 2 appendices, et index, Romae: Typis Collegii Urbani, 1839–1858.

Canones et Decreta Sacrosancti Oecumenici Concilii Tridentini, Editio Novissima ad Fidem Optimorum Exemplarium castigate Impressa (XIX reimpressio stereotypa), Taurini, 1913.

Canones Apostolorum et Conciliorum Saeculorum IV–VII, ed. H. T. Bruns, 2 vols., Berolini, 1839.

Codex Iuris Canonici Pii X Pontificis Maximi iussu digestus, Benedicti Papae XV auctoritate promulgatus, Romae: Typis Polyglottis Vaticanis, 1917.

Codicis Iuris Canonici Fontes, cura Emi Petri Card. Gasparri editi, 9 vols., Romae (postea, Civitate Vaticana): Typis Polyglottis Vaticanis, 1923–1939; Vols. VII–IX ed. cura et studio Emi Iustiniani Card. Serédi.

Corpus Iuris Canonici, editio Lipsiensis secunda, post Aemilii Ludovici Richteri curas instruxit Aemilius Friedberg, 1879–1881. Editio anastatice repetita, Lipsiae: Tauchnitz, 1928.

Corpus Iuris Civilis, 3 vols., Berolini, 1928–1929. *Institutiones,* quas recognovit P. Krueger, ed. stereotypa 15., 1928; *Digesta,* quas recognovit T. Mommsen et retractavit P. Krueger, ed. stereotypa 15., 1928; *Codex Iustinianus,* quem recognovit et retractavit P. Krueger, ed. stereotypa 10., 1929; *Novellae,* quas recognovit R. Schoell, et absolvit G. Kroll, ed. stereotypa 5., 1928.

Decretales D. Gregorii Papae IX, una cum glossis restitutae, 2 vols., Romae, 1582.

Decretum Gratiani emendatum et notationibus illustratum una cum glossis, 2 vols., Romae, 1582.

Jaffé, P., *Regesta Pontificum Romanorum ab condita Ecclesia ad annum post Christum natum 1198,* ed. secundam correctam et auctam auspiciis Guilelmi Wattenbach curaverunt S. Löwenfeld, F. Kaltenbrunner, P. Ewald, 2 vols. in 1, Lipsiae, 1885-1888.

Mansi, J. D., *Sacrorum Conciliorum Nova et Amplissima Collectio,* 53 vols. in 60, Paris—Arnhem—Leipzig, 1901-1927.

Monumenta Germaniae Historica, 188 vols., Hannoverae, 1826—*Legum Sectio II, Capitularia Regum Francorum,* Tom. I, ed. V. Krause, 1897.

S. Romanae Rotae Decisiones seu Sententiae quae . . . prodierunt anno 1909-1932, 24 vols., Romae: Typis Vaticanis, 1912-1940.

Schroeder, H. J., *Canons and Decrees of the Council of Trent,* St. Louis: Herder, 1941.

AUTHORS

Alberti, Josephus, *De Domicilio Ecclesiastico,* Romae, 1909.

Alphonsus Maria de Ligorio, St., *Theologia Moralis,* ed. nova cura et studio P. L. Gaudé, 4 vols., Romae: Typis Polyglottis Vaticanis, 1905-1912.

Augustine, Charles, *A Commentary on the New Code of Canon Law,* 8 vols., Vol. V., 5. ed., St. Louis, Herder, 1935.

Ballerini, A.-Palmieri, P., *Opus Theologicum Morale,* 3. ed., 7 vols., Prati, 1898-1901.

Benedictus XIV, *De Synodo Diocesana,* 2 vols., Romae: Typographia S. C. de Propaganda Fide, 1806.

———, *Institutiones Ecclesiasticae,* 3 vols., Lovanii, 1762.

Bertachinus, D., *Repertorium,* 5 vols., Venetiis, 1570.

Bouscaren, T. Lincoln, and Ellis, Adam C., *Canon Law, A Text and Commentary,* Milwaukee: The Bruce Publishing Co., 1946.

Bouscaren, T. Lincoln, *The Canon Law Digest, Officially Published Documents Affecting the Code of Canon Law,* 2 vols., Milwaukee: The Bruce Publishing Company, 1934-1943.

Buckland, W. W., *Elementary Principles of the Roman Private Law,* Cambridge: University Press, 1912.

Cappello, Felix, *Tractatus Canonico-Moralis De Sacramentis,* 3 vols., Vol. III, *De Matrimonio,* Romae: Marietti, 1923.

Chelodi, J., *Ius De Personis iuxta Codicem Iuris Canonici,* 2. ed., Tridenti, 1927.

———, *Ius Matrimoniale iuxta Codicem Iuris Canonici,* 3. ed., Tridenti: Libr. Edit. Tridentum, 1921.

———, *Ius Poenale et Ordo Procedendi in Iudiciis Criminalibus iuxta Codicem Iuris Canonici,* Tridenti: Libr. Edit. Tridentum, 1925.

Cocchi, Guidus, *Commentarium in Codicem Iuris Canonici,* 8 vols. in 5, Vol. II, *De Personis,* Taurninorum Augustae: Marietti, 1922.

Corbett, Percy Ellwood, *The Roman Law of Marriage,* Oxford: Clarendon Press, 1930.

Coronata, Matthaeus, Conte a, *Institutiones Iuris Canonici,* 5 vols., Taurini, Romae: Marietti, 1936-1945. Vols. I-II, 2. ed., 1938; Vol. III, 2. ed., 1941; Vol. IV, 2. ed., 1945; Vol. V, 1936.

———, *Institutiones Iuris Canonici ad usum utriusque cleri et scholarum De Sacramentis tractatus canonicus,* 3 vols., Taurini, Romae: Marietti, 1943–1946.

Costello, John Michael, *Domicile and Quasi-Domicile,* The Catholic University of America Canon Law Studies, n. 60, Washington, D. C.: The Catholic University of America, 1930.

Coyle, Paul R., *Judicial Exceptions,* The Catholic University of America Canon Law Studies, n. 193, Washington, D. C.: The Catholic University of America Press, 1944.

Cujas, J., *Opera Omnia,* 13 vols. in 12, Venetiis, 1758–1783.

D'Angelo, S., *Del Domicilio Ecclesiastico e dei suoi effetti,* Giare, 1916.

D'Annibale, Josephus, *Summula Theologiae Moralis,* 4. ed., 3 vols., Romae, 1894–1897.

De Meester, A., *Juris Canonici et Juris Canonico-Civilis Compendium,* nova editio, 3 vols. in 4, Burgis: sumptibus et typis Societatis S. Augustini, 1921–1928; Vol. I, 1921.

DeSmet, A., *Tractatus Theologico-Canonicus de Sponsalibus et Matrimonio,* ed. quarta inde a Codice altera, Burgis: Car. Beyaert, 1927.

Doheny, William J., *Canonical Procedure in Matrimonial Cases,* 2 vols., Milwaukee: Bruce Publishing Co., 1938–1944. Vol. I, *Formal Procedure,* 1938; Vol. II, *Informal Procedure,* 1944.

Durantis, Guilielmus, *Speculum Iuris,* 3 vols., Venetiis, 1760.

Fourneret, P., *Le Domicile Matrimonial,* Paris, 1906.

Funk, F. X., *A Manual of Church History,* 3. impression of authorized translation from 5. German edtion by Luigi Cappadelta, 2 vols., London, 1910.

Gasparri, Petrus, *Tractatus Canonicus de Matrimonio,* ed. nova ad mentem Codicis I. C., 2 vols., Typis Polyglottis Vaticanis, 1932.

———, *Tractatus Canonicus de Matrimonio,* 3. ed., 2 vols., Parisiis, 1904.

———, *Tractatus Canonicus de Sanctissima Eucharistia,* 2 vols., Parisiis: Delhomme et Briguet, 1897.

Genicot, Eduardus, et Salsmans, I., *Institutiones Theologiae Moralis,* 14. ed., 2 vols., Buenos Aires: Dedebec Ediciones Desclée, De Brouwer, 1939.

Hefele, Karl et Leclercq, Henri, *Histoire des Conciles,* 9 vols. in 18, Parisiis, 1907–1921.

Hostiensis (Henricus de Segusio), *Commentaria in Quinque Decretalium Libros,* 5 vols. in 3, Venetiis, 1581.

Joyce, G. H., *Christian Marriage, an Historical and Doctrinal Study,* Heythrop Series I, New York: Sheed and Ward, 1933.

Kay, Thomas Henry, *Competence in Matrimonial Procedure,* The Catholic University of America Canon Law Studies, n. 53, Washington, D. C.: The Catholic University of America, 1929.

Leage, R. W., *Roman Private Law,* 2. ed., by C. H. Zeigler, London: Macmillan & Co., 1942.

Mansella, Iosephus, *De Impedimentis Matrimonium Dirimentibus ac de Processu Iudiciali in Causis Matrimonialibus Notiones et Disceptationes Canonicae,* Romae: ex Typographia Polyglotta S. C. de Propaganda Fide, 1881.

Marx, Adolph, *The Declaration of Nullity of Marriages Contracted Outside the Church,* The Catholic University of America Canon Law Studies, n. 182, Washington, D. C.: The Catholic University of America Press, 1943.

McBride, James T., *Incardination and Excardination of Seculars,* The Catholic University of America Canon Law Studies, n. 145, Washington, D. C.: The Catholic University of America Press, 1942.

Merkelbach, Benedictus Henricus, *Summa Theologiae Moralis,* 3. ed., 3 vols., Parisiis: Typis Desclée De Brouwer et Soc., 1939.

Michiels, Gommarus, *Normae Generales Iuris Canonici,* 2 vols., Lublin, Polonia: Universitas Catholica, 1929.

———, *Principia Generalia De Personis in Ecclesia,* Lublin, Universitas Catholica, 1932.

Migne, Jacques Paul, *Patrologiae Cursus Completus, Series Graeca,* 161 Vols., Parisiis, 1856–1866.

———, *Patrologiae Cursus Completus, Series Latina,* 221 vols., Parisiis, 1844–1864.

Muirhead, J., *Historical Introduction to the Private Law of Rome,* 2. ed., London, 1899.

Noldin, H., et Schmitt, A., *Summa Theologiae Moralis,* 3 vols., Oeniponte: Typis et Sumptibus F. Rauch. Vol. I, 27. ed., 1940; Vol. II, 27. ed., 1941; Vol. II, 26. ed., 1940.

Noval, I, *Commentarius Codicis Iuris Canonici Libri IV de Processibus,* Pars I, *De Iudiciis,* Taurini, 1920.

Ojetti, B., *Commentarium in Codicem Iuris Canonici,* 4 vols., Romae: apud Aedes Universitatis Gregorianae, 1927–1931.

———, *Synopsis Rerum Moralium et Iuris Pontificii alphabetico ordine digesta,* 3 vols., et Index, Romae: 1909–1914.

Panormitanus, Abbas (Nicolaus de Tudeschis), *Commentaria super Quinque Libros Decretalium,* 5 vols. in 7, Venetiis, 1588.

Passerini, P. de Sextula (Passerinus), *Commentarium in Librum Sextum Decretalium,* 3 vols., Venetiis, 1698.

Payen, G., *De Matrimonio in Missionibus ac potissimum in Sinis,* 3 vols., Zi-ka-wei: In Typographia T'ou-se'-we', 1928–1929.

Petrovits, Joseph, *The New Church Law on Matrimony,* 2. ed., Philadelphia: McVey, 1926.

Pirhing, Enricus, *Ius Canonicum in Quinque Libros Decretalium Distributum Nova Methodo Explicatum,* ed. novissima, 5 vols. in 4, Dilingae, 1674–1678.

Poste, Edward, *Gaii Institutiones,* 4. ed., Oxford: Clarendon Press, 1904.

Reiffenstuel, A., *Ius Canonicum Universum,* 5 vols. in 7, Parisiis, 1864–1870.

Regatillo, Eduardus F., *Institutiones Iuris Canonici,* 2 vols., Santander: Sal Terrae, 1941–1942.

———, *Ius Sacramentarium,* 2 vols., Santander: Sal Terrae, 1945–1946.

Rice, Patrick William, *Proof of Death in Pre-Nuptial Investigation,* The Catholic University of America Canon Law Studies, n. 123, Washington, D. C.: The Catholic University of America Press, 1940.

Roberti, F., *De Processibus,* 2 vols., Romae: Apud Aedes Facultatis Iuridicae ad S. Apollinaris, 1926.

Sanchez, Thomas, *Disputationum de Sancto Matrimonii Sacramento Tomi Tres,* Antverpiae, 1626.

Schmalzgrueber, F., *Ius Ecclesiasticum Universum,* 5 vols. in 12, Romae, 1843–1845.

Sherman, Charles P., *Roman Law in the Modern World,* 2. ed., 3 vols., New York: Baker, Voorhis & Company, 1924.

Tanquerey, Adolphe A. (cooperantibus C. Belmon, A. Cance, F. Cimetier, et aliis), *Synopsis Theologiae Moralis et Pastoralis,* 3. ed. post Codicem recognovit, 3 vols., Parisiis: Typis Societatis Sancti Joannis Evangelistae, Desclée et Socii, 1936–1937.

Thomassinus Ludovicus, *Vetus et Nova Ecclesiae Disciplina circa Beneficia et Beneficarios,* Magontiaci, 1787.

Torre, Ioannes, *Instructio servanda a tribunalibus dioecesanis in pertractandis causis de nullitate matrimoniorum a Sacra Congregatione de Disciplina Sacramentorum edita Epitome cum explicita ad litteram mentione singulorum Codicis Iuris Canonici canonum nec non accuratissimo indice, analytico-alphabetico ac tabulis synopticis et brevi commentario de nonnullis articulis,* Neapoli, M. D'Auria, 1937.

Van Hove, A., *Commentarium Lovaniense in Codicem Iuris Canonici,* Vol. I, Tom. II, *De Legibus Ecclesiasticis,* Mechliniae: H. Dessain, 1930.

Vaughan, William E., *Constitutions for Diocesan Courts,* The Catholic University of America Canon Law Studies, n. 210, Washington, D. C.: The Catholic University of America Press, 1944.

Vermeersch, A.-Creusen, I., *Epitome Iuris Canonici,* 3 vols., Mechliniae-Romae: H. Dessain. Vol. I, 6. ed., 1937; Vol. II, 5. ed., 1934; Vol. III, 5. ed., 1936.

Vlaming, Th. N., *Praelectiones Iuris Canonici ad Normam Codicis Iuris Canonici,* 3. ed., 2 vols., Bussum in Hollandia: Sumptibus Societatis Editricis Anonymae olim Paulus Brand, 1919–1921.

Voet, I., *Commentariorum ad Pandectas Libri Quinquaginta,* 5. ed., 7 vols. in 4, Bassani: Typis Remondini, 1827.

Waldron, Joseph Francis, *The Minister of Baptism,* The Catholic University of America Canon Law Studies, n. 170, Washington, D. C.: The Catholic University of America Press, 1942.

Wernz, F. X., *Ius Decretalium,* 3. ed., 6 vols. in 10, Prati, 1913–1915.

Wernz, F. X.-Vidal, P., *Ius Canonicum, ad Codicis Normam Exactam,* 7 vols. in 8, Romae: apud Aedes Universitatis Gregorianae, 1923–

1938. Vol. II, *De Personis,* 3. ed. curavit P. Aguirre, 1943; Vol. V, *Ius Matrimoniale,* 2. ed., 1928; 3. ed. curavit P. Aguirre, 1946.

Woywod, S., *A Practical Commentary on the Code of Canon Law,* 7. ed., revised by Callistus Smith, 2 vols., New York, Joseph F. Wagner, Inc., 1943.

ARTICLES

Cattani-Amadori, F., "Supr. Tribunal Signaturae Ap., De Competentia ex Domicilio Legali in Causis Matrimonialibus"—*Jus Pontificium,* XIII (1933), 106–108.

Ciprotti, P., "Quaestiones de Competentia Ratione Contractus et Domicilii in Causis Matrimonialibus"—*Apollinaris,* XI (1938), 458–465.

Kelly, J. P., "Separation and Civil Divorce"—*The Jurist,* VI (1946), 187–238.

Rauscher, Card. Josephus, "Instructio Austrica"—*Analecta Iuris Pontificii,* II (1857), 2546–2565.

Roberti, F., "De Competentia Ratione Domicilii"—*Apollinaris,* III (1930), 458–459.

Schaaf, V. T., "Diocesan Tribunal Lacks Competence Over Marriages Between Non-Catholics"—*The Ecclesiastical Review,* XCI (1934), 75–84.

(Vindex), "Domicilium Et Quasi-Domicilium eorumque effectus in Codice Iuris Canonicis"—*Jus Pontificium,* VI (1926), 34–55, 112–126, 154–158.

PERIODICALS

Analecta Iuris Pontificii, Romae, 1855–1868; Parisiis, 1869–1890.

Apollinaris, Romae, 1928–

Ecclesiastical Review, The [originally *The American Ecclesiastical Review*], Philadelphia, 1889–1943; Baltimore, 1944–

Jurist, The, Washington, D. C., 1941–

Jus Pontificium, Romae, 1921–

ABBREVIATIONS

AAS—*Acta Apostolicae Sedis.*
ASS—*Acta Sanctae Sedis.*
C.—Codex (Iustinianus) vel *Causa.*
c.—canon seu caput (iuris antiqui).
cc.—canones seu capita (iuris antiqui).
can.—canon (novi Codicis).
cans.—canones (novi Codicis).
Conc. Trident.—Concilium Tridentinum.
D.—Digestum (Iustinianum).
Fontes—*Codicis Iuris Canonici Fontes.*
Instr.—Instructio.
J.P.—*Jus Pontificium.*
Mansi—Mansi, J. D., *Sacrorum Conciliorum Nova et Amplissima Collectio.*
MPG—(Migne, *Patrologia Graeca*) Migne, Jacques Paul, *Patrologiae Cursus Completus*—Series Graeca.
MPL—(Migne, *Patrologia Latina*) Migne, Jacques Paul, *Patrologiae Cursus Completus*—Series Latina.
Nov.—Novellae Constitutiones.
P.C.I.—Pontificia Commissio ad Codicis Canones Authentice Interpretandos.
S.C.C.—Sacra Congregatio Concilii.
S.C. de Prop. Fide—Sacra Congregatio de Propaganda Fide.
S.C.S.Off.—Sacra Congregatio Sancti Officii.
S.R.R.—Sacra Romana Rota.
s.v.—Sub verbo; sub verbis.

INDEX

BIOGRAPHICAL NOTE

Marion Leo Gibbons was born on August 15, 1908, in Jerseyville, Illinois. Having completed his grammar and high school education in that city, he entered the Saint Louis University, Saint Louis, Missouri, in 1926. He received his LL.B. degree from that university in 1931, and in the same year was duly admitted by license to the practice of law in the States of Missouri and Illinois. While teaching at De Paul Academy, Chicago, Illinois, he pursued graduate studies at De Paul University in the same city during the years 1935–1936. He entered the Novitiate of the Congregation of the Mission, Saint Mary's Seminary, Perryville, Missouri, on May 27, 1936. He pronounced his vows in this Congregation on May 31, 1938, and after completing his philosophical and theological training received his B. A. degree. He was ordained to the Holy Priesthood on June 3, 1943, and was assigned to the faculty of Saint John's Seminary, San Antonio, Texas. He was sent to the Catholic University of America in September, 1944. There he entered the Graduate School of Canon Law, from which he received the degree of the Baccaulaureate in Canon Law in June, 1945, and the degree of the Licentiate in Canon Law in June, 1946.

Canon Law Studies *

1. Freriks, Rev. Celestine A., C.PP.S., J.C.D., Religious Congregations in Their External Relations, 121 pp., 1916.
2. Galliher, Rev. Daniel M., O.P., J.C.D., Canonical Elections, 117 pp., 1917.
3. Borkowski, Rev. Aurelius L., O.F.M., J.C.D., De Confraternitatibus Ecclesiasticis, 136 pp., 1918.
4. Castillo, Rev. Cayo, J.C.D., Disertacion Historico-Canonica sobre la Potestad del Cabildo en Sede Vacante o Impedida del Vicario Capitular, 99 pp., 1919 (1918).
5. Kubelbeck, Rev. William J., S.T.B., J.C.D., The Sacred Penitentiaria and Its Relation to Faculties of Ordinaries and Priests, 129 pp., 1918.
6. Petrovits, Rev. Joseph J. C., S.T.D., J.C.D., The New Church Law on Matrimony, X-461 pp., 1919.
7. Hickey, Rev. John J., S.T.B., J.C.D., Irregularities and Simple Impediments in the New Code of Canon Law, 100 pp., 1920.
8. Klekotka, Rev. Peter J., S.T.B., J.C.D., Diocesan Consultors, 179 pp., 1920.
9. Wanenmacher, Rev. Francis, J.C.D., The Evidence in Ecclesiastical Procedure Affecting the Marriage Bond, 1920 (Printed 1935).
10. Golden, Rev. Henry Francis, J.C.D., Parochial Benefices in the New Code, IV-119 pp., 1921 (Printed 1925).
11. Koudelka, Rev. Charles J., J.C.D., Pastors, Their Rights and Duties According to the New Code of Canon Law, 211 pp., 1921.
12. Melo, Rev. Antonius, O.F.M., J.C.D., De Exemptione Regularium, X-188 pp., 1921.
13. Schaaf, Rev. Valentine Theodore, O.F.M., S.T.B., J.C.D., The Cloister, X-180 pp., 1921.
14. Burke, Rev. Thomas Joseph, S.T.D., J.C.D., Competence in Ecclesiastical Tribunals, IV-117 pp., 1922.
15. Leech, Rev. George Leo, J.C.D., A Comparative Study of the Constitution "Apostolicae Sedis" and the "Codex Juris Canonici," 179 pp., 1922.
16. Motry, Rev. Hubert Louis, S.T.D., J.C.D., Diocesan Faculties According to the Code of Canon Law, II-167 pp., 1922.
17. Murphy, Rev. George Lawrence, J.C.D., Delinquencies and Penalties in the Administration and the Reception of the Sacraments, IV-121 pp., 1923.

* From nn. 1–100 inclusive only n. 25 is still obtainable. From n. 101 onward all numbers are available except the following: 101–114, 116, 118, 120, 122, 123 and 162.

18. O'Reilly, Rev. John Anthony, S.T.B., J.C.D., Ecclesiastical Sepulture in the New Code of Canon Law, II-129 pp., 1923.
19. Michalicka, Rev. Wenceslas Cyrill, O.S.B., J.C.D., Judicial Procedure in Dismissal of Clerical Exempt Religious, 107 pp., 1923.
20. Dargin, Rev. Edward Vincent, S.T.B., J.C.D., Reserved Cases According to the Code of Canon Law, IV-103 pp., 1924.
21. Godfrey, Rev. John A., S.T.B., J.C.D., The Right of Patronage According to the Code of Canon Law, 153 pp., 1924.
22. Hagedorn, Rev. Francis Edward, J.C.D., General Legislation on Indulgences, II-154 pp., 1924.
23. King, Rev. James Ignatius, J.C.D., The Administration of the Sacraments to Dying Non-Catholics, V-141 pp., 1924.
24. Winslow, Rev. Francis Joseph, M.M., J.C.D., Vicars and Prefects Apostolic, IV-149 pp., 1924.
25. Correa, Rev. Jose Servelion, S.T.L., J.C.D., La Potestad Legislativa de la Iglesia Catolica, IV-127 pp., 1925.
26. Dugan, Rev. Henry Francis, A.M., J.C.D., The Judiciary Department of the Diocesan Curia, 87 pp., 1925.
27. Keller, Rev. Charles Frederick, S.T.B., J.C.D., Mass Stipends, 167 pp., 1925.
28. Paschang, Rev. John Linus, J.C.D., The Sacramentals According to the Code of Canon Law, 129 pp., 1925.
29. Piontek, Rev. Cyrillus, O.F.M., S.T.B., J.C.D., De Indulto Exclaustrationis necnon Saecularizationis, XIII-289 pp., 1925.
30. Kearney, Rev. Richard Joseph, S.T.B., J.C.D., Sponsors at Baptism According to the Code of Canon Law, IV-127 pp., 1925.
31. Bartlett, Rev. Chester Joseph, A.M., LL.B., J.C.D., The Tenure of Parochial Property in the United States of America, V-108 pp., 1926.
32. Kilker, Rev. Adrian Jerome, J.C.D., Extreme Unction, V-425 pp., 1926.
33. McCormick, Rev. Robert Emmett, J.C.D., Confessors of Religious, VIII-266 pp., 1926.
34. Miller, Rev. Newton Thomas, J.C.D., Founded Masses According to the Code of Canon Law, VII-93 pp., 1926.
35. Roelker, Rev. Edward G., S.T.D., J.C.D., Principles of Privilege According to the Code of Canon Law, XI-166 pp., 1926.
36. Bakalarczyk, Rev. Richardus, M.I.C., J.U.D., De Novitiatu, VIII-208 pp., 1927.
37. Pizzuti, Rev. Lawrence, O.F.M., J.U.L., De Parochis Religiosis, 1927. (Not Printed.)
38. Bliley, Rev. Nicholas Martin, O.S.B., J.C.D., Altars According to the Code of Canon Law, XIX-132 pp., 1927.
39. Brown, Mr. Brendan Francis, A.B., LL.M., J.U.D., The Canonical Juristic Personality with Special Reference to its Status in the United States of America, V-212 pp., 1927.

40. Cavanaugh, Rev. William Thomas, C.P., J.U.D., The Reservation of the Blessed Sacrament, VIII-101 pp., 1927.
41. Doheny, Rev. William J., C.S.C., A.B., J.U.D., Church Property: Modes of Acquisition, X-118 pp., 1927.
42. Feldhaus, Rev. Aloysius H., C.PP.S., J.C.D., Oratories, IX-141 pp., 1927.
43. Kelly, Rev. James Patrick, A.B., J.C.D., The Jurisdiction of the Simple Confessor, X-208 pp., 1927.
44. Neuberger, Rev. Nicholas J., J.C.D., Canon 6 or the Relation of the Codex Juris Canonici to the Preceding Legislation, V-95 pp., 1927.
45. O'Keefe, Rev. Gerald Michael, J.C.D., Matrimonial Dispensations, Powers of Bishops, Priests, and Confessors, VIII-232 pp., 1927.
46. Quigley, Rev. Joseph A. M., A.B., J.C.D., Condemned Societies, 139 pp., 1927.
47. Zaplotnik, Rev. Johannes Leo, J.C.D., De Vicariis Foraneis, X-142 pp., 1927.
48. Duskie, Rev. John Aloysius, A.B., J.C.D., The Canonical Status of the Orientals in the United States, VIII-196 pp., 1928.
49. Hyland, Rev. Francis Edward, J.C.D., Excommunication, Its Nature, Historical Development and Effects, VIII-181 pp., 1928.
50. Reinmann, Rev. Gerald Joseph, O.M.C., J.C.D., The Third Order Secular of Saint Francis, 201 pp., 1928.
51. Schenk, Rev. Francis J., J.C.D., The Matrimonial Impediments of Mixed Religion and Disparity of Cult, XVI-318 pp., 1929.
52. Coady, Rev. John Joseph, S.T.D., J.U.D., A.M., The Appointment of Pastors, VIII-150 pp., 1929.
53. Kay, Rev. Thomas Henry, J.C.D., Competence in Matrimonial Procedure, VIII-164 pp., 1929.
54. Turner, Rev. Sidney Joseph, C.P., J.U.D., The Vow of Poverty, XLIX-217 pp., 1929.
55. Kearney, Rev. Raymond A., A.B., S.T.D., J.C.D., The Principles of Delegation, VII-149 pp., 1929.
56. Conran, Rev. Edward James, A.B., J.C.D., The Interdict, V-163 pp., 1930.
57. O'Neill, Rev. William H., J.C.D., Papal Rescripts of Favor, VII-218 pp., 1930.
58. Bastnagel, Rev. Clement Vincent, J.U.D., The Appointment of Parochial Adjutants and Assistants, XV-257 pp., 1930.
59. Ferry, Rev. William A., A.B., J.C.D., Stole Fees, V-136 pp., 1930.
60. Costello, Rev. John Michael, A.B., J.C.D., Domicile and Quasi-Domicile, VII-201 pp., 1930.
61. Kremer, Rev. Michael Nicholas, A.B., S.T.B., J.C.D., Church Support in the United States, VI-136 pp., 1930.
62. Angulo, Rev. Luis, C.M., J.C.D., Legislation de la Iglesia sobre la intencion en la application de la Santa Misa, VII-104 pp., 1931.

63. Frey, Rev. Wolfgang Norbert, O.S.B., A.B., J.C.D., The Act of Religious Profession, VIII-174 pp., 1931.
64. Roberts, Rev. James Brendan, A.B., J.C.D., The Banns of Marriage, XIV-140 pp., 1931.
65. Ryder, Rev. Raymond Aloysius, A.B., J.C.D., Simony, IX-151 pp., 1931.
66. Campagna, Rev. Angelo, Ph.D., J.U.D., Il Vicario Generale del Vescovo, VII-205 pp., 1931.
67. Cox, Rev. Joseph Godfrey, A.B., J.C.D., The Administration of Seminaries, VI-124 pp., 1931.
68. Gregory, Rev. Donald J., J.U.D., The Pauline Privilege, XV-165 pp., 1931.
69. Donohue, Rev. John F., J.C.D., The Impediment of Crime, VII-110 pp., 1931.
70. Dooley, Rev. Eugene A., O.M.I., J.C.D., Church Law on Sacred Relics, IX-143 pp., 1931.
71. Orth, Rev. Clement Raymond, O.M.C., J.C.D., The Approbation of Religious Institutes, 171 pp., 1931.
72. Pernicone, Rev. Joseph M., A.B., J.C.D., The Ecclesiastical Prohibition of Books, XII-267 pp., 1932.
73. Clinton, Rev. Connell, A.B., J.C.D., The Paschal Precept, IX-108 pp., 1932.
74. Donnelly, Rev. Francis B., A.M., S.T.L., J.C.D., The Diocesan Synod, VIII-125 pp., 1932.
75. Torrente, Rev. Camilo, C.M.F., J.C.D., Las Procesiones Sagradas, V-145 pp., 1932.
76. Murphy, Rev. Edwin J., C.PP.S., J.C.D., Suspension Ex Informata Conscientia, XI-122 pp., 1932.
77. MacKenzie, Rev. Eric F., A.M., S.T.L., J.C.D., The Delict of Heresy in its Commission, Penalization, Absolution, VII-124 pp., 1932.
78. Lyons, Rev. Avitus E., S.T.B., J.C.D., The Collegiate Tribunal of First Instance, XI-147 pp., 1932.
79. Connolly, Rev. Thomas A., J.C.D., Appeals, XI-195 pp., 1932.
80. Sangmeister, Rev. Joseph V., A.B., J.C.D., Force and Fear as Precluding Matrimonial Consent, V-211 pp., 1932.
81. Jaeger, Rev. Leo A., A.B., J.C.D., The Administration of Vacant and Quasi-Vacant Episcopal Sees in the United States, IX-229 pp., 1932.
82. Rimlinger, Rev. Herbert T., J.C.D., Error Invalidating Matrimonial Consent, VII-79 pp., 1932.
83. Barrett, Rev. John D. M., S.S., J.C.D., A Comparative Study of the Third Plenary Council of Baltimore and the Code, IX-221 pp., 1932.
84. Carberry, Rev. John J., Ph.D., S.T.D., J.C.D., The Juridical Form of Marriage, X-177 pp., 1934.
85. Dolan, Rev. John L., A.B., J.C.D., The Defensor Vinculi, XII-157 pp., 1934.

86. Hannan, Rev. Jerome D., A.M., S.T.D., LL.B., J.C.D., The Canon Law of Wills, IX-517 pp., 1934.
87. Lemieux, Rev. Delise A., A.M., J.C.D., The Sentence in Ecclesiastical Procedure, IX-131 pp., 1934.
88. O'Rourke, Rev. James J., A.B., J.C.D., Parish Registers, VII-109 pp., 1934.
89. Timlin, Rev. Bartholomew, O.F.M., A.M., J.C.D., Conditional Matrimonial Consent, X-381 pp., 1934.
90. Wahl, Rev. Francis X., A.B., J.C.D., The Matrimonial Impediments of Consanguinity and Affinity, VI-125 pp., 1934.
91. White, Rev. Robert J., A.B., LL.B., S.T.B., J.C.D., Canonical Ante-Nuptial Promises and the Civil Law, VI-152 pp., 1934.
92. Herrera, Rev. Antonio Parra, O.C.D., J.C.D., Legislacion Ecclesiastica sobra el Ayuno y la Abstinencia, XI-191 pp., 1935.
93. Kennedy, Rev. Edwin J., J.C.D., The Special Matrimonial Process in Cases of Evident Nullity, X-165 pp., 1935.
94. Manning, Rev. John J., A.B., J.C.D., Presumption of Law in Matrimonial Procedure, XI-111 pp., 1935.
95. Moeder, Rev. John M., J.C.D., The Proper Bishop for Ordination and Dimissorial Letters, VII-135 pp., 1935.
96. O'Mara, Rev. William A., A.B., J.C.D., Canonical Causes for Matrimonial Dispensations, IX-155 pp., 1935.
97. Reilly, Rev. Peter, J.C.D., Residence of Pastors, IX-81 pp., 1935.
98. Smith, Rev. Mariner T., O.P., S.T.Lr., J.C.D., The Penal Law for Religious, VII-169 pp., 1935.
99. Whalen, Rev. Donald W., A.M., J.C.D., The Value of Testimonial Evidence in Matrimonial Procedure, XIII-297 pp., 1935.
100. Cleary, Rev. Joseph F., J.C.D., Canonical Limitations on the Alienation of Church Property, VIII-141 pp., 1936.
101. Glynn, Rev. John C., J.C.D., The Promoter of Justice, XX-337 pp., 1936.
102. Brennan, Rev. James H., S.S., M.A., S.T.B., J.C.D., The Simple Convalidation of Marriage, VI-135 pp., 1937.
103. Brunini, Rev. Joseph Bernard, J.C.D., The Clerical Obligations of Canons 139 and 142, X-121 pp., 1937.
104. Connor, Rev. Maurice, A.B., J.C.D., The Administrative Removal of Pastors, VIII-159 pp., 1937.
105. Guilfoyle, Rev. Merlin Joseph, J.C.D., Custom, XI-144 pp., 1937.
106. Hughes, Rev. James Austin, A.B., A.M., J.C.D., Witnesses in Criminal Trials of Clerics, IX-140 pp., 1937.
107. Jansen, Rev. Raymond J., A.B., S.T.L., J.C.D., Canonical Provisions for Catechetical Instruction, VII-153 pp., 1937.
108. Kealy, Rev. John James, A.B., J.C.D., The Introductory Libellus in Church Court Procedure, XI-121 pp., 1937.

109. McManus, Rev. James Edward, C.SS.R., J.C.D., The Administration of Temporal Goods in Religious Institutes, XVI-196 pp., 1937.

110. Moriarty, Rev. Eugene James, J.C.D., Oaths in Ecclesiastical Courts, X-115 pp., 1937.

111. Rainer, Rev. Eligius George, C.SS.R., J.C.D., Suspension of Clerics, XVII-249 pp., 1937.

112. Reilly, Rev. Thomas F., C.SS.R., J.C.D., Visitation of Religious, VI-195 pp., 1938.

113. Moriarity, Rev. Francis E., C.SS.R., J.C.D., The Extraordinary Absolution from Censures, XV-334 pp., 1938.

114. Connolly, Rev. Nicholas P., J.C.D., The Canonical Erection of Parishes, X-132 pp., 1938.

115. Donovan, Rev. James Joseph, J.C.D., The Pastor's Obligation in Prenuptial Investigation, XII-322 pp., 1938.

116. Harrigan, Rev. Robert J., M.A., S.T.B., J.C.D., The Radical Sanation of Invalid Marriages, VIII-208 pp., 1938.

117. Boffa, Rev. Conrad Humbert, J.C.D., Canonical Provisions for Catholic Schools, VII-211 pp., 1939.

118. Parsons, Rev. Anscar John, O.M.Cap., J.C.D., Canonical Elections, XII-236 pp., 1939.

119. Reilly, Rev. Edward Michael, A.B., J.C.D., The General Norms of Dispensation, XII-156 pp., 1939.

120. Ryan, Rev. Gerald Aloysius, A.B., J.C.D., Principles of Episcopal Jurisdiction, XII-172 pp., 1939.

121. Burton, Rev. Francis James, C.S.C., A.B., J.C.D., A Commentary on Canon 1125, X-222 pp., 1940.

122. Miaskiewicz, Rev. Francis Sigismund, J.C.D., Supplied Jurisdiction According to Canon 209, XII-340 pp., 1940.

123. Rice, Rev. Patrick William, A.B., J.C.D., Proof of Death in Prenuptial Investigation, VIII-156 pp., 1940.

124. Anglin, Rev. Thomas Francis, M.S., J.C.D., The Eucharistic Fast, VIII-183 pp., 1941.

125. Coleman, Rev. John Jerome, J.C.D., The Minister of Confirmation, VI-153 pp., 1941.

126. Downs, Rev. Joseph Emmanuel, A.B., J.C.D., The Concept of Clerical Immunity, XI-163 pp., 1941.

127. Esswein, Rev. Anthony Albert, J.C.D., Extrajudicial Penal Powers of Ecclesiastical Superiors, X-144 pp., 1941.

128. Farrell, Rev. Benjamin Francis, M.A., S.T.L., J.C.D., The Rights and Duties of the Local Ordinary Regarding Congregations of Women Religious of Pontifical Approval, V-195 pp., 1941.

129. Feeney, Rev. Thomas John, A.B., S.T.L., J.C.D., Restitutio in Integrum, VI-169 pp., 1941.

130. Findlay, Rev. Stephen William, O.S.B., A.B., J.C.D., Canonical

Norms Governing the Deposition and Degradation of Clerics, XVII-279 pp., 1941.

131. GOODWINE, REV. JOHN, A.B., S.T.L., J.C.D., The Right of the Church to Acquire Property, VIII-119 pp., 1941.

132. HESTON, REV. EDWARD LOUIS, C.S.C., Ph.D., S.T.D., J.C.D., The Alienation of Church Property in the United States, XII-222 pp., 1941.

133. HOGAN, REV. JAMES JOHN, A.B., S.T.L., J.C.D., Judicial Advocates and Procurators, XIII-200 pp., 1941.

134. KEALY, REV. THOMAS M., A.B., Litt.B., J.C.D., Dowry of Women Religious, IX-152 pp., 1941.

135. KEENE, REV. MICHAEL JAMES, O.S.B., J.C.D., Religious Ordinaries and Canon 198, V-164 pp., 1942.

136. KERIN, REV. CHARLES A., S.S., M.A., S.T.B., J.C.D., The Privation of Christian Burial, XVI-279 pp., 1941.

137. LOUIS, REV. WILLIAM FRANCIS, M.A., J.C.D., Diocesan Archives, X-101 pp., 1941.

138. MCDEVITT, REV. GILBERT JOSEPH, A.B., J.C.D., Legitimacy and Legitimation, X-247 pp., 1941.

139. MCDONOUGH, REV. THOMAS JOSEPH, A.B., J.C.D., Apostolic Administrators, X-217 pp., 1941.

140. **MEIER, REV. CARL ANTHONY, A.B., J.C.D., Penal Administrative Pro**cedure Against Negligent Pastors, XI-240 pp., 1941.

141. SCHMIDT, REV. JOHN ROGG, A.B., J.C.D., The Principles of Authentic Interpretation in Canon 17 of the Code of Canon Law, XII-331 pp., 1941.

142. SLAFKOSKY, REV. ANDREW LEONARD, A.B., J.C.D., The Canonical Episcopal Visitation of the Diocese, X-197 pp., 1941.

143. SWOBODA, REV. INNOCENT ROBERT, O.F.M., J.C.D., Ignorance in Relation to the Imputability of Delicts, IX-271 pp., 1941.

144. DUBÉ, REV. ARTHUR JOSEPH, A.B., J.C.D., The General Principles for the Reckoning of Time in Canon Law, VIII-299 pp., 1941.

145. MCBRIDE, REV. JAMES T., A.B., J.C.D., Incardination and Excardination of Seculars, XX-585 pp., 1941.

146. KRÓL, REV. JOHN T., J.C.D., The Defendant in Contentious Trials, XII-207 pp., 1942.

147. COMYNS, REV. JOSEPH J., C.SS.R., A.B., J.C.D., Papal and Episcopal Administration of Church Property, XIV-155 pp., 1942.

148. BARRY, REV. GARRETT FRANCIS, O.M.I., J.C.D., Violation of the Cloister, XII-260 pp., 1942.

149. BOLDUC, REV. GATIEN, C.S.V., A.B., S.T.L., J.C.D., Les Études dans les Religions Cléricales, VIII-155 pp., 1942.

150. BOYLE, REV. DAVID JOHN, M.A., J.C.D., The Juridic Effects of Moral Certitude on Pre-Nuptial Guarantees, XII-188 pp., 1942.

151. **CANAVAN, REV. WALTER JOSEPH, M.A., Litt.D., J.C.D., The Profes**sion of Faith, XII-143 pp., 1942.

152. Desrochers, Rev. Bruno, A.B., Ph.L., S.T.B., J.C.D., Le Premier Concile Plénier de Québec et le Code de Droit Canonique, XIV-186 pp., 1942.
153. Dillon, Rev. Robert Edward, A.B., J.C.D., Common Law Marriage, X-148 pp., 1942.
154. Dodwell, Rev. Edward John, Ph.D., S.T.B., J.C.D., The Time and Place for the Celebration of Marriage, X-156 pp., 1942.
155. Donnellan, Rev. Thomas Andrew, A.B., J.C.D., The Obligation of the Missa pro Populo, VII-131 pp., 1942.
156. Eltz, Rev. Louis Anthony, A.B., J.C.D., Cooperation in Crime, XII-208 pp., 1942.
157. Gass, Rev. Sylvester Francis, M.A., J.C.D., Ecclesiastical Pensions, XI-206 pp., 1942.
158. Guiniven, Rev. John Joseph, C.SS.R., J.C.D., The Precept of Hearing Mass, XIV-188 pp., 1942.
159. Gulcynski, Rev. John Theophilus, J.C.D., The Desecration and Violation of Churches, X-126 pp., 1942.
160. Hammill, Rev. John Leo, M.A., J.C.D., The Obligations of the Traveler According to Canon 14, VIII-204 pp., 1942.
161. Haydt, Rev. John Joseph, A.B., J.C.D., Reserved Benefices, XI-148 pp., 1942.
162. Huser, Rev. Roger John, O.F.M., A.B., J.C.D., The Crime of Abortion in Canon Law, XII-187 pp., 1942.
163. Kearney, Rev. Francis Patrick, A.B., S.T.L., J.C.D., The Principles of Canon 1127, X-162 pp., 1942.
164. Linahen, Rev. Leo James, S.T.L., J.C.D., De Absolutione Complicis In Peccato Turpi, 114 pp., 1942.
165. McCloskey, Rev. Joseph Aloysius, A.B., J.C.D., The Subject of Ecclesiastical Law According to Canon 12, XVII-246 pp., 1942.
166. O'Neill, Rev. Francis Joseph, C.SS.R., J.C.D., The Dismissal of Religious in Temporary Vows, XIII-220 pp., 1942.
167. Prince, Rev. John Edward, A.B., S.T.B., J.C.D., The Diocesan Chancellor, X-136 pp., 1942.
168. Riesner, Rev. Albert Joseph, C.SS.R., J.C.D., Apostates and Fugitives from Religious Institutes, IX-168 pp., 1942.
169. Stenger, Rev. Joseph Bernard, J.C.D., The Mortgaging of Church Property, 186 pp., 1942.
170. Waldron, Rev. Joseph Francis, A.B., J.C.D., The Minister of Baptism, XII-197 pp., 1942.
171. Willett, Rev. Robert Albert, J.C.D., The Probative Value of Documents in Ecclesiastical Trials, X-124 pp., 1942.
172. Woeber, Rev. Edward Martin, M.A., J.C.D., The Interpellations, XII-161 pp., 1942.
173. Benko, Rev. Matthew Aloysius, O.S.B., M.A., J.C.D., The Abbot *Nullius*, XIV-148 pp., 1943.

174. CHRIST, REV. JOSEPH JAMES, M.A., S.T.L., J.C.D., Dispensation from Vindicative Penalties, XIV-285 pp., 1943.
175. CLANCY, REV. PATRICK M. J., O.P., A.B., S.T.Lr., J.C.D., The Local Religious Superior, X-229 pp., 1943.
176. CLARKE, REV. THOMAS JAMES, J.C.D., Parish Societies, XII-147 pp., 1943.
177. CONNOLLY, REV. JOHN PATRICK, S.T.L., J.C.D., Synodal Examiners and Parish Priest Consultors, X-223 pp., 1943.
178. DRUMM, REV. WILLIAM MARTIN, A.B., J.C.D., Hospital Chaplains, XII-175 pp., 1943.
179. FLANAGAN, REV. BERNARD JOSEPH, A.B., S.T.L., J.C.D., The Canonical Erection of Religious Houses, X-147 pp., 1943.
180. KELLEHER, REV. STEPHEN JOSEPH, A.B., S.T.B., J.C.D., Discussions with Non-Catholics: Canonical Legislation, X-93 pp., 1943.
181. LEWIS, REV. GORDIAN, C.P., J.C.D., Chapters in Religious Institutes, XII-169 pp., 1943.
182. MARX, REV. ADOLPH, J.C.D., The Declaration of Nullity of Marriages Contracted Outside the Church, X-151 pp., 1943.
183. MATULENAS, REV. RAYMOND ANTHONY, O.S.B., A.B., J.C.D., Communication, a Source of Privileges, XII-225 pp., 1943.
184. O'LEARY, REV. CHARLES GERARD, C.SS.R., J.C.D., Religious Dismissed After Perpetual Profession, X-213 pp., 1943.
185. POWER, REV. CORNELIUS MICHAEL, J.C.D., The Blessing of Cemeteries, XII-231 pp., 1943.
186. SHUHLER, REV. RALPH VINCENT, O.S.A., J.C.D., Privileges of Regulars to Absolve and Dispense, XII-195 pp., 1943.
187. ZIOLKOWSKI, REV. THADDEUS STANISLAUS, A.B., J.C.D., The Consecration and Blessing of Churches, XII-151 pp., 1943.
188. HENEGHAN, REV. JOHN JOSEPH, S.T.D., J.C.D., The Marriages of Unworthy Catholics: Canons 1065 and 1066, XVI-213 pp., 1944.
189. CARROLL, REV. COLEMAN FRANCIS, M.A., S.T.L., J.C.L., Charitable Institutions.
190. CIESLUK, REV. JOSEPH EDWARD, Ph.B., S.T.L., J.C.L., National Parishes in the United States.
191. COBURN, REV. VINCENT PAUL, A.B., J.C.D., Marriages of Conscience, XII-172 pp., 1944.
192. CONNORS, REV. CHARLES PAUL, C.S.Sp., A.B., J.C.D., Extra-Judicial Procurators in the Code of Canon Law, X-94 pp., 1944.
193. COYLE, REV. PAUL RAYMOND, A.B., J.C.D., Judicial Exceptions, X-142 pp., 1944.
194. FAIR, REV. BARTHOLOMEW FRANCIS, A.B., S.T.L., J.C.D., The Impediment of Abduction, XII-122 pp., 1944.
195. GALLAGHER, REV. THOMAS RAPHAEL, O.P., A.B., S.T.Lr., J.C.D., The Examination of the Qualities of the Ordinand, X-166 pp., 1944.
196. GANNON, REV. JOHN MARK, S.T.L., J.C.D., The Interstices Required for the Promotion to Orders, XII-100 pp., 1944.

197. Goldsmith, Rev. J. William, B.C.S., S.T.L., J.C.D., The Competence of Church and State over Marriage—Disputed Points, X-128 pp., 1944.
198. Goodwine, Rev. Joseph Gerard, A.B., S.T.B., J.C.D., The Receptioı of Converts, XIV-326 pp., 1944.
199. Kowalski, Rev. Romuald Eugene, O.F.M., A.B., J.C.D., Sustenance of Religious Houses of Regulars, X-174 pp., 1944.
200. McCoy, Rev. Alan Edward, O.F.M., J.C.D., Force and Fear in Relation to Delictual Imputability and Penal Responsibility, XII-160 pp., 1944.
201. McDevitt, Rev. Vincent John, Ph.B., S.T.L., J.C.L., Perjury.
202. Martin, Rev. Thomas Owen, Ph.D., S.T.D., J.C.D., Adverse Possession, Prescription and Limitation of Actions: The Canonical "Praescriptio," XX-208 pp., 1944.
203. Miklosovic, Rev. Paul John, A.B., J.C.L., Attempted Marriages and Their Consequent Juridic Effects.
204. Mundy, Rev. Thomas Maurice, A.B., S.T.L., J.C.D., The Union of Parishes, X—164 pp., 1944.
205. O'Dea, Rev. John Coyle, A.B., J.C.D., The Matrimonial Impediment of Nonage, VIII-126 pp., 1944.
206. Olalia, Rev. Alexander Ayson, S.T.L., J.C.D., A Comparative Study of the Christian Constitution of States and the Constitution of the Philippine Commonwealth, XII—136 pp., 1944.
207. Poisson, Rev. Pierre-Marie, C.S.C., A.B., Ph.L., Th.L., J.C.L., Droits Patrimoniaux des Maisons et des Églises Religieuses.
208. Stadalnikas, Rev. Casimir Joseph, M.I.C., J.C.D., Reservation of Censures, X-141 pp., 1944.
209. Sullivan, Rev. Eugene Henry, S.T.L., J.C.D., Proof of the Reception of the Sacraments, X—165 pp., 1944.
210. Vaughan, Rev. William Edward, J.C.D., Constitutions for Diocesan Courts, X-210 pp., 1944.
211. Paro, Rev. Gino, S.T.D., J.C.L., The Right of Apostolic Legation.
212. Balzer, Rev. Ralph Francis, C.P., J.C.D., The Computation of Time in a Canonical Novitiate, X—227 pp., 1945.
213. Dougherty, Rev. John Whelan, A.B., S.T.L., J.C.D., De Inquisitione Speciali, XII—195 pp., 1945.
214. Dziob, Rev. Michael Walter, J.C.D., The Sacred Congregation for the Oriental Church, XII—181 pp., 1945.
215. Eidenschink, Rev. John Albert, O.S.B., B.A., J.C.D, The Election of Bishops in the Letters of Pope Gregory the Great, VII—200 pp., 1945.
216. Gill, Rev. Nicholas, C.P., J.C.D., The Spiritual Prefect in Clerical Religious Houses of Study, X—140 pp., 1945.
217. Hynes, Rev. Harry Gerard, S.T.L., J.C.D., The Privileges of Cardinals, XII-183 pp., 1945.
218. McDevitt, Rev. Gerald Vincent, S.T.L., J.C.D., The Renunciation of an Ecclesiastical Office, XIV—179 pp., 1945.

219. Manning, Rev. Joseph Leroy, J.C.D., The Free Conferral of Offices, VIII—116 pp., 1945.
220. Meyer, Rev. Louis G., O.S.B., A.B., S.T.B., J.C.D., Alms-Gathering by Religious, XII—163 pp., 1945.
221. O'Donnell, Rev. Cletus Francis, M.A., J.C.L., The Marriage of Minors, XII—268 pp., 1945.
222. Prunskis, Rev. Joseph, J.C.D., Comparative Law, Ecclesiastical and Civil, in Lithuanian Concordat, X—161 pp., 1945.
223. Sweeney, Rev. Francis Patrick, C.SS.R., J.C.D., The Reduction of Clerics to the Lay State, X—199 pp., 1945.
224. Vogelpohl, Rev. Henry John, J.C.D., The Simple Impediments to Holy Orders, XVI—190 pp., 1945.
225. Brockhaus, Rev. Thomas Aquinas, O.S.B., A.B., J.C.D., Religious who Are Known as *Conversi,* X—127 pp., 1945.
226. Griese, Rev. N. Orville, S.T.D., J.C.D., The Marriage Contract and the Procreation of Offspring, XVI-224 pp., 1946.
227. Boudreaux, Rev. Warren Louis, J.C.L., The "*ab acatholicis nati*" of Canon 1099, § 2.
228. Bowe, Rev. Thomas Joseph, A.B., J.C.D., Religious Superioresses, VIII-206 pp., 1946.
229. Diederichs, Rev. Michael Ferdinand, S.C.J., J.C.D., The Jurisdiction of the Latin Ordinaries over their Oriental Subjects, XIV-153 pp., 1946.
230. Dingman, Rev. Maurice John, A.B., S.T.L., J.C.L., The Plaintiff in Contentious Trials.
231. Frison, Rev. Basil, C.M.F., M.Mus., J.C.D., The Retroactivity of Law, X-221 pp., 1946.
232. Galvin, Rev. William Anthony, M.A., J.C.D., The Administrative Transfer of Pastors, XII-288 pp., 1946.
233. Goracy, Rev. Joseph C., J.C.L., The Diriment Matrimonial Impediment of Major Orders.
234. Hale, Rev. Joseph Francis, M.A., S.T.L., J.C.L., The Pastor of Burial.
235. Henry, Rev. Joseph Arthur, A.B., J.C.D., The Mass and Holy Communion: Inter-Ritual Law, XII-138 pp., 1946.
236. Linenberger, Rev. Herbert, C.PP.S., J.C.L., The False Denunciation of an Innocent Confessor.
237. Lowry, Rev. James Martin, A.B., J.C.D., Dispensation from Private Vows, XII-266 pp., 1946.
238. Lynch, Rev. George Edward, A.B., S.T.L., J.C.D., Coadjutors and Auxiliaries of Bishops, X-107 pp., 1947.
239. Lynch, Rev. Timothy, M.S.SS.T., J.C.D., Contracts between Bishops and Religious Congregations, XIV-232 pp., 1946.
240. McClunn, Rev. Justin David, A.B., S.T.L., J.C.D., Administrative Recourse, VII-142 pp., 1946.

241. Lohmuller, Rev. Martin Nicholas, A.B., J.C.D., The Promulgation of Law, XII-140 pp., 1947.
242. McGrath, Rev. James, A.B., J.C.D., The Privilege of the Canon, XII-156 pp., 1946.
243. Marbach, Rev. Joseph Francis, A.B., J.C.D., Marriage Legislation for the Catholics of the Oriental Rites in the United States and Canada, XIV-314 pp., 1946.
244. Shimkus, Rev. Bernard Aloyius, A.B., J.C.L., The Determination and Transfer of Rite.
245. Smith, Rev. Vincent Michael, A.B., S.T.L., J.C.L., Ignorance Affecting Matrimonial Consent.
246. Wachtrle, Rev. Paul Anthony, A.B., J.C.L., The Baptism of the Children of Non-Catholics.
247. Crotty, Rev. Matthew Michael, J.C.L., The Recipient of First Holy Communion.
248. Eagleton, Rev. George, J.C.L., The Quinquennial Faculties, Formula IV.
249. Gibbons, Rev. Marion Leo, C.M., J.C.L., Domicile of the Wife Unlawfully Separated from Her Husband.
250. Kelly, Rev. Bernard Matthew, J.C.L., The Functions Reserved to Pastors.
251. Kilcullen, Rev. Thomas John, J.C.L., The Collegiate Moral Person as Party Litigant.
252. Lafontaine, Rev. Germain Joseph, W.F., J.C.L., Relations Canoniques entre le Missionaire et Ses Superieurs.
253. Lane, Rev. Loras Thomas, J.C.L., Matrimonial Procedure in Ordinary Court of Second Instance.
254. Lover, Rev. James Francis, C.Ss.R., J.C.L., The Master of Novices.
255. McNicholas, Rev. Timothy Joseph, J.C.L., The *Septimae Manus* Witness.
256. Marositz, Rev. Joseph John, M.S.C., J.C.L., Obligations and Privileges of Religious Promoted to the Episcopal or Cardinalitial Dignities.
257. Murphy, Rev. Francis Joseph, J.C.L., Legislative Powers of the Provincial Council.
258. O'Brien, Rev. Romaeus William, O.Carm., J.C.L., The Provincial Superior in Religious Orders of Men.
259. Pfaller, Rev. Benedict Augustine, O.S.B., J.C.L., The *ipso facto* Effected Dismissal of Religious.
260. Popek, Rev. Alphonse Sylvester, J.C.L., The Rights and Obligations of Metropolitans.
261. Ristuccia, Rev. Bernard Joseph, C.M., J.C.L., Quasi-Religious.
262. Sonntag, Rev. Nathaniel Louis, O.F.M.Cap., J.C.L., Censorship of Special Classes of Books.
263. Stadler, Rev. Joseph Nicholas, J.C.L., Frequent Holy Communion.

264. Szal, Rev. Ignatius Joseph, J.C.L., The Communication of Catholics with Schismatics.
265. Wagner, Rev. Urban Stanley, O.F.M.Conv., J.C.L., Parochial Substitute Vicars and Supplying Priests.

www.ingramcontent.com/pod-product-compliance
Lightning Source LLC
LaVergne TN
LVHW050231080826
844660LV00012B/514

* 9 7 8 0 8 1 3 2 2 4 2 7 5 *